JUDGE DREDD®

TOXIC

Become our fan on Facebook **facebook.com/idwpublishing**
Follow us on Twitter **@idwpublishing**
Subscribe to us on YouTube **youtube.com/idwpublishing**
See what's new on Tumblr **tumblr.idwpublishing.com**
Check us out on Instagram **instagram.com/idwpublishing**

IDW
www.IDWPUBLISHING.com

2000 AD

COVER ARTIST
MARK BUCKINGHAM

COVER COLORIST
CHRIS BLYTHE

COLLECTION EDITORS
JUSTIN EISINGER
AND **ALONZO SIMON**

COLLECTION DESIGNER
CLAUDIA CHONG

Chris Ryall, President, Publisher, & CCO
John Barber, Editor-In-Chief
Robbie Robbins, EVP & Sr. Art Director
Cara Morrison, Chief Financial Officer
Matthew Ruzicka, Chief Accounting Officer
Anita Frazier, SVP of Sales and Marketing
David Hedgecock, Associate Publisher
Jerry Bennington, VP of New Product Development
Lorelei Bunjes, VP of Digital Services
Justin Eisinger, Editorial Director, Graphic Novels & Collections
Eric Moss, Sr. Director, Licensing & Business Development

Ted Adams, IDW Founder

ISBN: 978-1-68405-475-6   22 21 20 19   1 2 3 4

Originally published as JUDGE DREDD: TOXIC issues #1–4.

Special thanks to Ben Smith and Matt Smith for their invaluable
assistance.

For international rights, contact licensing@idwpublishing.com

JUDGE DREDD
TOXIC

WRITTEN BY
PAUL JENKINS

ART BY
MARCO CASTIELLO

ASSISTANT INKS BY
VINCENZO ACUNZO

COLORS BY
JASON MILLET

LETTERS BY
SHAWN LEE

SERIES ASSISTANT EDITS BY
ELIZABETH BREI AND **ANNI PERHEENTUPA**

SERIES EDITS BY
CHASE MAROTZ

GROUP EDITOR
DENTON J. TIPTON

JUDGE DREDD CREATED BY JOHN WAGNER AND CARLOS EZQUERRA

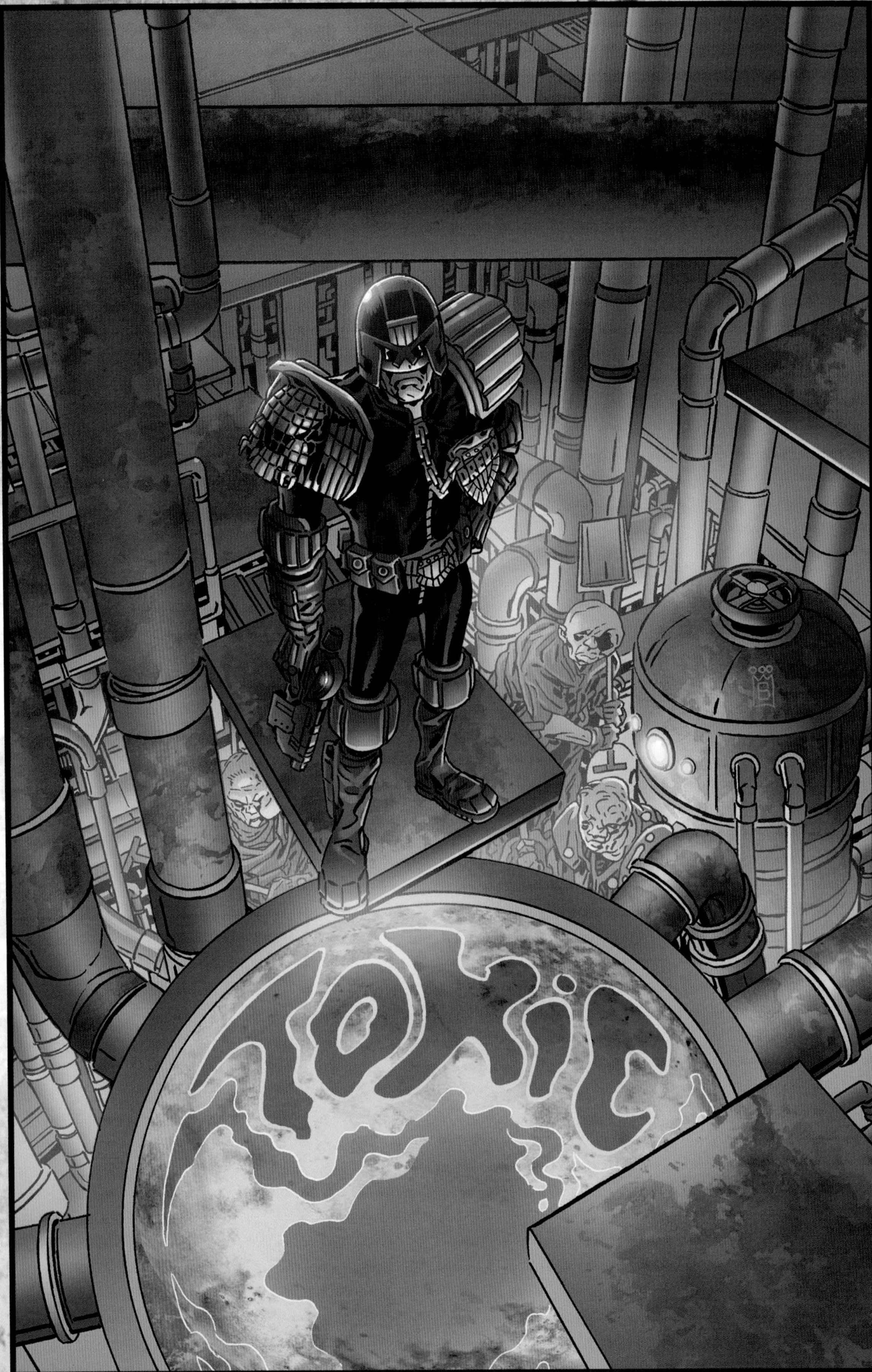
TOXIC

ART BY **MARK BUCKINGHAM** COLORS BY **CHRIS BLYTHE**

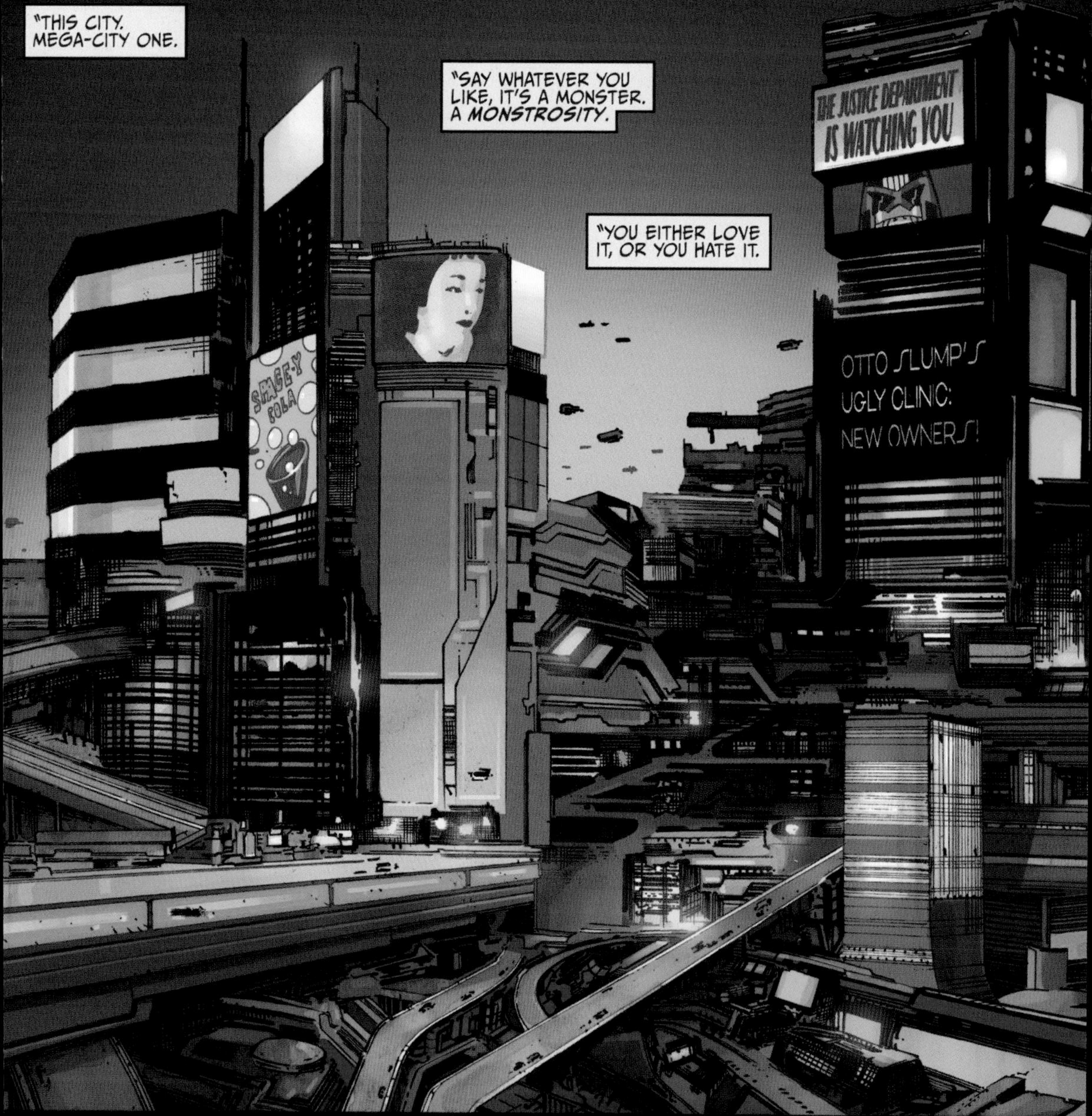
"THIS CITY. MEGA-CITY ONE.
"SAY WHATEVER YOU LIKE, IT'S A MONSTER. A *MONSTROSITY*.
THE JUSTICE DEPARTMENT IS WATCHING YOU
"YOU EITHER LOVE IT, OR YOU HATE IT.
OTTO SLUMP'S UGLY CLINIC: NEW OWNERS!
COLA

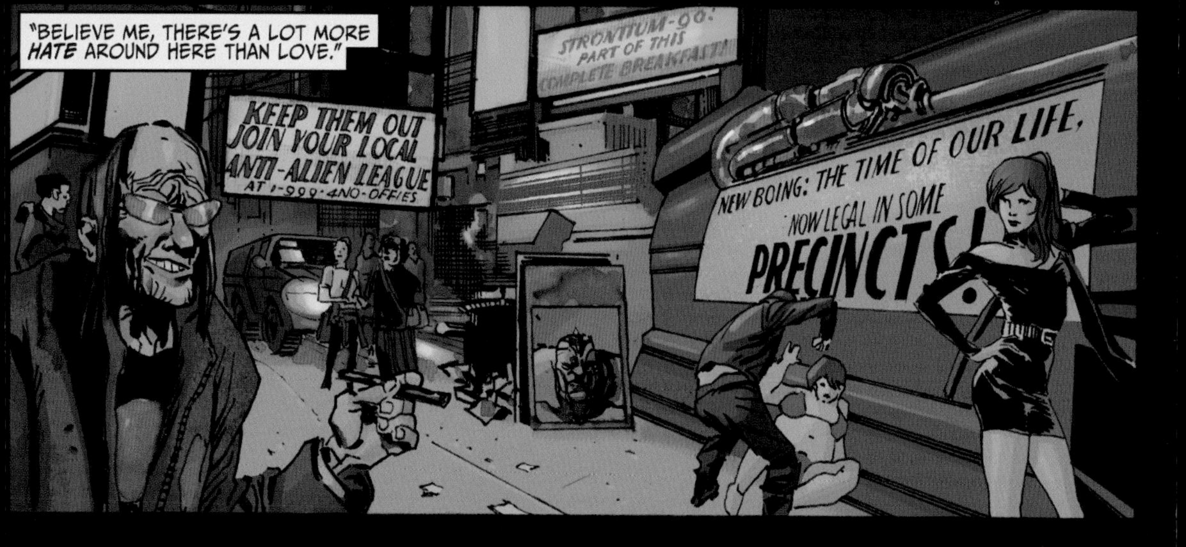
"BELIEVE ME, THERE'S A LOT MORE *HATE* AROUND HERE THAN LOVE."
STRONTIUM-90: PART OF THIS COMPLETE BREAKFAST!
KEEP THEM OUT JOIN YOUR LOCAL ANTI-ALIEN LEAGUE AT 1-999-4NO-OFFIES
NEW BOING: THE TIME OF OUR LIFE, NOW LEGAL IN SOME PRECINCTS!

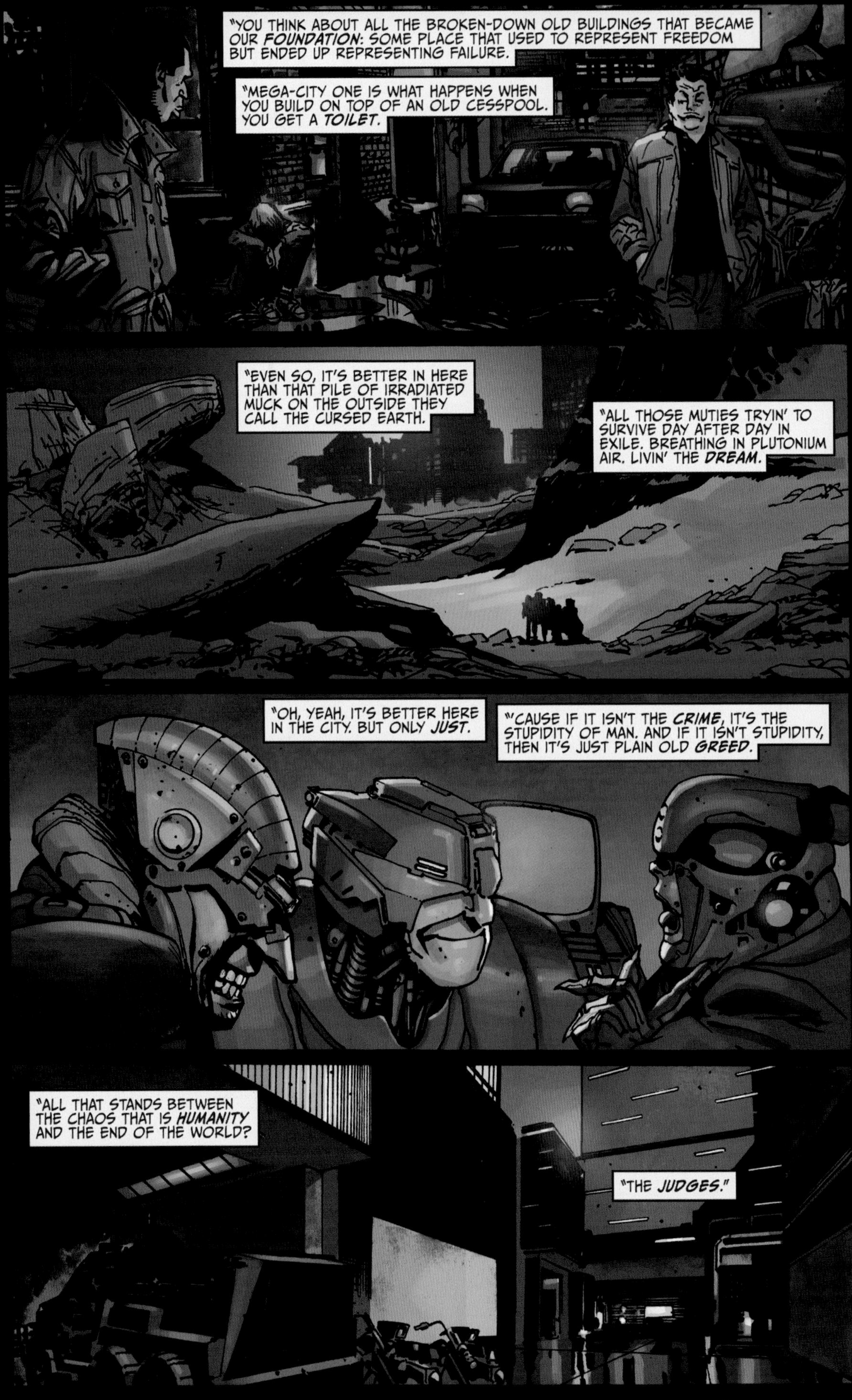
"YOU THINK ABOUT ALL THE BROKEN-DOWN OLD BUILDINGS THAT BECAME OUR FOUNDATION: SOME PLACE THAT USED TO REPRESENT FREEDOM BUT ENDED UP REPRESENTING FAILURE.
"MEGA-CITY ONE IS WHAT HAPPENS WHEN YOU BUILD ON TOP OF AN OLD CESSPOOL. YOU GET A TOILET.
"EVEN SO, IT'S BETTER IN HERE THAN THAT PILE OF IRRADIATED MUCK ON THE OUTSIDE THEY CALL THE CURSED EARTH.
"ALL THOSE MUTIES TRYIN' TO SURVIVE DAY AFTER DAY IN EXILE. BREATHING IN PLUTONIUM AIR. LIVIN' THE DREAM.
"OH, YEAH, IT'S BETTER HERE IN THE CITY. BUT ONLY JUST.
"'CAUSE IF IT ISN'T THE CRIME, IT'S THE STUPIDITY OF MAN. AND IF IT ISN'T STUPIDITY, THEN IT'S JUST PLAIN OLD GREED.
"ALL THAT STANDS BETWEEN THE CHAOS THAT IS HUMANITY AND THE END OF THE WORLD?
"THE JUDGES."

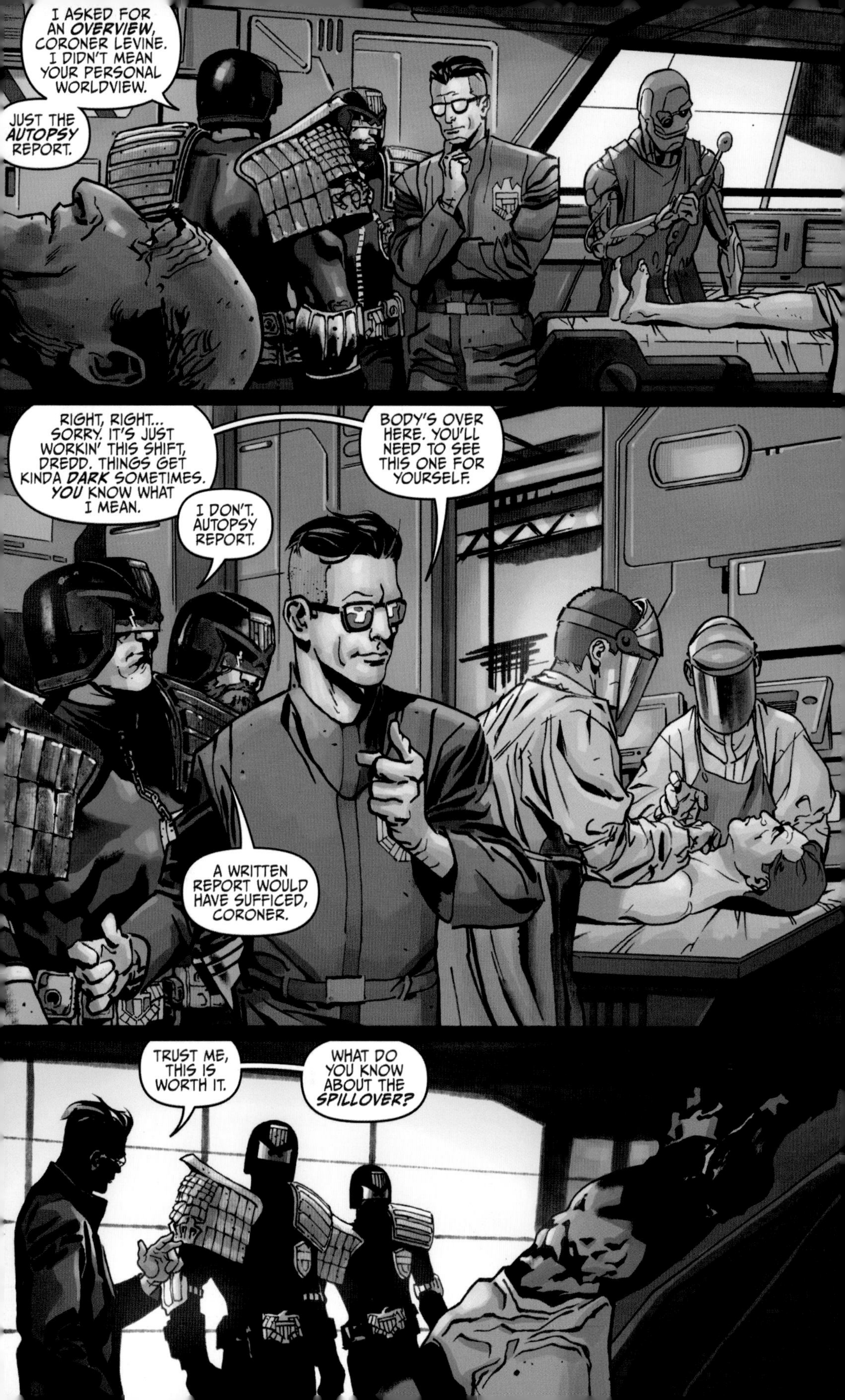
I ASKED FOR AN *OVERVIEW*, CORONER LEVINE. I DIDN'T MEAN YOUR PERSONAL WORLDVIEW.
JUST THE *AUTOPSY* REPORT.
RIGHT, RIGHT... SORRY. IT'S JUST WORKIN' THIS SHIFT, DREDD. THINGS GET KINDA *DARK* SOMETIMES. *YOU* KNOW WHAT I MEAN.
BODY'S OVER HERE. YOU'LL NEED TO SEE THIS ONE FOR YOURSELF.
I DON'T. AUTOPSY REPORT.
A WRITTEN REPORT WOULD HAVE SUFFICED, CORONER.
TRUST ME, THIS IS WORTH IT.
WHAT DO YOU KNOW ABOUT THE *SPILLOVER?*

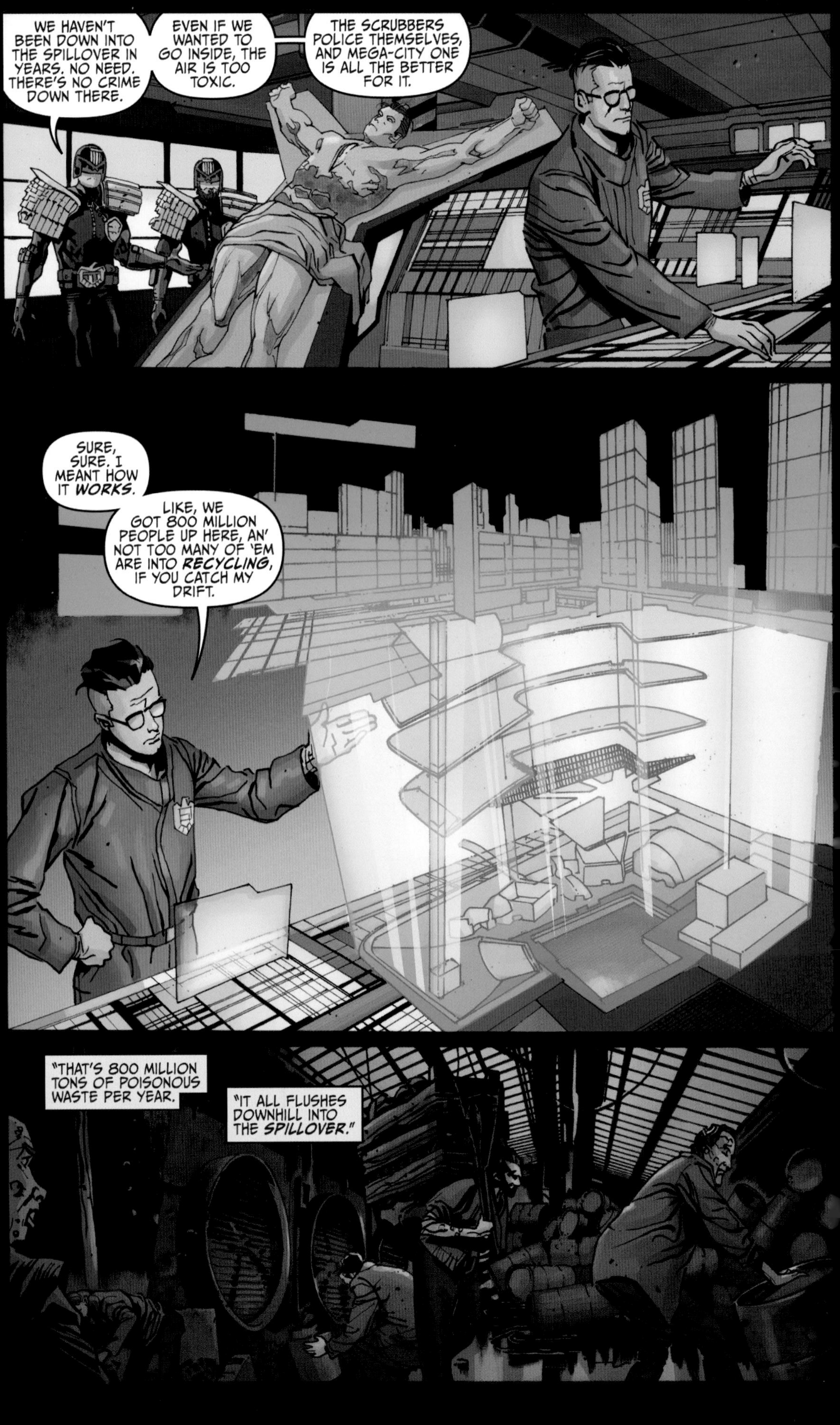
WE HAVEN'T BEEN DOWN INTO THE SPILLOVER IN YEARS. NO NEED. THERE'S NO CRIME DOWN THERE.
EVEN IF WE WANTED TO GO INSIDE, THE AIR IS TOO TOXIC.
THE SCRUBBERS POLICE THEMSELVES, AND MEGA-CITY ONE IS ALL THE BETTER FOR IT.
SURE, SURE. I MEANT HOW IT *WORKS*.
LIKE, WE GOT 800 MILLION PEOPLE UP HERE, AN' NOT TOO MANY OF 'EM ARE INTO *RECYCLING*, IF YOU CATCH MY DRIFT.
"THAT'S 800 MILLION TONS OF POISONOUS WASTE PER YEAR.
"IT ALL FLUSHES DOWNHILL INTO THE *SPILLOVER*."

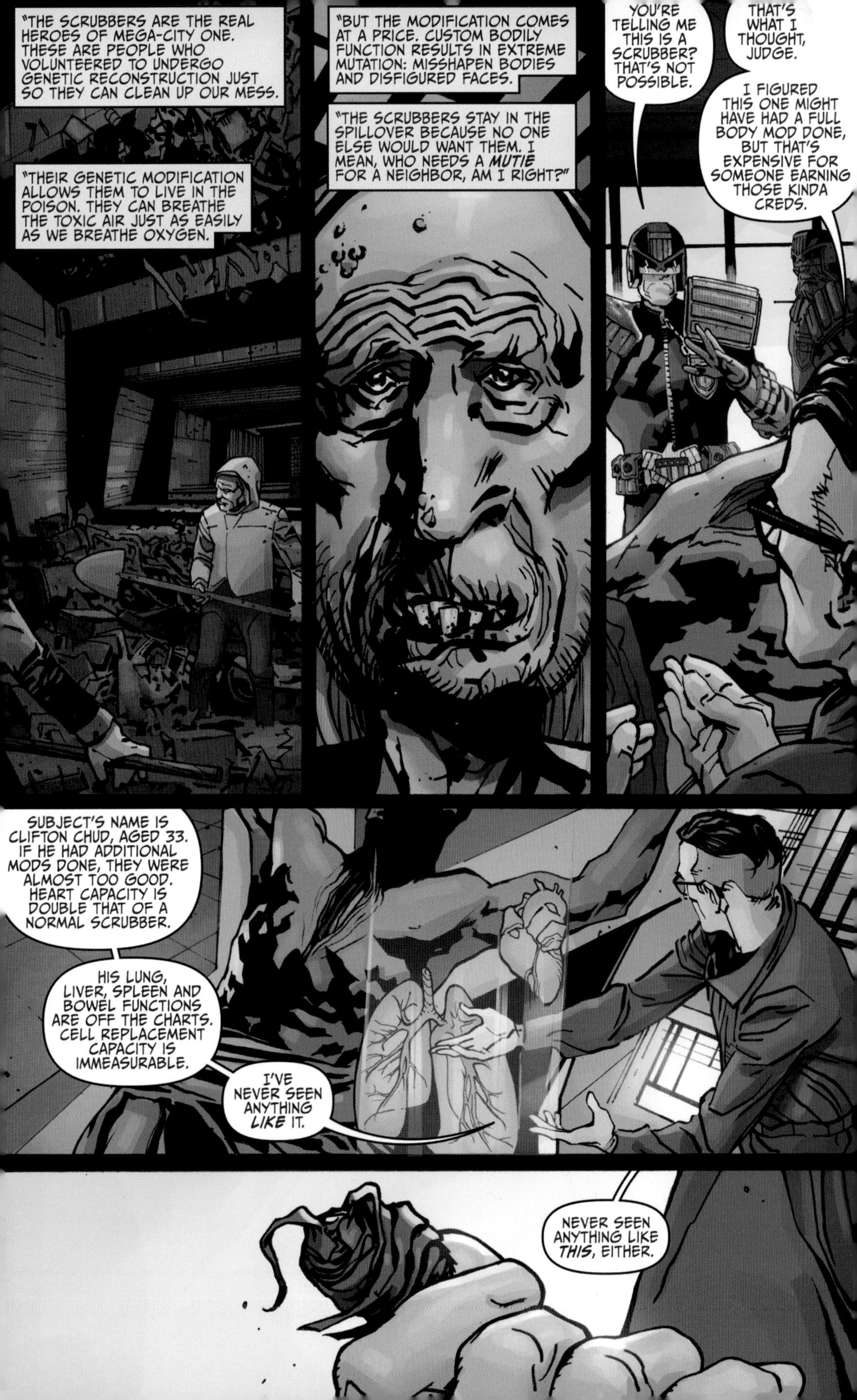
"THE SCRUBBERS ARE THE REAL HEROES OF MEGA-CITY ONE. THESE ARE PEOPLE WHO VOLUNTEERED TO UNDERGO GENETIC RECONSTRUCTION JUST SO THEY CAN CLEAN UP OUR MESS.
"THEIR GENETIC MODIFICATION ALLOWS THEM TO LIVE IN THE POISON. THEY CAN BREATHE THE TOXIC AIR JUST AS EASILY AS WE BREATHE OXYGEN.
"BUT THE MODIFICATION COMES AT A PRICE. CUSTOM BODILY FUNCTION RESULTS IN EXTREME MUTATION: MISSHAPEN BODIES AND DISFIGURED FACES.
"THE SCRUBBERS STAY IN THE SPILLOVER BECAUSE NO ONE ELSE WOULD WANT THEM. I MEAN, WHO NEEDS A *MUTIE* FOR A NEIGHBOR, AM I RIGHT?"
YOU'RE TELLING ME THIS IS A SCRUBBER? THAT'S NOT POSSIBLE.
THAT'S WHAT I THOUGHT, JUDGE.
I FIGURED THIS ONE MIGHT HAVE HAD A FULL BODY MOD DONE, BUT THAT'S EXPENSIVE FOR SOMEONE EARNING THOSE KINDA CREDS.
SUBJECT'S NAME IS CLIFTON CHUD, AGED 33. IF HE HAD ADDITIONAL MODS DONE, THEY WERE ALMOST TOO GOOD. HEART CAPACITY IS DOUBLE THAT OF A NORMAL SCRUBBER.
HIS LUNG, LIVER, SPLEEN AND BOWEL FUNCTIONS ARE OFF THE CHARTS. CELL REPLACEMENT CAPACITY IS IMMEASURABLE.
I'VE NEVER SEEN ANYTHING *LIKE* IT.
NEVER SEEN ANYTHING LIKE *THIS*, EITHER.

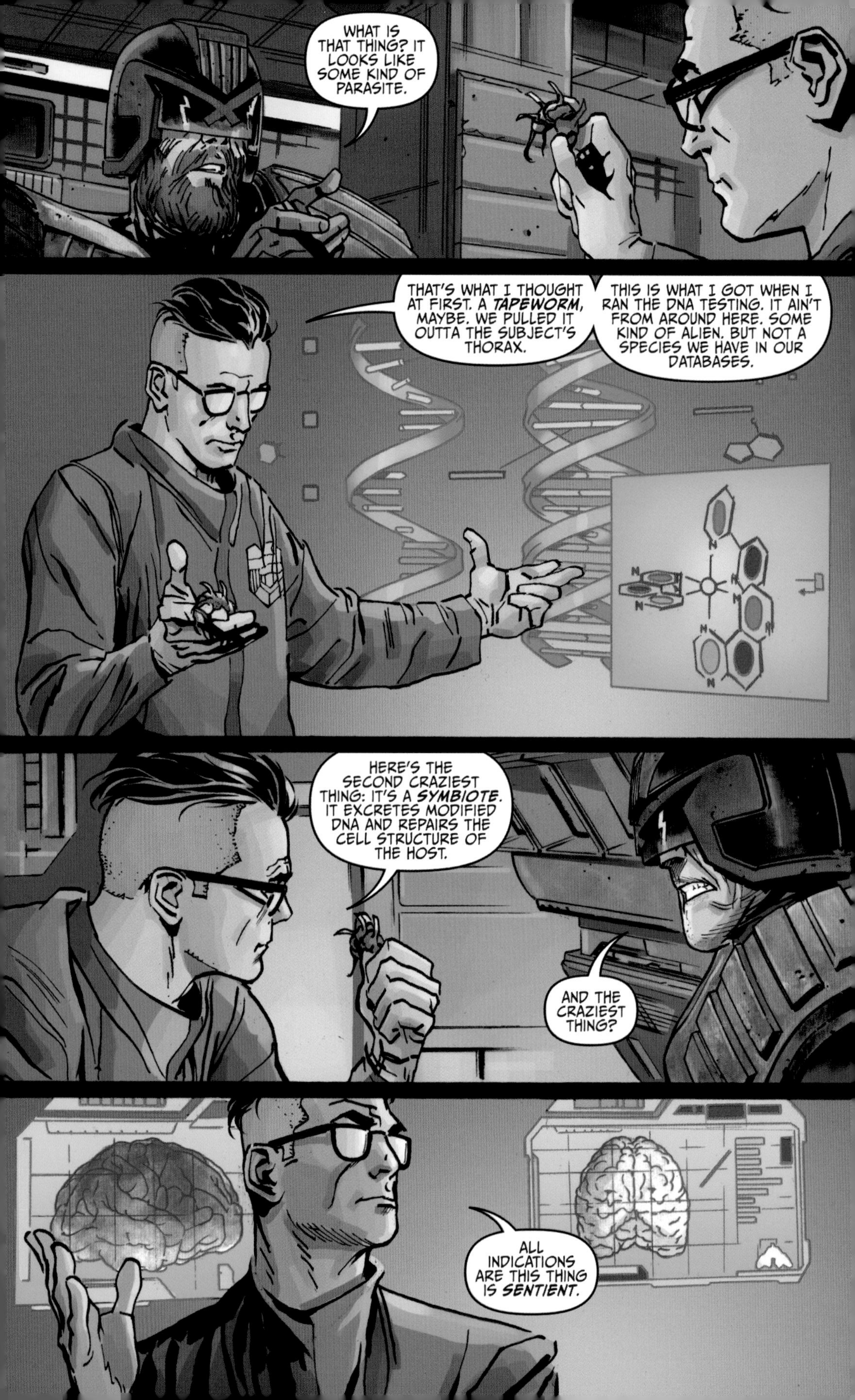
WHAT IS THAT THING? IT LOOKS LIKE SOME KIND OF PARASITE.
THAT'S WHAT I THOUGHT AT FIRST. A *TAPEWORM*, MAYBE. WE PULLED IT OUTTA THE SUBJECT'S THORAX.
THIS IS WHAT I GOT WHEN I RAN THE DNA TESTING. IT AIN'T FROM AROUND HERE. SOME KIND OF ALIEN. BUT NOT A SPECIES WE HAVE IN OUR DATABASES.
HERE'S THE SECOND CRAZIEST THING: IT'S A *SYMBIOTE*. IT EXCRETES MODIFIED DNA AND REPAIRS THE CELL STRUCTURE OF THE HOST.
AND THE CRAZIEST THING?
ALL INDICATIONS ARE THIS THING IS *SENTIENT*.

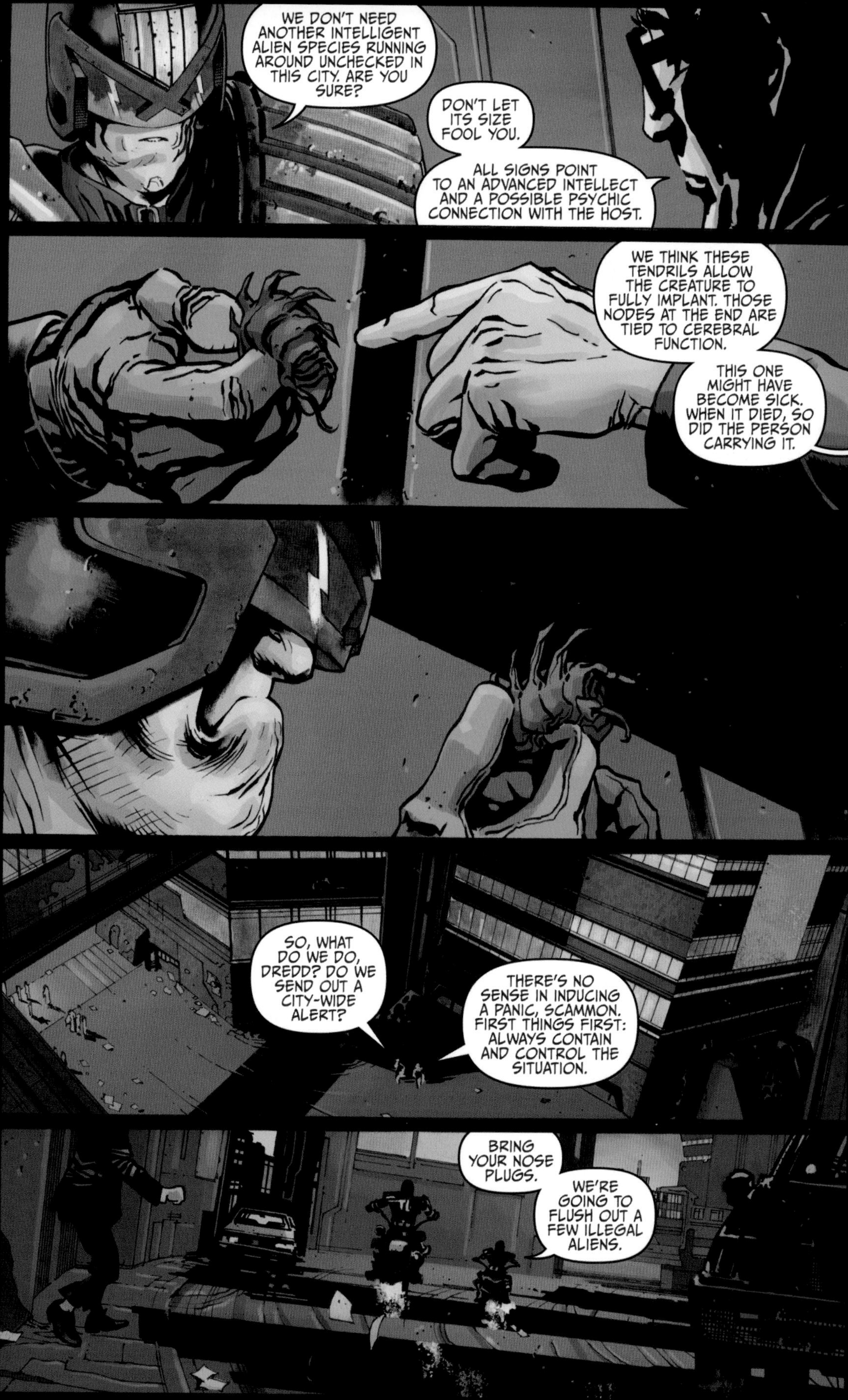
WE DON'T NEED ANOTHER INTELLIGENT ALIEN SPECIES RUNNING AROUND UNCHECKED IN THIS CITY. ARE YOU SURE?
DON'T LET ITS SIZE FOOL YOU.
ALL SIGNS POINT TO AN ADVANCED INTELLECT AND A POSSIBLE PSYCHIC CONNECTION WITH THE HOST.
WE THINK THESE TENDRILS ALLOW THE CREATURE TO FULLY IMPLANT. THOSE NODES AT THE END ARE TIED TO CEREBRAL FUNCTION.
THIS ONE MIGHT HAVE BECOME SICK. WHEN IT DIED, SO DID THE PERSON CARRYING IT.
SO, WHAT DO WE DO, DREDD? DO WE SEND OUT A CITY-WIDE ALERT?
THERE'S NO SENSE IN INDUCING A PANIC, SCAMMON. FIRST THINGS FIRST: ALWAYS CONTAIN AND CONTROL THE SITUATION.
BRING YOUR NOSE PLUGS.
WE'RE GOING TO FLUSH OUT A FEW ILLEGAL ALIENS.

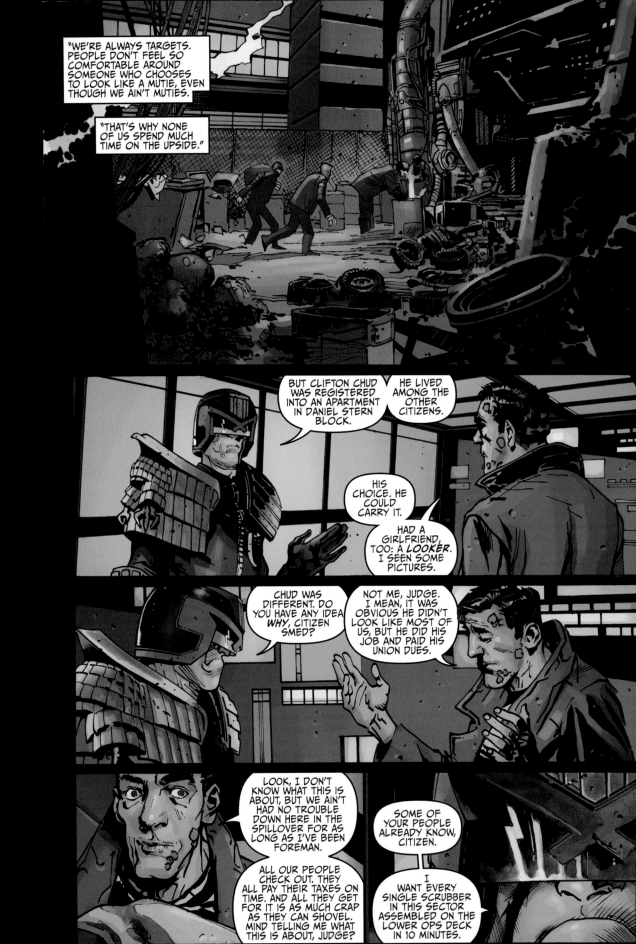

"WE'RE ALWAYS TARGETS. PEOPLE DON'T FEEL SO COMFORTABLE AROUND SOMEONE WHO CHOOSES TO LOOK LIKE A MUTIE, EVEN THOUGH WE AIN'T MUTIES."

"THAT'S WHY NONE OF US SPEND MUCH TIME ON THE UPSIDE."

BUT CLIFTON CHUD WAS REGISTERED INTO AN APARTMENT IN DANIEL STERN BLOCK.

HE LIVED AMONG THE OTHER CITIZENS.

HIS CHOICE. HE COULD CARRY IT.

HAD A GIRLFRIEND, TOO: A *LOOKER*. I SEEN SOME PICTURES.

CHUD WAS DIFFERENT. DO YOU HAVE ANY IDEA *WHY*, CITIZEN SMED?

NOT ME, JUDGE. I MEAN, IT WAS OBVIOUS HE DIDN'T LOOK LIKE MOST OF US, BUT HE DID HIS JOB AND PAID HIS UNION DUES.

LOOK, I DON'T KNOW WHAT THIS IS ABOUT, BUT WE AIN'T HAD NO TROUBLE DOWN HERE IN THE SPILLOVER FOR AS LONG AS I'VE BEEN FOREMAN.

ALL OUR PEOPLE CHECK OUT. THEY ALL PAY THEIR TAXES ON TIME. AND ALL THEY GET FOR IT IS AS MUCH CRAP AS THEY CAN SHOVEL. MIND TELLING ME WHAT THIS IS ABOUT, JUDGE?

SOME OF YOUR PEOPLE ALREADY KNOW, CITIZEN.

I WANT EVERY SINGLE SCRUBBER IN THIS SECTOR ASSEMBLED ON THE LOWER OPS DECK IN 10 MINUTES.

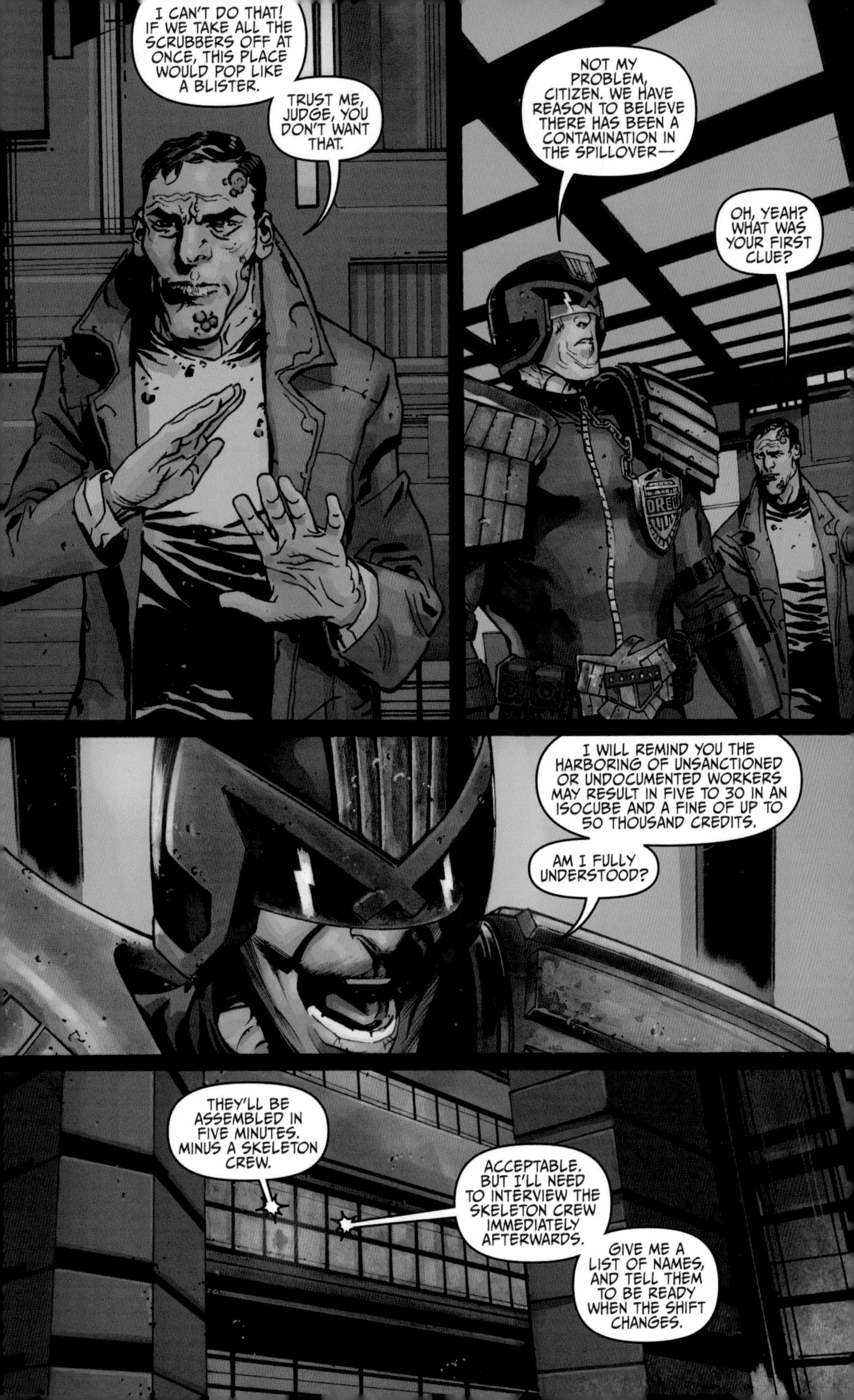
I CAN'T DO THAT! IF WE TAKE ALL THE SCRUBBERS OFF AT ONCE, THIS PLACE WOULD POP LIKE A BLISTER.
TRUST ME, JUDGE, YOU DON'T WANT THAT.
NOT MY PROBLEM, CITIZEN. WE HAVE REASON TO BELIEVE THERE HAS BEEN A CONTAMINATION IN THE SPILLOVER—
OH, YEAH? WHAT WAS YOUR FIRST CLUE?
I WILL REMIND YOU THE HARBORING OF UNSANCTIONED OR UNDOCUMENTED WORKERS MAY RESULT IN FIVE TO 30 IN AN ISOCUBE AND A FINE OF UP TO 50 THOUSAND CREDITS.
AM I FULLY UNDERSTOOD?
THEY'LL BE ASSEMBLED IN FIVE MINUTES. MINUS A SKELETON CREW.
ACCEPTABLE. BUT I'LL NEED TO INTERVIEW THE SKELETON CREW IMMEDIATELY AFTERWARDS.
GIVE ME A LIST OF NAMES, AND TELL THEM TO BE READY WHEN THE SHIFT CHANGES.

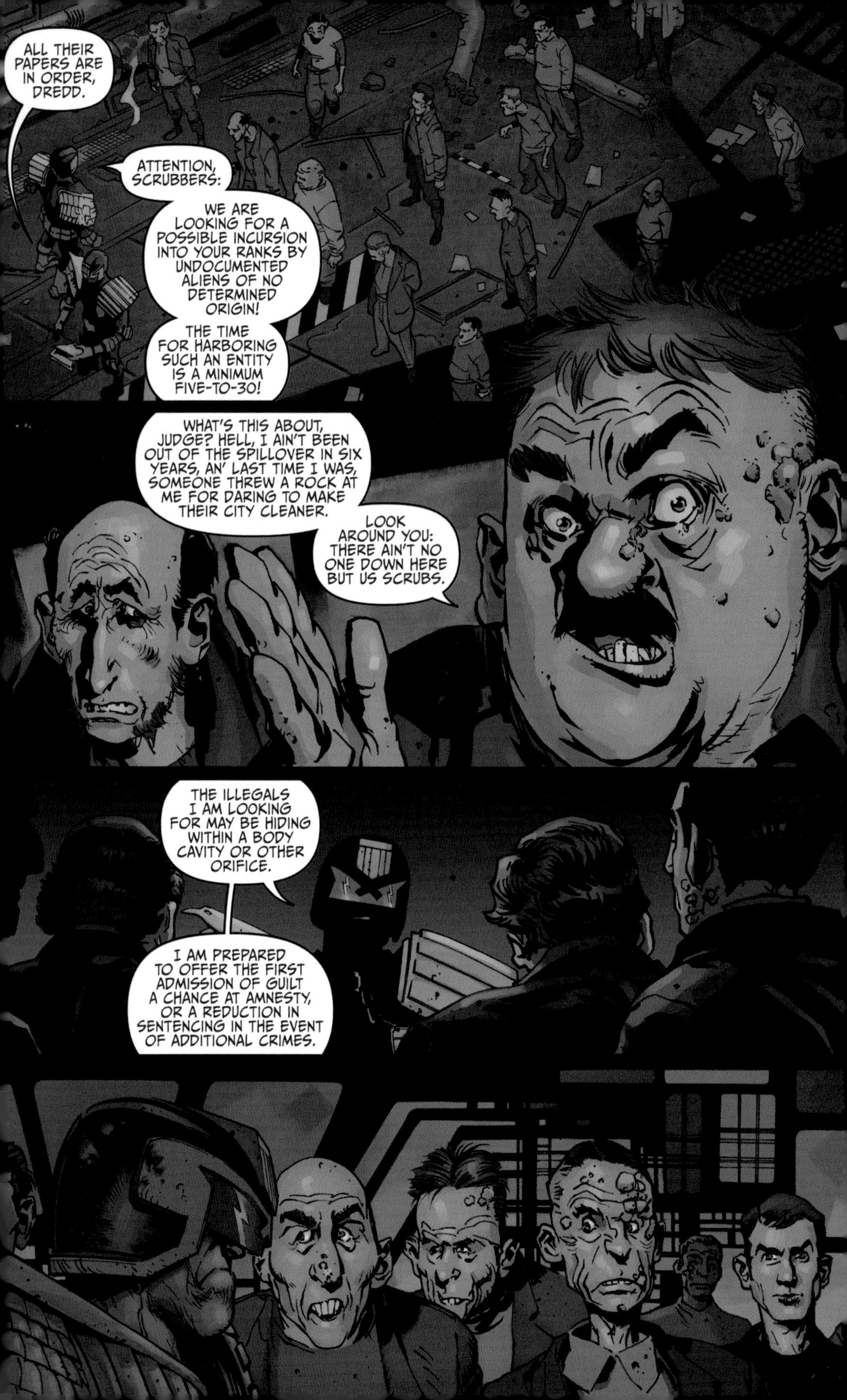

ALL THEIR PAPERS ARE IN ORDER, DREDD.
ATTENTION, SCRUBBERS:
WE ARE LOOKING FOR A POSSIBLE INCURSION INTO YOUR RANKS BY UNDOCUMENTED ALIENS OF NO DETERMINED ORIGIN!
THE TIME FOR HARBORING SUCH AN ENTITY IS A MINIMUM FIVE-TO-30!
WHAT'S THIS ABOUT, JUDGE? HELL, I AIN'T BEEN OUT OF THE SPILLOVER IN SIX YEARS, AN' LAST TIME I WAS, SOMEONE THREW A ROCK AT ME FOR DARING TO MAKE THEIR CITY CLEANER.
LOOK AROUND YOU: THERE AIN'T NO ONE DOWN HERE BUT US SCRUBS.
THE ILLEGALS I AM LOOKING FOR MAY BE HIDING WITHIN A BODY CAVITY OR OTHER ORIFICE.
I AM PREPARED TO OFFER THE FIRST ADMISSION OF GUILT A CHANCE AT AMNESTY, OR A REDUCTION IN SENTENCING IN THE EVENT OF ADDITIONAL CRIMES.

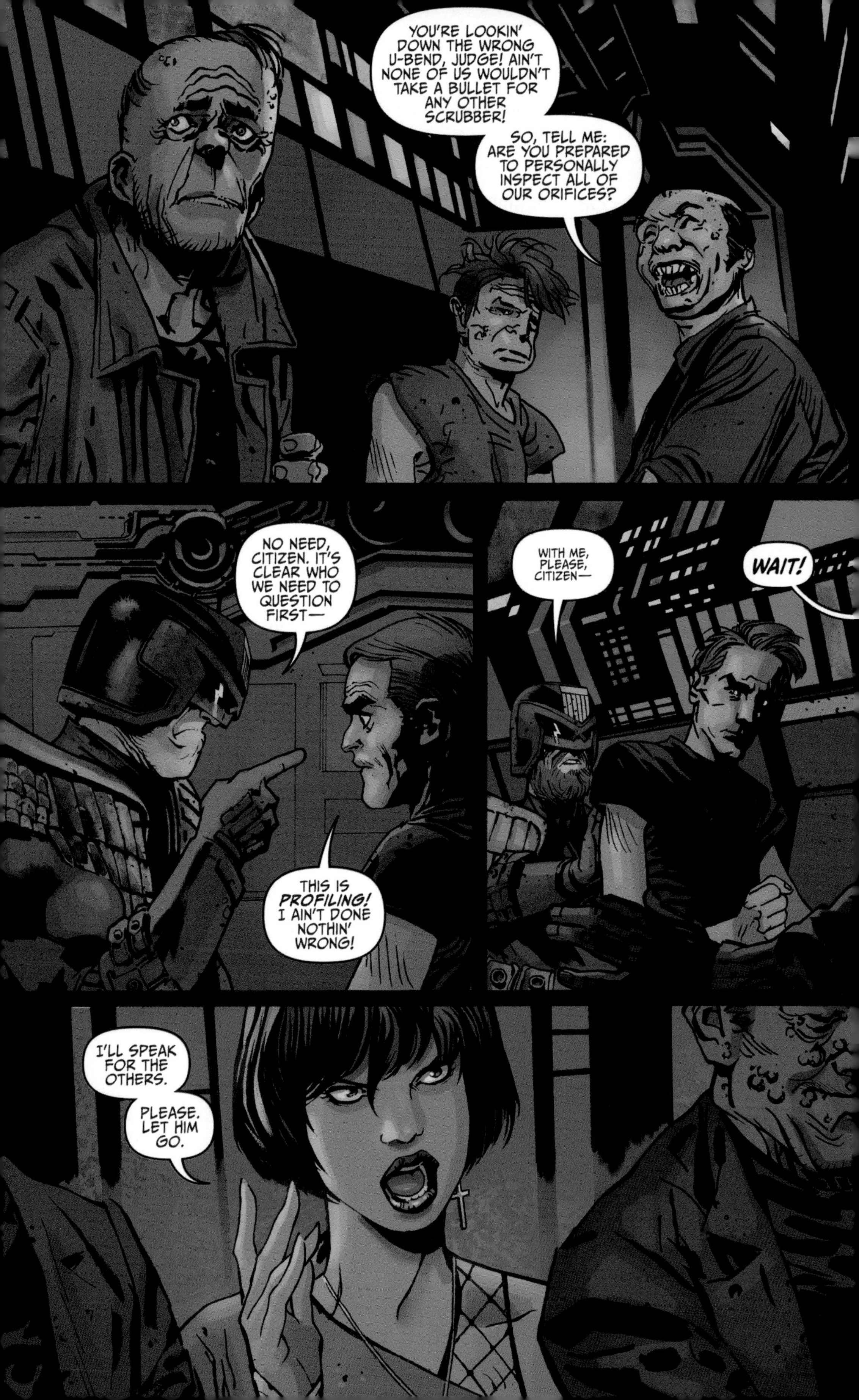
YOU'RE LOOKIN' DOWN THE WRONG U-BEND, JUDGE! AIN'T NONE OF US WOULDN'T TAKE A BULLET FOR ANY OTHER SCRUBBER!
SO, TELL ME: ARE YOU PREPARED TO PERSONALLY INSPECT ALL OF OUR ORIFICES?
NO NEED, CITIZEN. IT'S CLEAR WHO WE NEED TO QUESTION FIRST—
THIS IS PROFILING! I AIN'T DONE NOTHIN' WRONG!
WITH ME, PLEASE, CITIZEN—
WAIT!
I'LL SPEAK FOR THE OTHERS.
PLEASE. LET HIM GO.

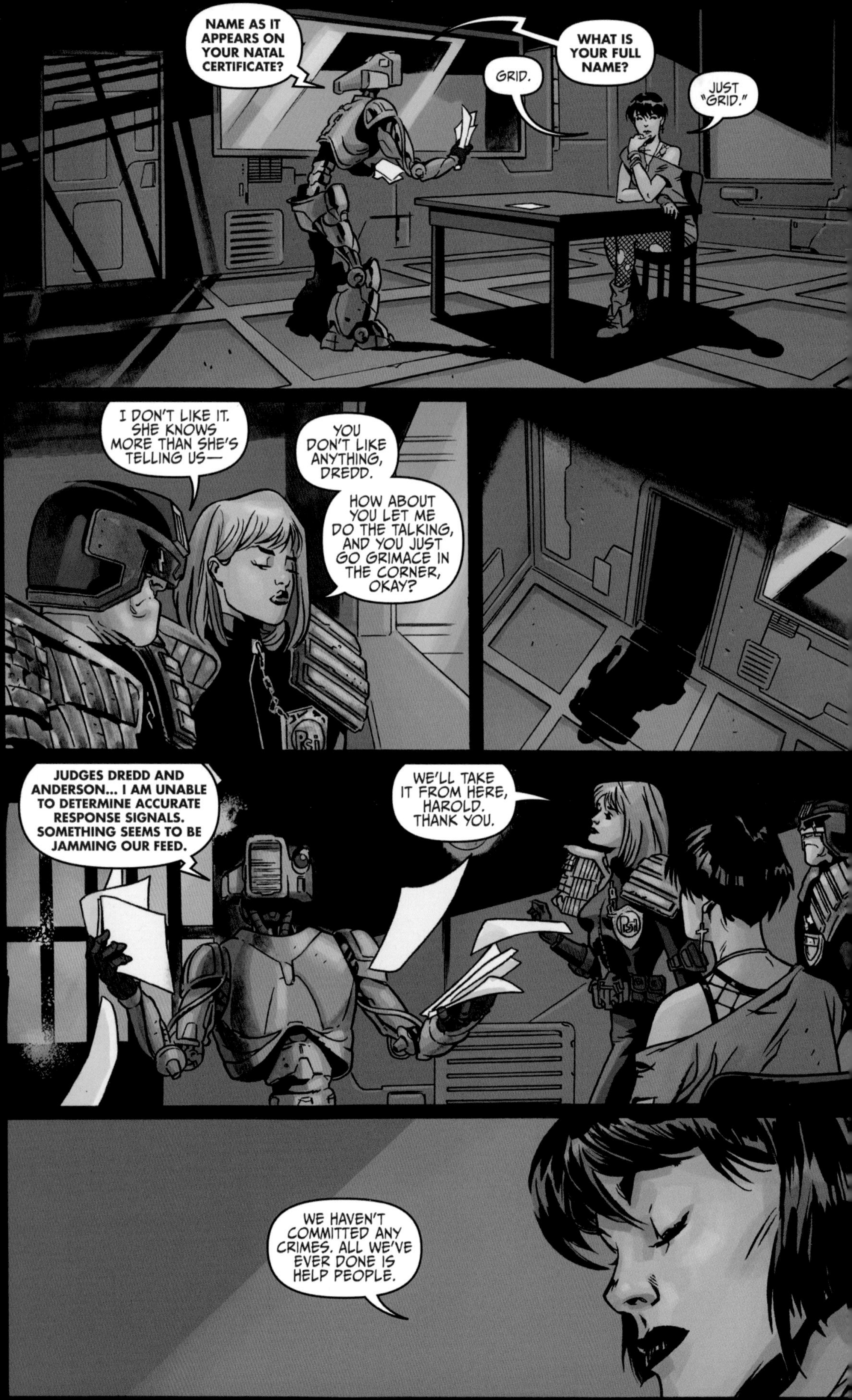

WHAT IS YOUR FULL NAME?
GRID.
NAME AS IT APPEARS ON YOUR NATAL CERTIFICATE?
JUST "GRID."
I DON'T LIKE IT. SHE KNOWS MORE THAN SHE'S TELLING US—
YOU DON'T LIKE ANYTHING, DREDD.
HOW ABOUT YOU LET ME DO THE TALKING, AND YOU JUST GO GRIMACE IN THE CORNER, OKAY?
JUDGES DREDD AND ANDERSON... I AM UNABLE TO DETERMINE ACCURATE RESPONSE SIGNALS. SOMETHING SEEMS TO BE JAMMING OUR FEED.
WE'LL TAKE IT FROM HERE, HAROLD. THANK YOU.
WE HAVEN'T COMMITTED ANY CRIMES. ALL WE'VE EVER DONE IS HELP PEOPLE.

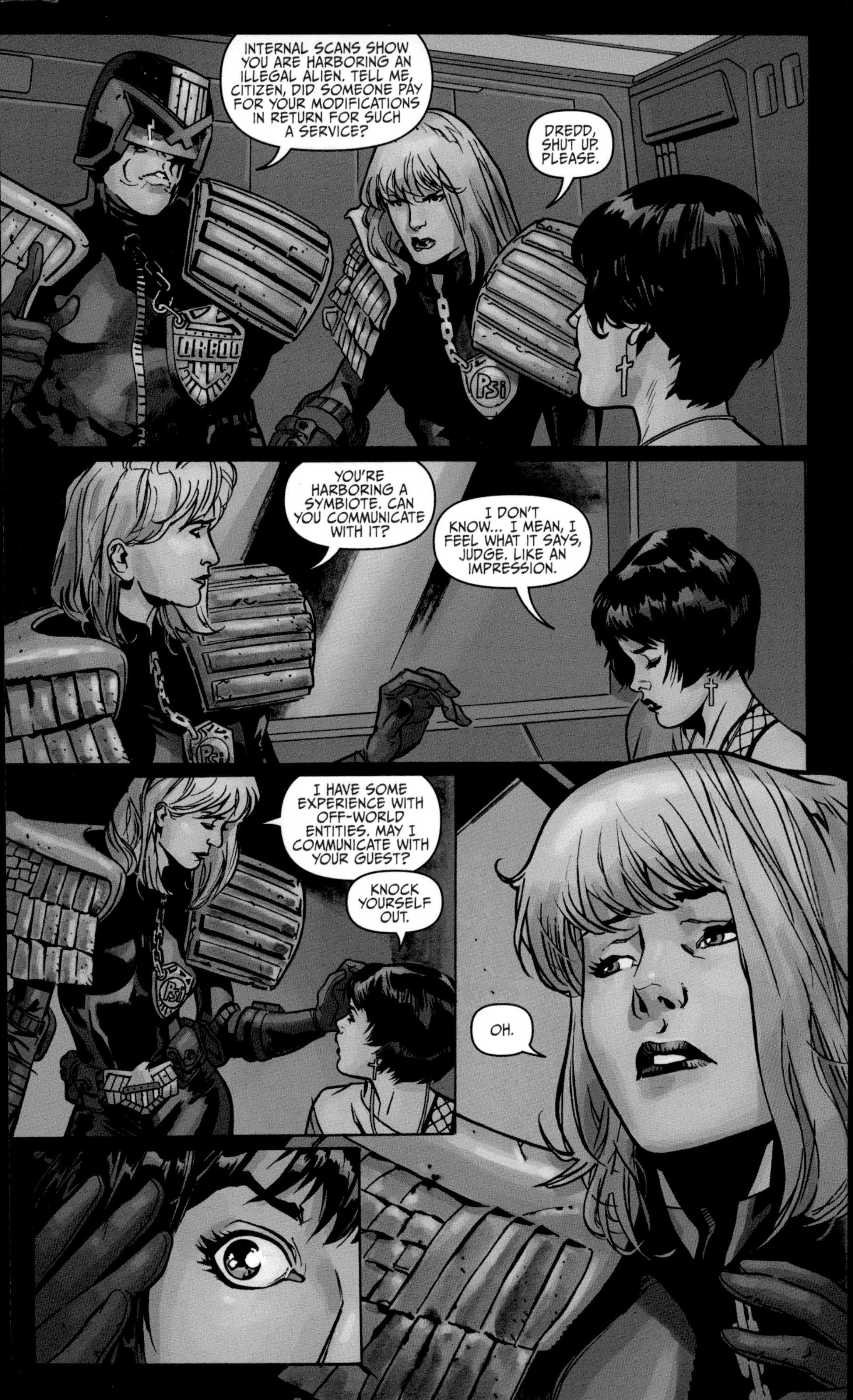
INTERNAL SCANS SHOW YOU ARE HARBORING AN ILLEGAL ALIEN. TELL ME, CITIZEN, DID SOMEONE PAY FOR YOUR MODIFICATIONS IN RETURN FOR SUCH A SERVICE?
DREDD, SHUT UP. PLEASE.
YOU'RE HARBORING A SYMBIOTE. CAN YOU COMMUNICATE WITH IT?
I DON'T KNOW... I MEAN, I FEEL WHAT IT SAYS, JUDGE. LIKE AN IMPRESSION.
I HAVE SOME EXPERIENCE WITH OFF-WORLD ENTITIES. MAY I COMMUNICATE WITH YOUR GUEST?
KNOCK YOURSELF OUT.
OH.

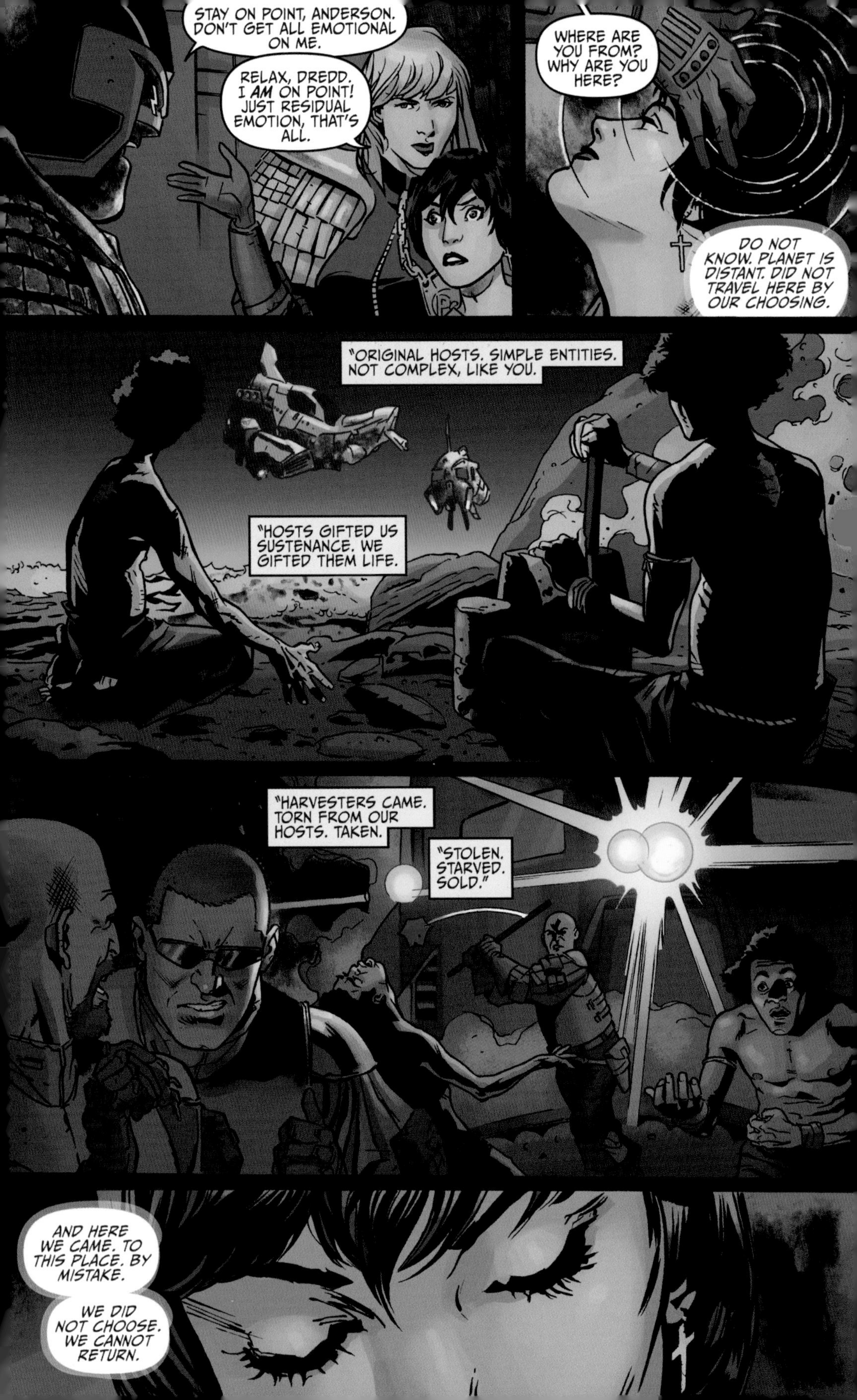
STAY ON POINT, ANDERSON. DON'T GET ALL EMOTIONAL ON ME.
RELAX, DREDD. I *AM* ON POINT! JUST RESIDUAL EMOTION, THAT'S ALL.
WHERE ARE YOU FROM? WHY ARE YOU HERE?
DO NOT KNOW. PLANET IS DISTANT. DID NOT TRAVEL HERE BY OUR CHOOSING.
"ORIGINAL HOSTS. SIMPLE ENTITIES. NOT COMPLEX, LIKE YOU.
"HOSTS GIFTED US SUSTENANCE. WE GIFTED THEM LIFE.
"HARVESTERS CAME. TORN FROM OUR HOSTS. TAKEN.
"STOLEN. STARVED. SOLD."
AND HERE WE CAME. TO THIS PLACE. BY MISTAKE.
WE DID NOT CHOOSE. WE CANNOT RETURN.

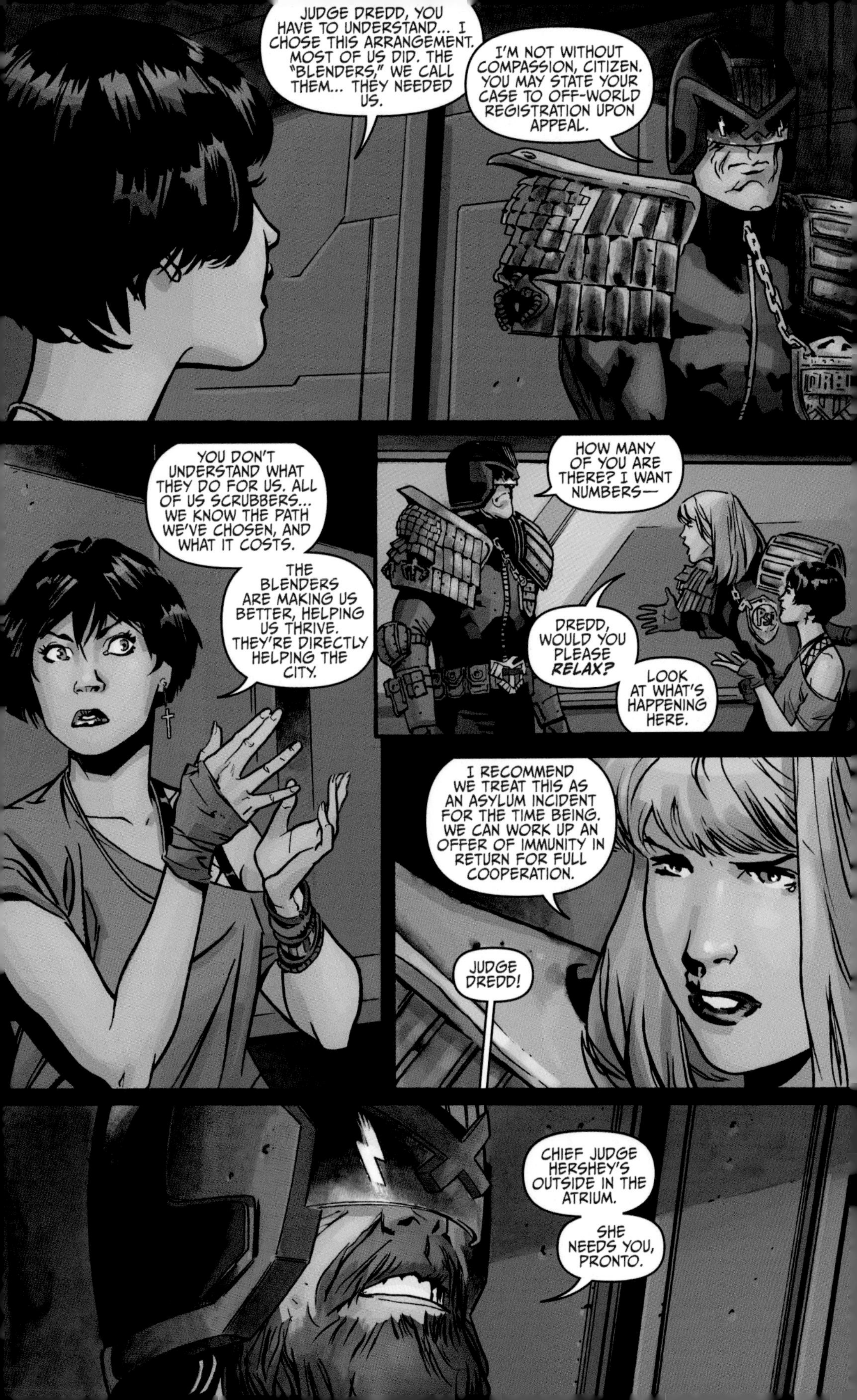
JUDGE DREDD, YOU HAVE TO UNDERSTAND... I CHOSE THIS ARRANGEMENT. MOST OF US DID. THE "BLENDERS," WE CALL THEM... THEY NEEDED US.
I'M NOT WITHOUT COMPASSION, CITIZEN. YOU MAY STATE YOUR CASE TO OFF-WORLD REGISTRATION UPON APPEAL.
YOU DON'T UNDERSTAND WHAT THEY DO FOR US. ALL OF US SCRUBBERS... WE KNOW THE PATH WE'VE CHOSEN, AND WHAT IT COSTS.
THE BLENDERS ARE MAKING US BETTER, HELPING US THRIVE. THEY'RE DIRECTLY HELPING THE CITY.
HOW MANY OF YOU ARE THERE? I WANT NUMBERS—
DREDD, WOULD YOU PLEASE *RELAX?*
LOOK AT WHAT'S HAPPENING HERE.
I RECOMMEND WE TREAT THIS AS AN ASYLUM INCIDENT FOR THE TIME BEING. WE CAN WORK UP AN OFFER OF IMMUNITY IN RETURN FOR FULL COOPERATION.
JUDGE DREDD!
CHIEF JUDGE HERSHEY'S OUTSIDE IN THE ATRIUM.
SHE NEEDS YOU, PRONTO.

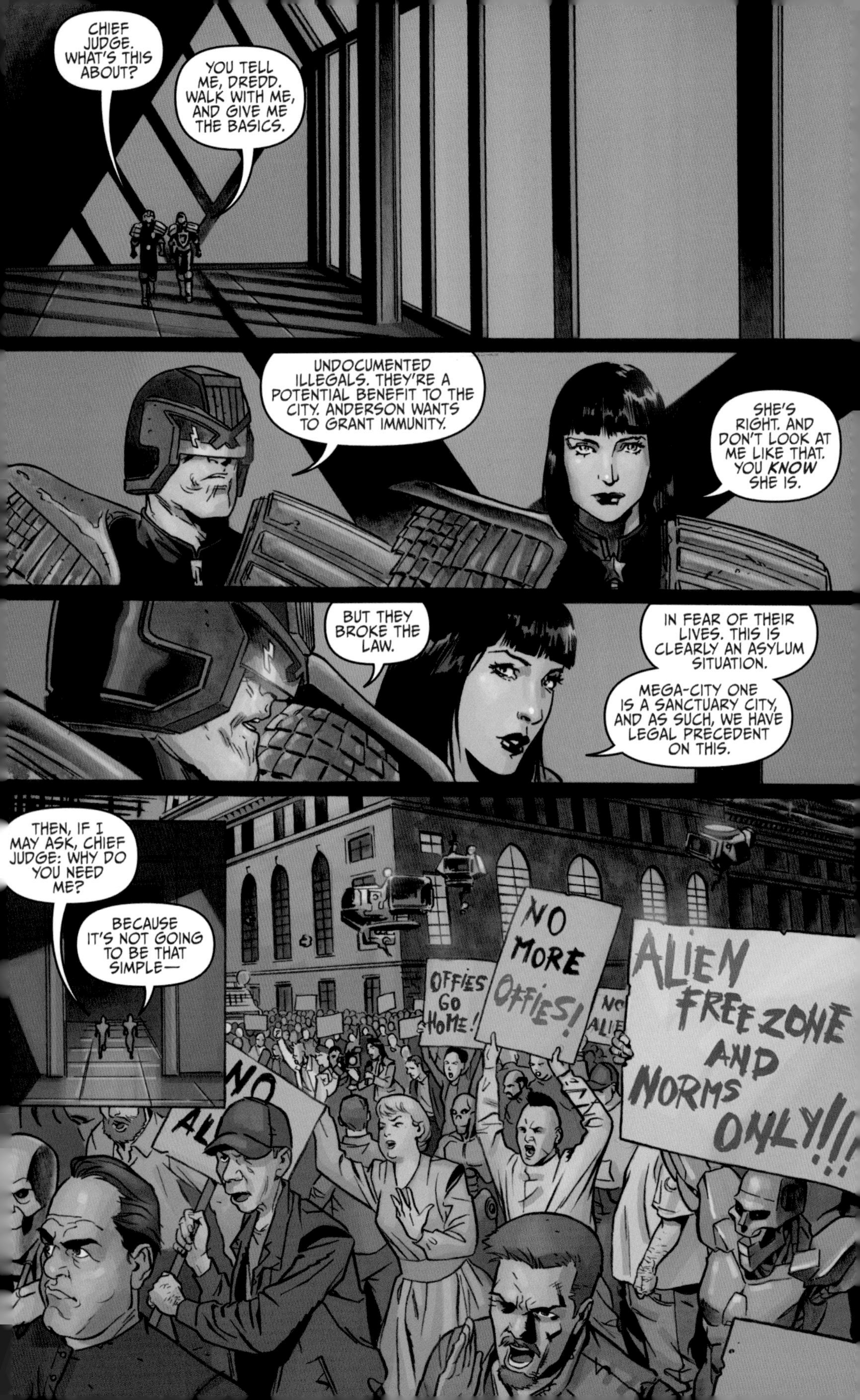
CHIEF JUDGE. WHAT'S THIS ABOUT?
YOU TELL ME, DREDD. WALK WITH ME, AND GIVE ME THE BASICS.
UNDOCUMENTED ILLEGALS. THEY'RE A POTENTIAL BENEFIT TO THE CITY. ANDERSON WANTS TO GRANT IMMUNITY.
SHE'S RIGHT. AND DON'T LOOK AT ME LIKE THAT. YOU *KNOW* SHE IS.
BUT THEY BROKE THE LAW.
IN FEAR OF THEIR LIVES. THIS IS CLEARLY AN ASYLUM SITUATION.
MEGA-CITY ONE IS A SANCTUARY CITY, AND AS SUCH, WE HAVE LEGAL PRECEDENT ON THIS.
THEN, IF I MAY ASK, CHIEF JUDGE: WHY DO YOU NEED ME?
BECAUSE IT'S NOT GOING TO BE THAT SIMPLE—
OFFIES GO HOME!
NO MORE OFFIES!
ALIEN FREE ZONE AND NORMS ONLY!!!

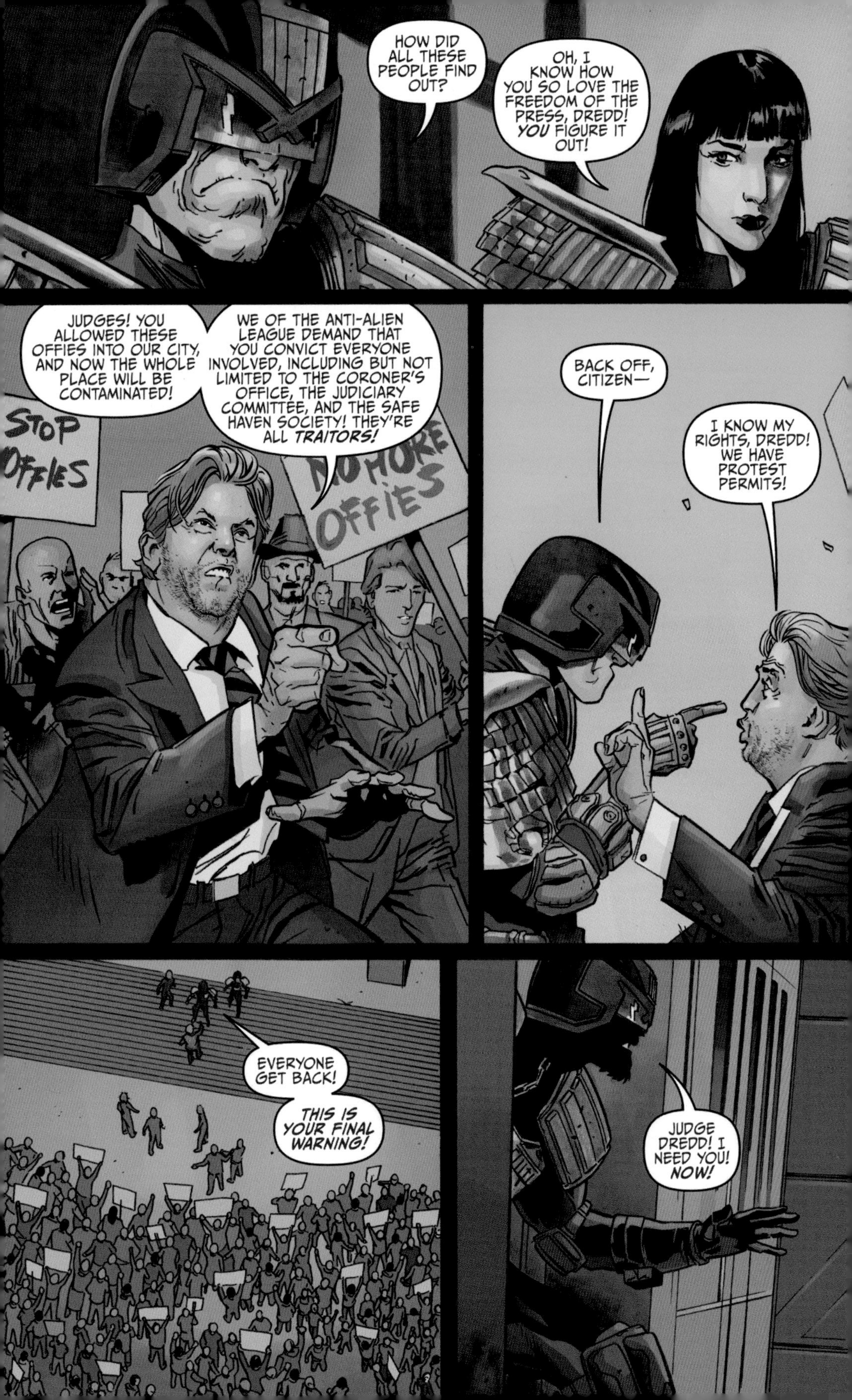

HOW DID ALL THESE PEOPLE FIND OUT?
OH, I KNOW HOW YOU SO LOVE THE FREEDOM OF THE PRESS, DREDD! *YOU* FIGURE IT OUT!
JUDGES! YOU ALLOWED THESE OFFIES INTO OUR CITY, AND NOW THE WHOLE PLACE WILL BE CONTAMINATED!
WE OF THE ANTI-ALIEN LEAGUE DEMAND THAT YOU CONVICT EVERYONE INVOLVED, INCLUDING BUT NOT LIMITED TO THE CORONER'S OFFICE, THE JUDICIARY COMMITTEE, AND THE SAFE HAVEN SOCIETY! THEY'RE ALL *TRAITORS!*
STOP OFFIES
NO MORE OFFIES
BACK OFF, CITIZEN—
I KNOW MY RIGHTS, DREDD! WE HAVE PROTEST PERMITS!
EVERYONE GET BACK!
THIS IS YOUR FINAL WARNING!
JUDGE DREDD! I NEED YOU! *NOW!*

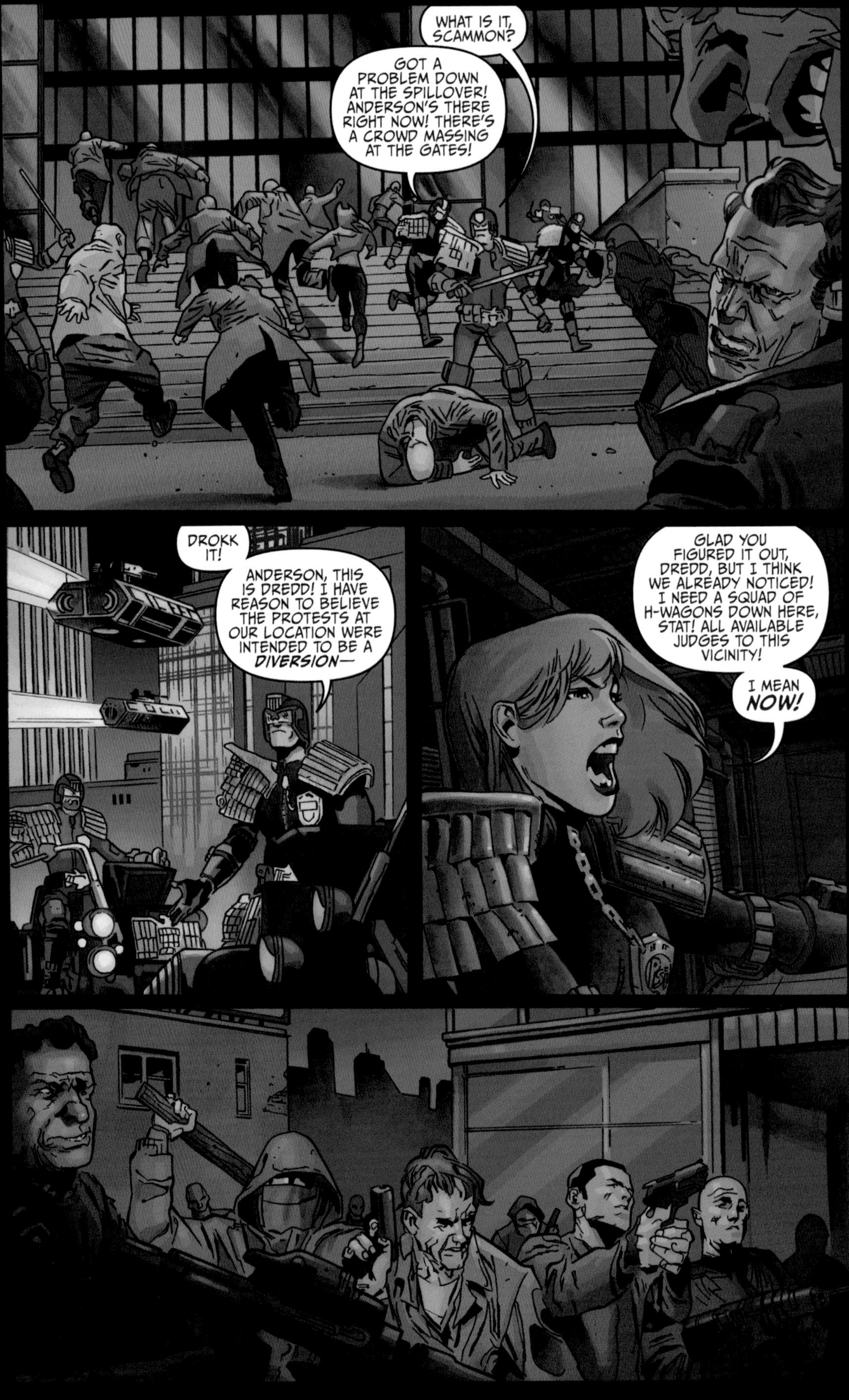
WHAT IS IT, SCAMMON?
GOT A PROBLEM DOWN AT THE SPILLOVER! ANDERSON'S THERE RIGHT NOW! THERE'S A CROWD MASSING AT THE GATES!
DROKK IT!
ANDERSON, THIS IS DREDD! I HAVE REASON TO BELIEVE THE PROTESTS AT OUR LOCATION WERE INTENDED TO BE A DIVERSION—
GLAD YOU FIGURED IT OUT, DREDD, BUT I THINK WE ALREADY NOTICED! I NEED A SQUAD OF H-WAGONS DOWN HERE, STAT! ALL AVAILABLE JUDGES TO THIS VICINITY!
I MEAN NOW!

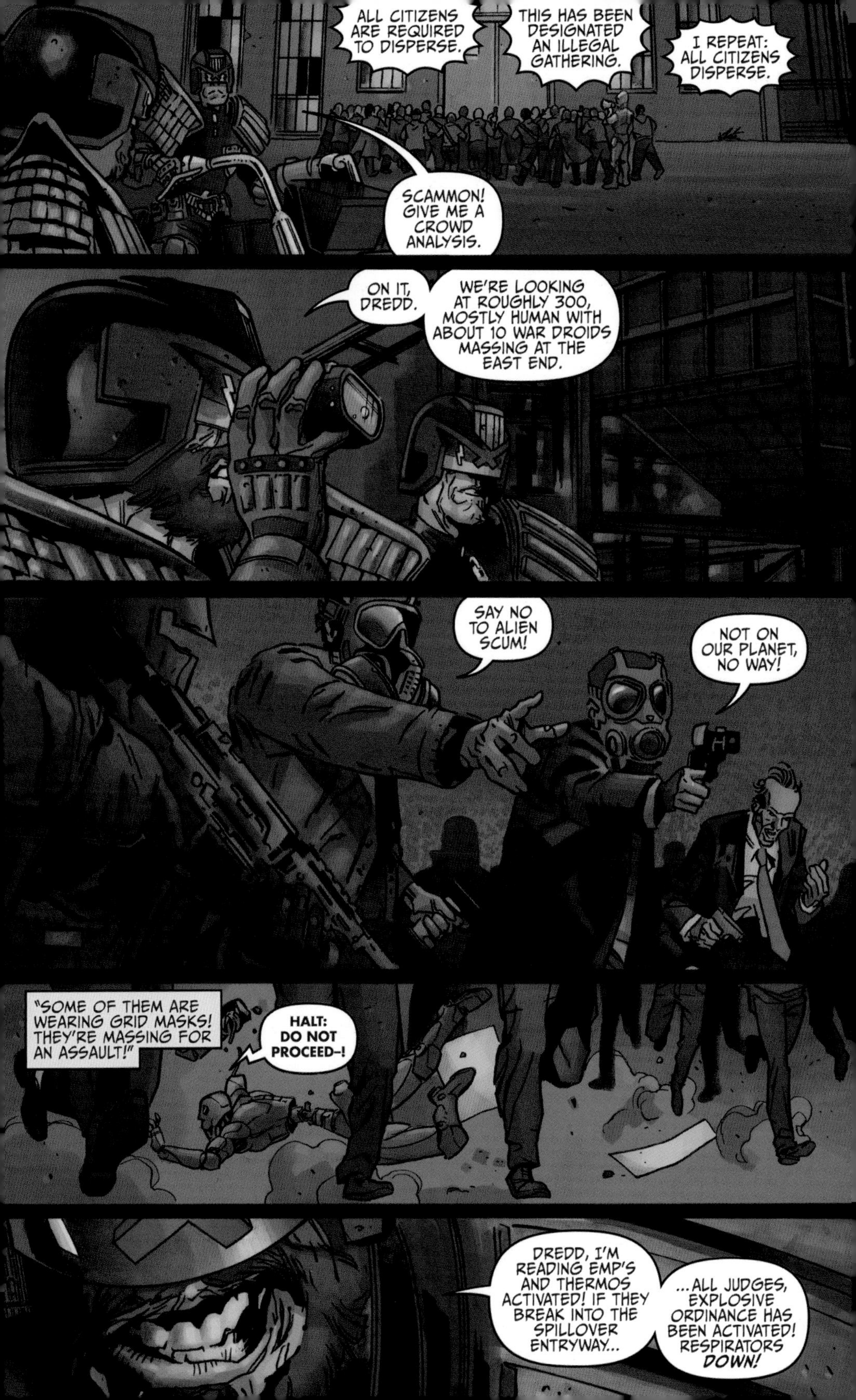
ALL CITIZENS ARE REQUIRED TO DISPERSE.
THIS HAS BEEN DESIGNATED AN ILLEGAL GATHERING.
I REPEAT: ALL CITIZENS DISPERSE.
SCAMMON! GIVE ME A CROWD ANALYSIS.
ON IT, DREDD.
WE'RE LOOKING AT ROUGHLY 300, MOSTLY HUMAN WITH ABOUT 10 WAR DROIDS MASSING AT THE EAST END.
SAY NO TO ALIEN SCUM!
NOT ON OUR PLANET, NO WAY!
"SOME OF THEM ARE WEARING GRID MASKS! THEY'RE MASSING FOR AN ASSAULT!"
HALT: DO NOT PROCEED-!
DREDD, I'M READING EMP'S AND THERMOS ACTIVATED! IF THEY BREAK INTO THE SPILLOVER ENTRYWAY...
...ALL JUDGES, EXPLOSIVE ORDINANCE HAS BEEN ACTIVATED! RESPIRATORS DOWN!

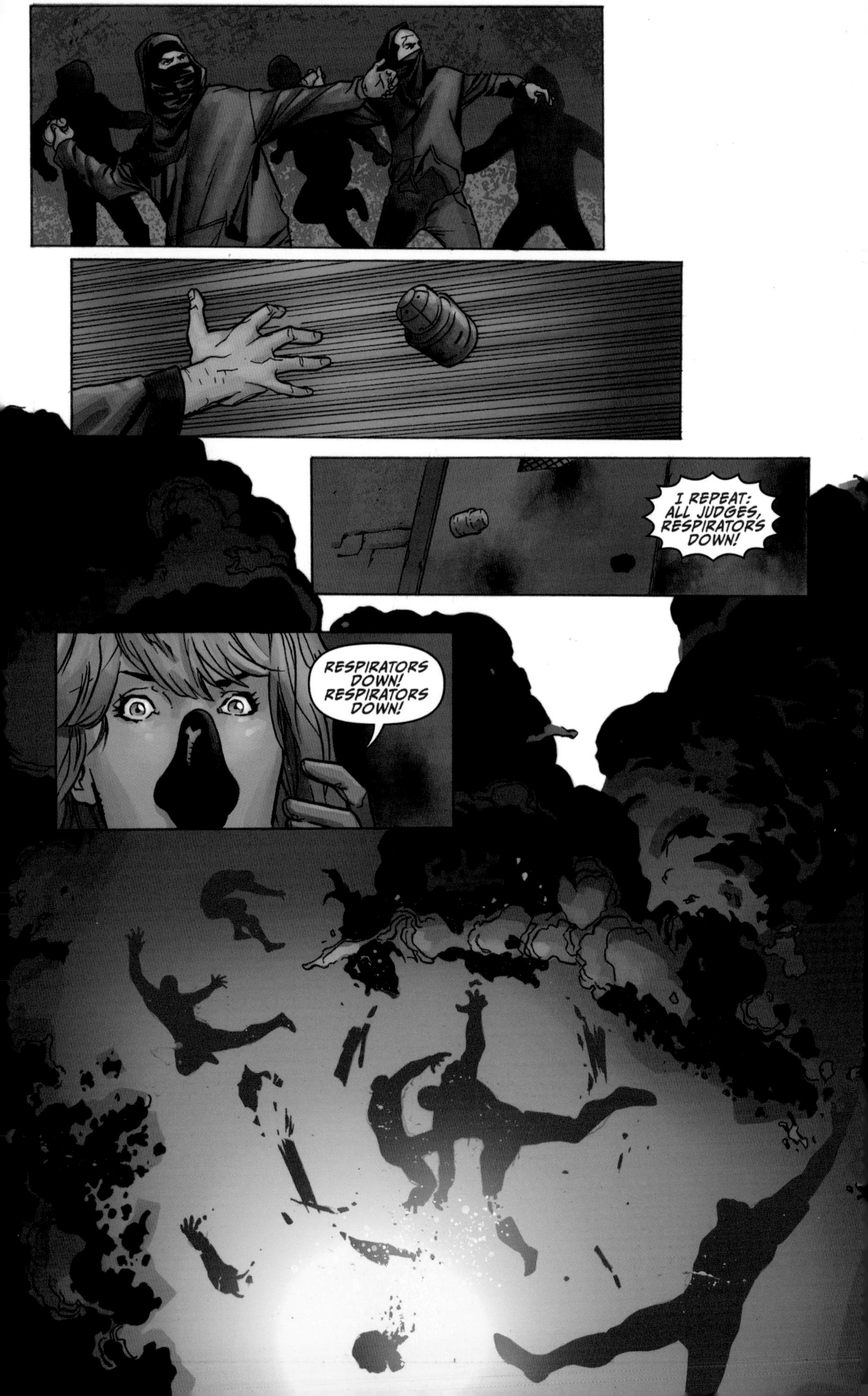
I REPEAT: ALL JUDGES, RESPIRATORS DOWN!
RESPIRATORS DOWN! RESPIRATORS DOWN!

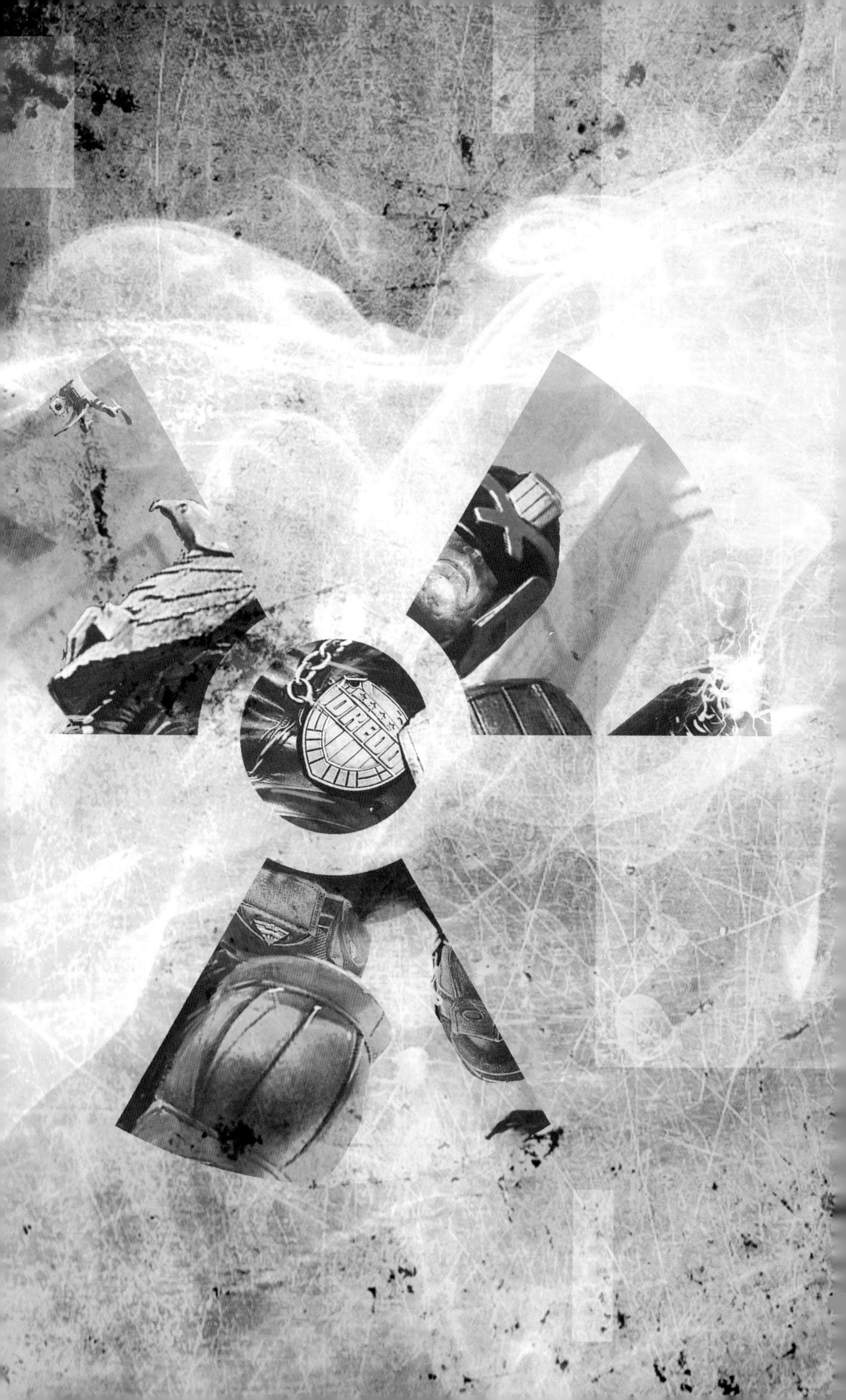
DREDD

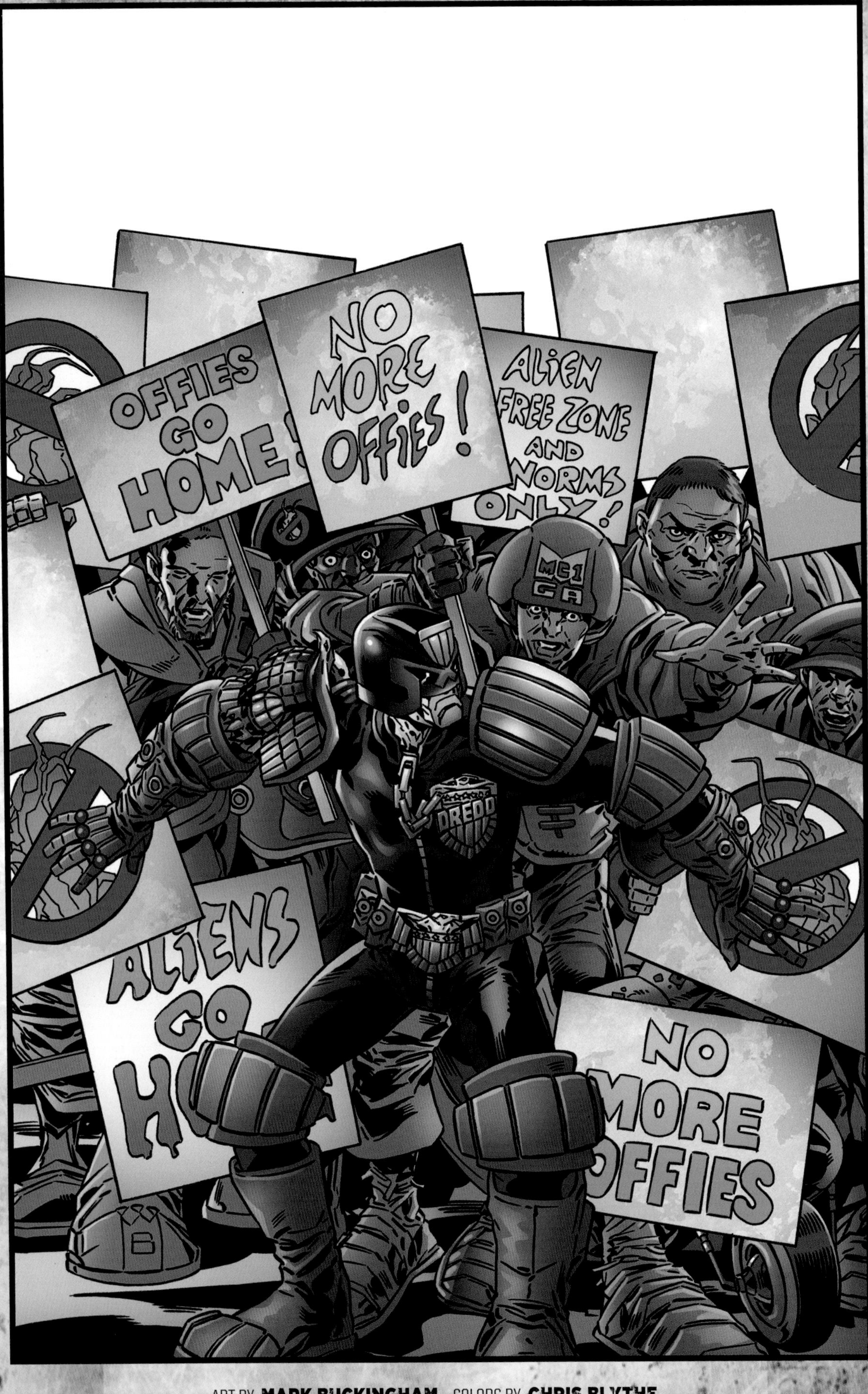

OFFIES GO HOME!
NO MORE OFFIES!
ALIEN FREE ZONE AND NORMS ONLY!
MC1 GA
DREDD
ALIENS GO HO
NO MORE OFFIES

ART BY **MARK BUCKINGHAM** COLORS BY **CHRIS BLYTHE**

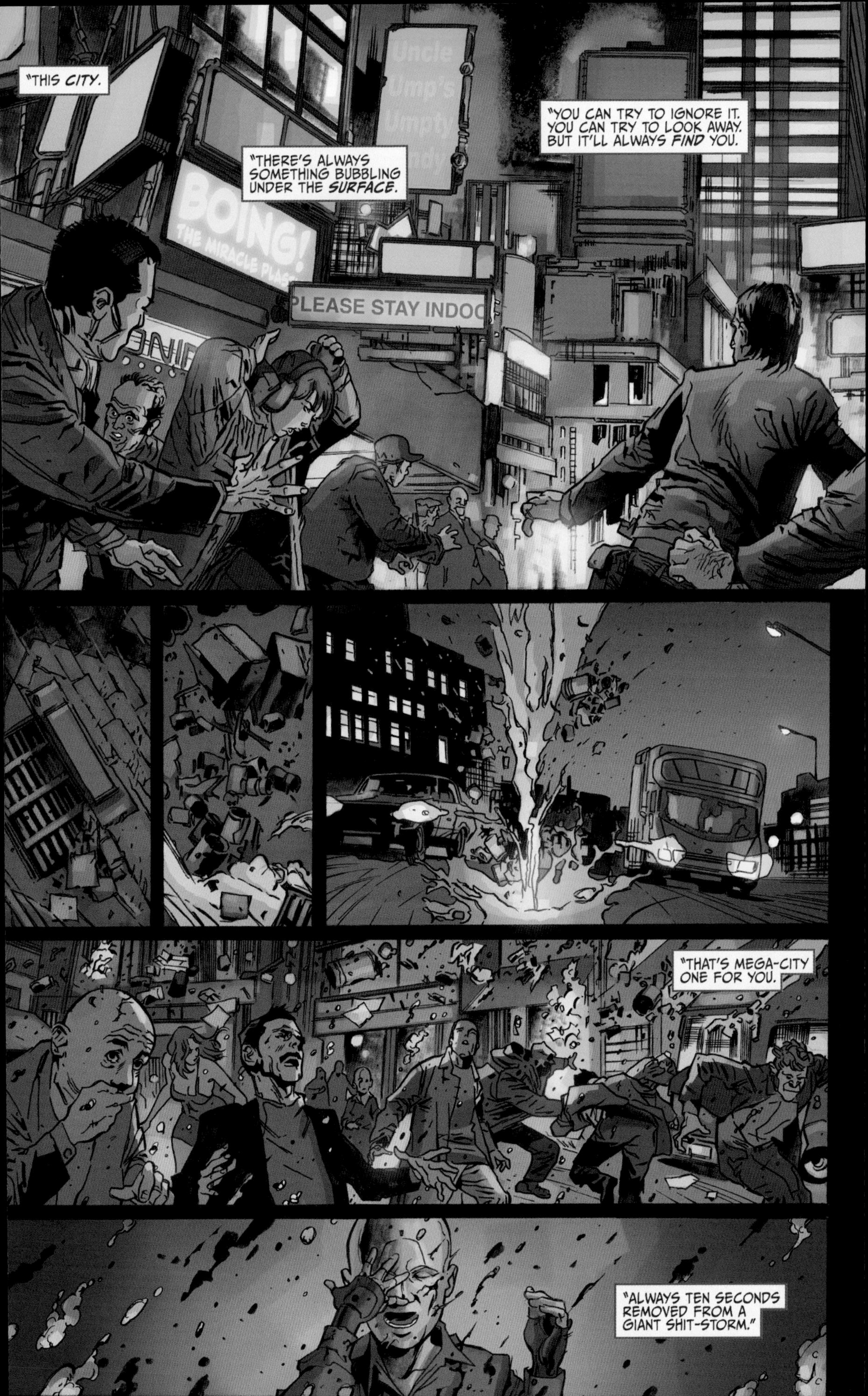
"THIS CITY.
"THERE'S ALWAYS SOMETHING BUBBLING UNDER THE SURFACE.
"YOU CAN TRY TO IGNORE IT. YOU CAN TRY TO LOOK AWAY. BUT IT'LL ALWAYS FIND YOU.
Uncle Ump's Umpty
BOING!
"THAT'S MEGA-CITY ONE FOR YOU.
"ALWAYS TEN SECONDS REMOVED FROM A GIANT SHIT-STORM."

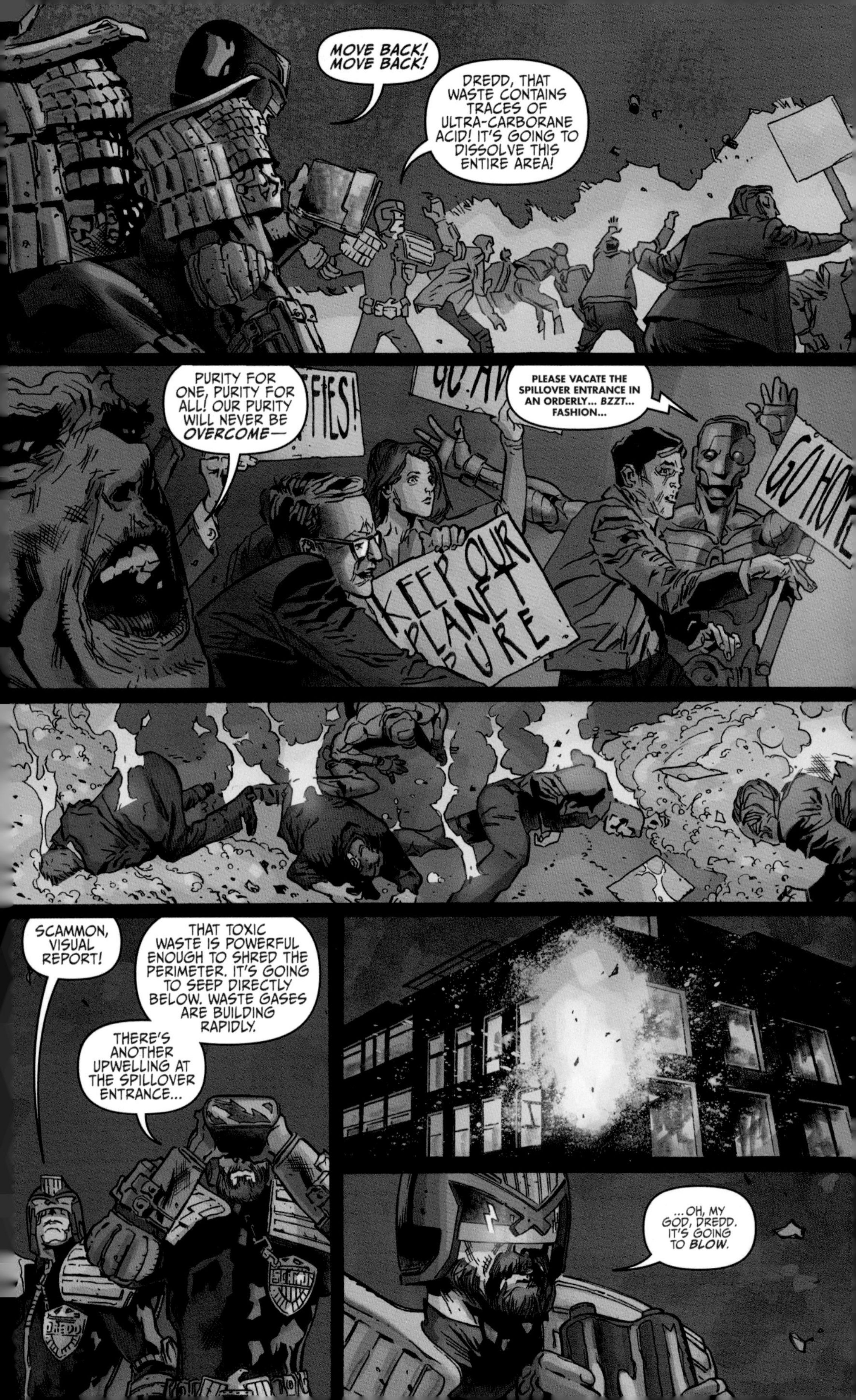
MOVE BACK! MOVE BACK!
DREDD, THAT WASTE CONTAINS TRACES OF ULTRA-CARBORANE ACID! IT'S GOING TO DISSOLVE THIS ENTIRE AREA!
PURITY FOR ONE, PURITY FOR ALL! OUR PURITY WILL NEVER BE *OVERCOME*—
PLEASE VACATE THE SPILLOVER ENTRANCE IN AN ORDERLY... *BZZT*... FASHION...
KEEP OUR PLANET PURE
GO HOME
SCAMMON, VISUAL REPORT!
THAT TOXIC WASTE IS POWERFUL ENOUGH TO SHRED THE PERIMETER. IT'S GOING TO SEEP DIRECTLY BELOW. WASTE GASES ARE BUILDING RAPIDLY.
THERE'S ANOTHER UPWELLING AT THE SPILLOVER ENTRANCE...
...OH, MY GOD, DREDD. IT'S GOING TO *BLOW*.

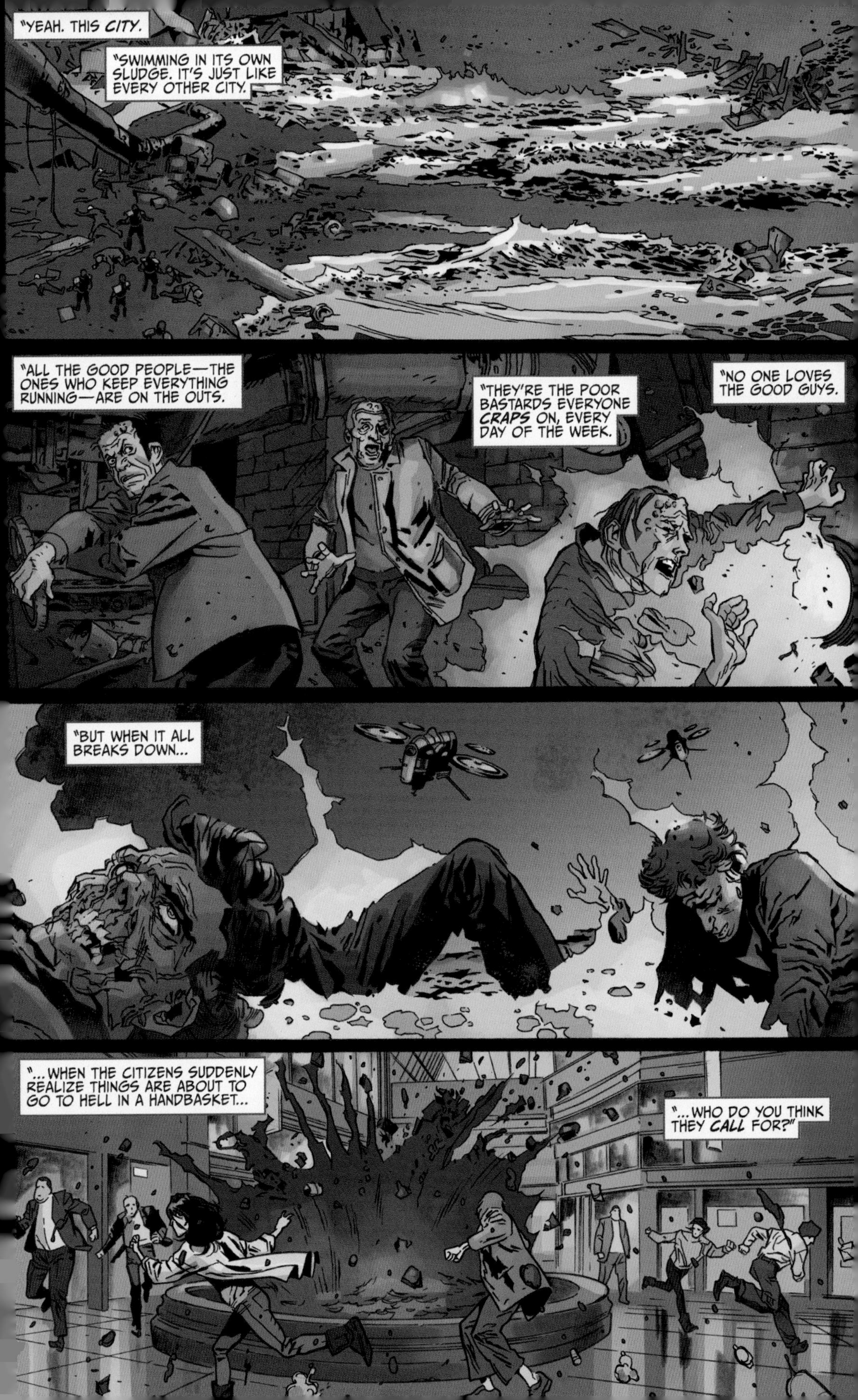
"YEAH. THIS CITY.
"SWIMMING IN ITS OWN SLUDGE. IT'S JUST LIKE EVERY OTHER CITY.
"ALL THE GOOD PEOPLE—THE ONES WHO KEEP EVERYTHING RUNNING—ARE ON THE OUTS.
"THEY'RE THE POOR BASTARDS EVERYONE CRAPS ON, EVERY DAY OF THE WEEK.
"NO ONE LOVES THE GOOD GUYS.
"BUT WHEN IT ALL BREAKS DOWN...
"...WHEN THE CITIZENS SUDDENLY REALIZE THINGS ARE ABOUT TO GO TO HELL IN A HANDBASKET...
"...WHO DO YOU THINK THEY CALL FOR?"

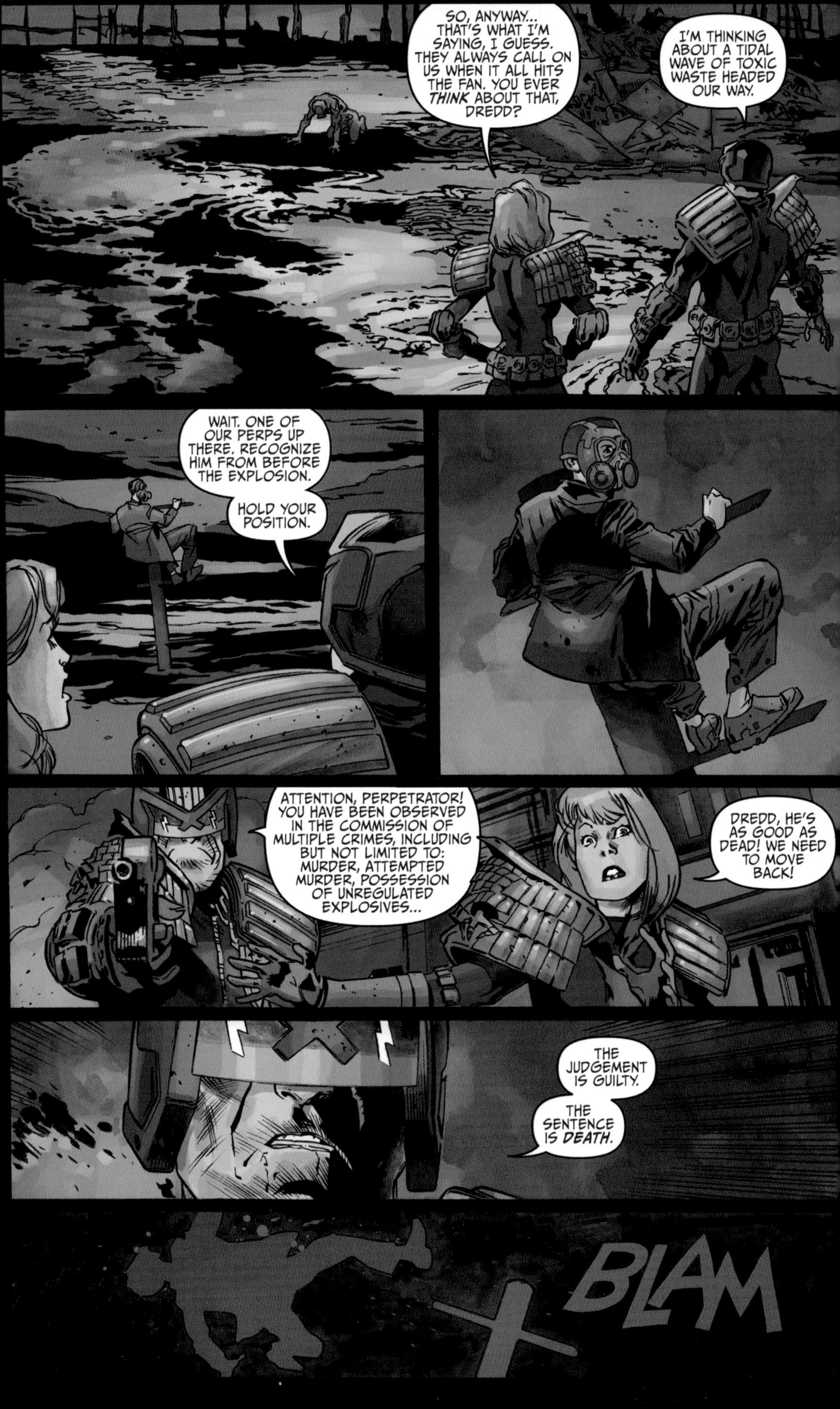
SO, ANYWAY... THAT'S WHAT I'M SAYING, I GUESS. THEY ALWAYS CALL ON US WHEN IT ALL HITS THE FAN. YOU EVER *THINK* ABOUT THAT, DREDD?
I'M THINKING ABOUT A TIDAL WAVE OF TOXIC WASTE HEADED OUR WAY.
WAIT. ONE OF OUR PERPS UP THERE. RECOGNIZE HIM FROM BEFORE THE EXPLOSION.
HOLD YOUR POSITION.
ATTENTION, PERPETRATOR! YOU HAVE BEEN OBSERVED IN THE COMMISSION OF MULTIPLE CRIMES, INCLUDING BUT NOT LIMITED TO: MURDER, ATTEMPTED MURDER, POSSESSION OF UNREGULATED EXPLOSIVES...
DREDD, HE'S AS GOOD AS DEAD! WE NEED TO MOVE BACK!
THE JUDGEMENT IS GUILTY.
THE SENTENCE IS *DEATH*.
BLAM

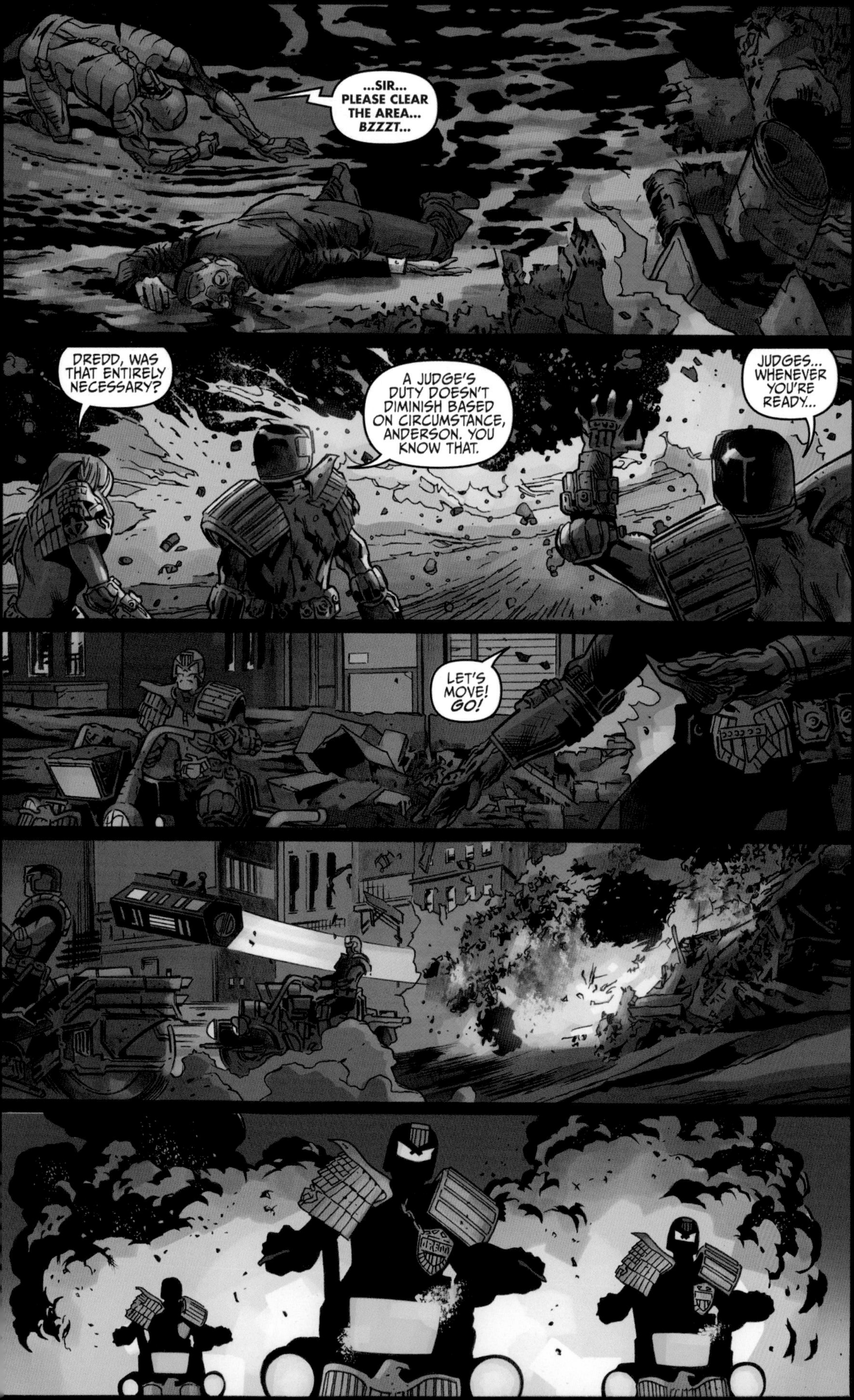
...SIR... PLEASE CLEAR THE AREA... BZZZT...
DREDD, WAS THAT ENTIRELY NECESSARY?
A JUDGE'S DUTY DOESN'T DIMINISH BASED ON CIRCUMSTANCE, ANDERSON. YOU KNOW THAT.
JUDGES... WHENEVER YOU'RE READY...
LET'S MOVE! GO!

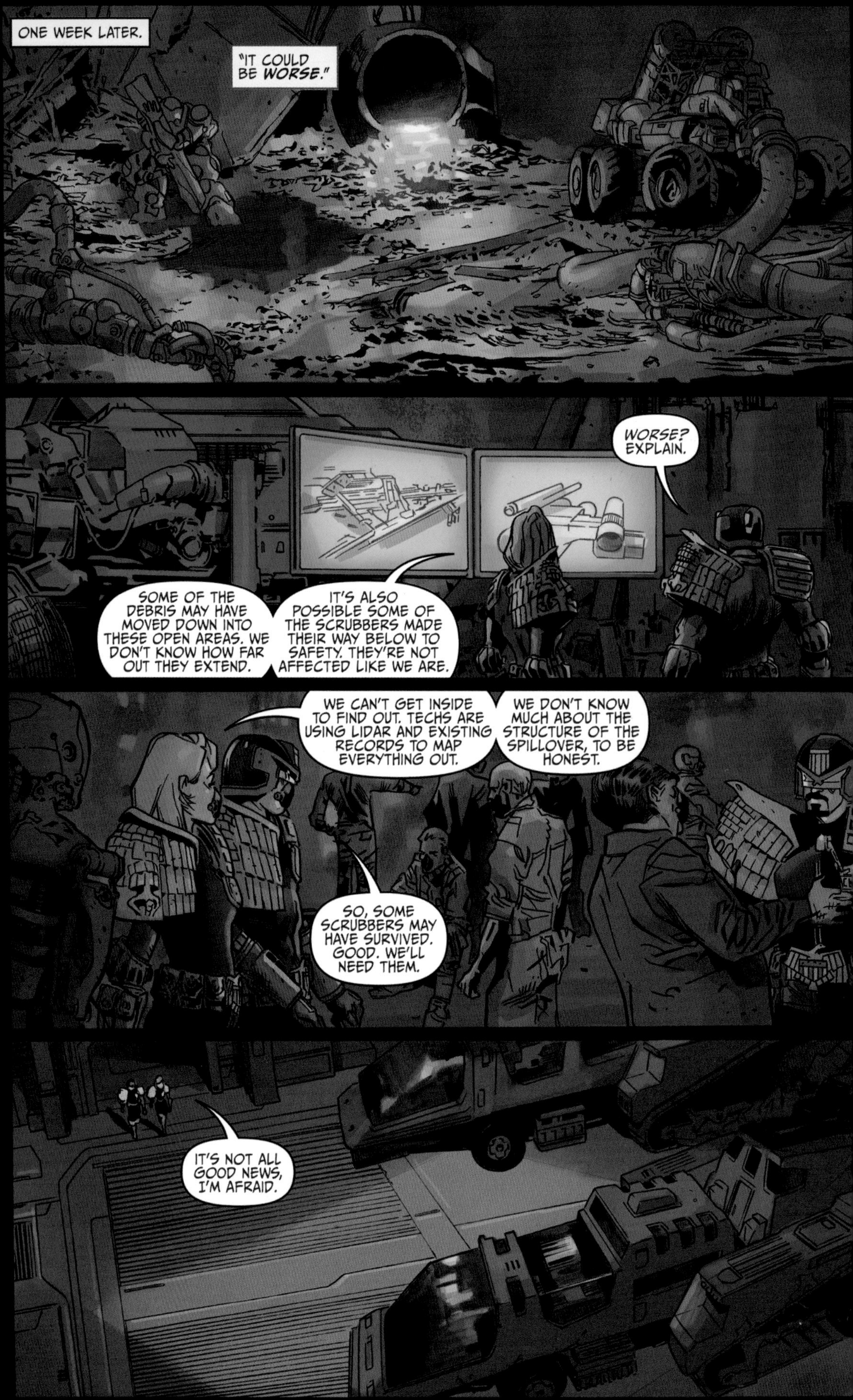

ONE WEEK LATER.
"IT COULD BE WORSE."
WORSE? EXPLAIN.
SOME OF THE DEBRIS MAY HAVE MOVED DOWN INTO THESE OPEN AREAS. WE DON'T KNOW HOW FAR OUT THEY EXTEND.
IT'S ALSO POSSIBLE SOME OF THE SCRUBBERS MADE THEIR WAY BELOW TO SAFETY. THEY'RE NOT AFFECTED LIKE WE ARE.
WE CAN'T GET INSIDE TO FIND OUT. TECHS ARE USING LIDAR AND EXISTING RECORDS TO MAP EVERYTHING OUT.
WE DON'T KNOW MUCH ABOUT THE STRUCTURE OF THE SPILLOVER, TO BE HONEST.
SO, SOME SCRUBBERS MAY HAVE SURVIVED. GOOD. WE'LL NEED THEM.
IT'S NOT ALL GOOD NEWS, I'M AFRAID.

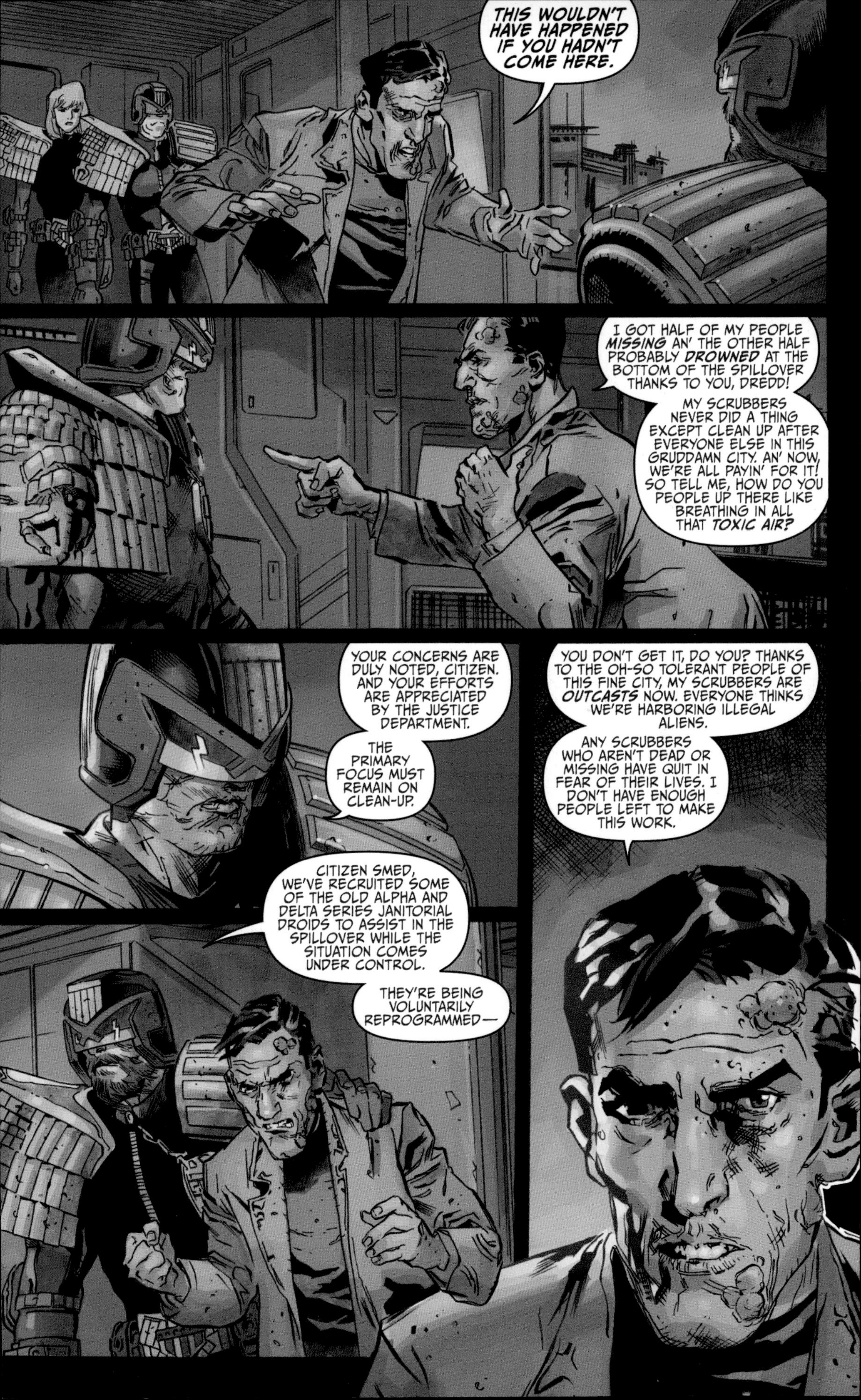
THIS WOULDN'T HAVE HAPPENED IF YOU HADN'T COME HERE.
I GOT HALF OF MY PEOPLE MISSING AN' THE OTHER HALF PROBABLY DROWNED AT THE BOTTOM OF THE SPILLOVER THANKS TO YOU, DREDD!
MY SCRUBBERS NEVER DID A THING EXCEPT CLEAN UP AFTER EVERYONE ELSE IN THIS GRUDDAMN CITY. AN' NOW, WE'RE ALL PAYIN' FOR IT! SO TELL ME, HOW DO YOU PEOPLE UP THERE LIKE BREATHING IN ALL THAT TOXIC AIR?
YOUR CONCERNS ARE DULY NOTED, CITIZEN. AND YOUR EFFORTS ARE APPRECIATED BY THE JUSTICE DEPARTMENT.
THE PRIMARY FOCUS MUST REMAIN ON CLEAN-UP.
YOU DON'T GET IT, DO YOU? THANKS TO THE OH-SO TOLERANT PEOPLE OF THIS FINE CITY, MY SCRUBBERS ARE OUTCASTS NOW. EVERYONE THINKS WE'RE HARBORING ILLEGAL ALIENS.
ANY SCRUBBERS WHO AREN'T DEAD OR MISSING HAVE QUIT IN FEAR OF THEIR LIVES. I DON'T HAVE ENOUGH PEOPLE LEFT TO MAKE THIS WORK.
CITIZEN SMED, WE'VE RECRUITED SOME OF THE OLD ALPHA AND DELTA SERIES JANITORIAL DROIDS TO ASSIST IN THE SPILLOVER WHILE THE SITUATION COMES UNDER CONTROL.
THEY'RE BEING VOLUNTARILY REPROGRAMMED—

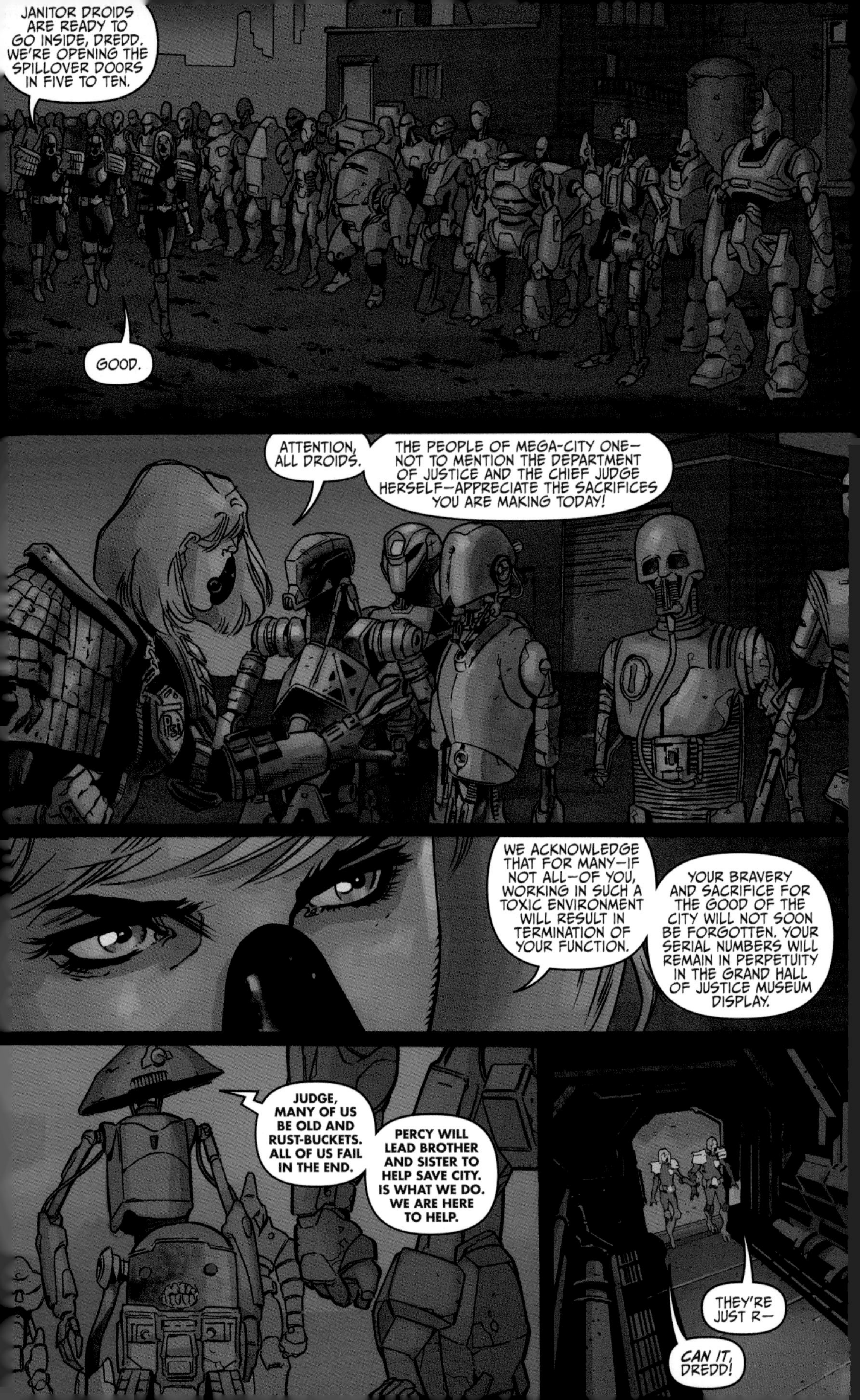
JANITOR DROIDS ARE READY TO GO INSIDE, DREDD. WE'RE OPENING THE SPILLOVER DOORS IN FIVE TO TEN.
GOOD.
ATTENTION, ALL DROIDS.
THE PEOPLE OF MEGA-CITY ONE—NOT TO MENTION THE DEPARTMENT OF JUSTICE AND THE CHIEF JUDGE HERSELF—APPRECIATE THE SACRIFICES YOU ARE MAKING TODAY!
WE ACKNOWLEDGE THAT FOR MANY—IF NOT ALL—OF YOU, WORKING IN SUCH A TOXIC ENVIRONMENT WILL RESULT IN TERMINATION OF YOUR FUNCTION.
YOUR BRAVERY AND SACRIFICE FOR THE GOOD OF THE CITY WILL NOT SOON BE FORGOTTEN. YOUR SERIAL NUMBERS WILL REMAIN IN PERPETUITY IN THE GRAND HALL OF JUSTICE MUSEUM DISPLAY.
JUDGE, MANY OF US BE OLD AND RUST-BUCKETS. ALL OF US FAIL IN THE END.
PERCY WILL LEAD BROTHER AND SISTER TO HELP SAVE CITY. IS WHAT WE DO. WE ARE HERE TO HELP.
THEY'RE JUST R—
CAN IT, DREDD!

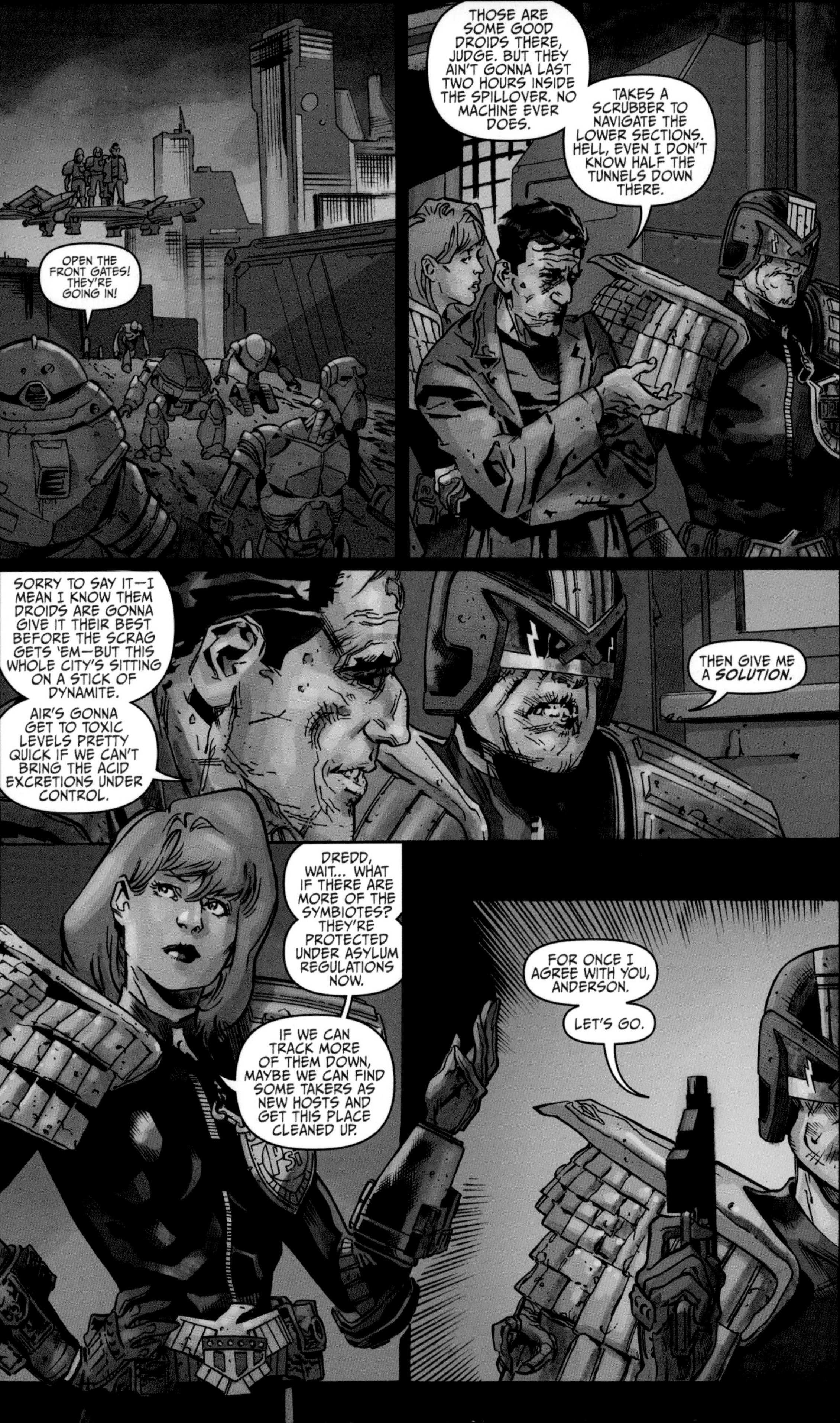
OPEN THE FRONT GATES! THEY'RE GOING IN!
THOSE ARE SOME GOOD DROIDS THERE, JUDGE. BUT THEY AIN'T GONNA LAST TWO HOURS INSIDE THE SPILLOVER. NO MACHINE EVER DOES.
TAKES A SCRUBBER TO NAVIGATE THE LOWER SECTIONS. HELL, EVEN I DON'T KNOW HALF THE TUNNELS DOWN THERE.
SORRY TO SAY IT—I MEAN I KNOW THEM DROIDS ARE GONNA GIVE IT THEIR BEST BEFORE THE SCRAG GETS 'EM—BUT THIS WHOLE CITY'S SITTING ON A STICK OF DYNAMITE.
AIR'S GONNA GET TO TOXIC LEVELS PRETTY QUICK IF WE CAN'T BRING THE ACID EXCRETIONS UNDER CONTROL.
THEN GIVE ME A *SOLUTION*.
DREDD, WAIT... WHAT IF THERE ARE MORE OF THE SYMBIOTES? THEY'RE PROTECTED UNDER ASYLUM REGULATIONS NOW.
IF WE CAN TRACK MORE OF THEM DOWN, MAYBE WE CAN FIND SOME TAKERS AS NEW HOSTS AND GET THIS PLACE CLEANED UP.
FOR ONCE I AGREE WITH YOU, ANDERSON.
LET'S GO.

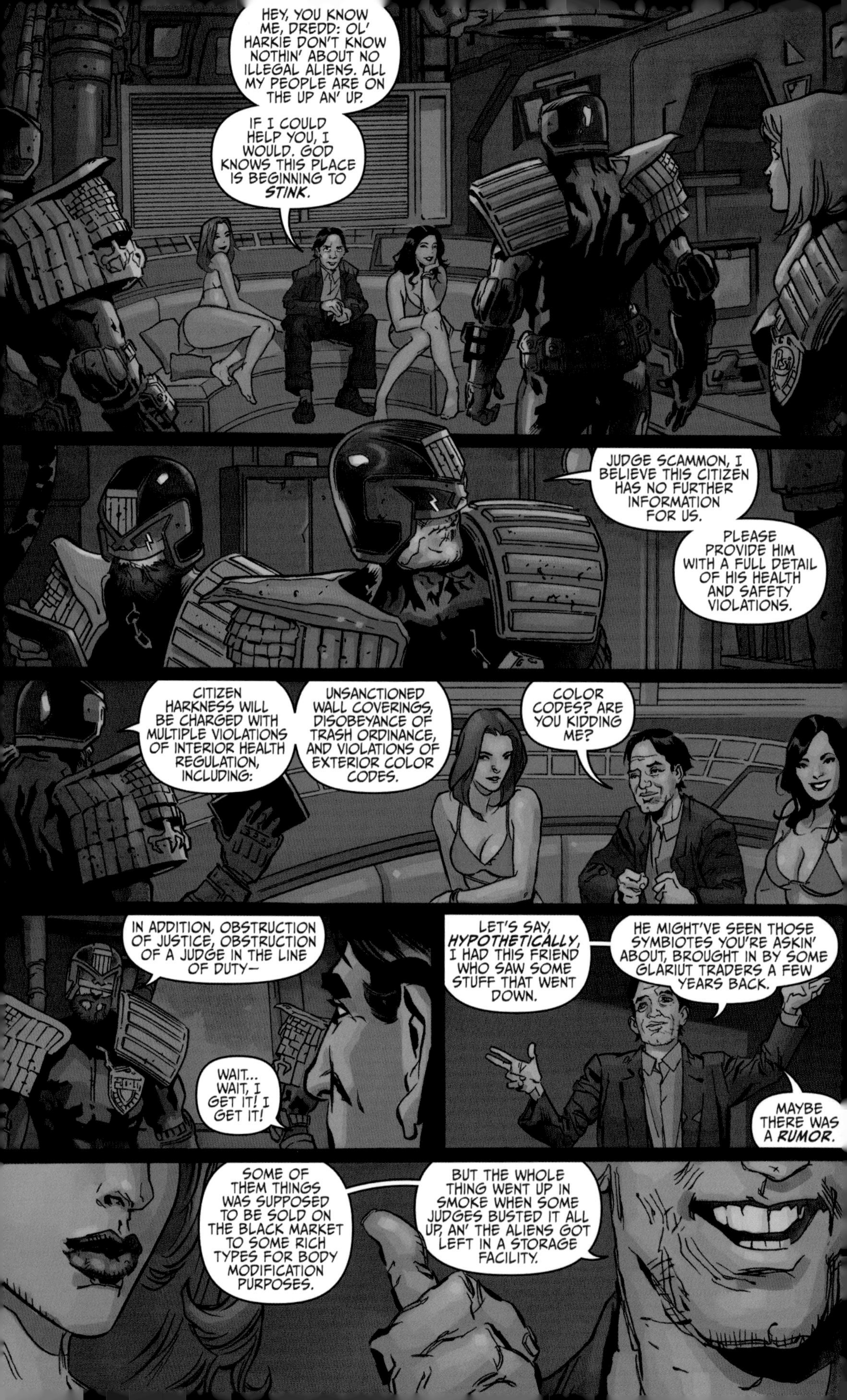
HEY, YOU KNOW ME, DREDD: OL' HARKIE DON'T KNOW NOTHIN' ABOUT NO ILLEGAL ALIENS. ALL MY PEOPLE ARE ON THE UP AN' UP.
IF I COULD HELP YOU, I WOULD. GOD KNOWS THIS PLACE IS BEGINNING TO *STINK*.
JUDGE SCAMMON, I BELIEVE THIS CITIZEN HAS NO FURTHER INFORMATION FOR US.
PLEASE PROVIDE HIM WITH A FULL DETAIL OF HIS HEALTH AND SAFETY VIOLATIONS.
CITIZEN HARKNESS WILL BE CHARGED WITH MULTIPLE VIOLATIONS OF INTERIOR HEALTH REGULATION, INCLUDING:
UNSANCTIONED WALL COVERINGS, DISOBEYANCE OF TRASH ORDINANCE, AND VIOLATIONS OF EXTERIOR COLOR CODES.
COLOR CODES? ARE YOU KIDDING ME?
IN ADDITION, OBSTRUCTION OF JUSTICE, OBSTRUCTION OF A JUDGE IN THE LINE OF DUTY—
WAIT... WAIT, I GET IT! I GET IT!
LET'S SAY, ***HYPOTHETICALLY***, I HAD THIS FRIEND WHO SAW SOME STUFF THAT WENT DOWN.
HE MIGHT'VE SEEN THOSE SYMBIOTES YOU'RE ASKIN' ABOUT, BROUGHT IN BY SOME GLARIUT TRADERS A FEW YEARS BACK.
MAYBE THERE WAS A ***RUMOR***.
SOME OF THEM THINGS WAS SUPPOSED TO BE SOLD ON THE BLACK MARKET TO SOME RICH TYPES FOR BODY MODIFICATION PURPOSES.
BUT THE WHOLE THING WENT UP IN SMOKE WHEN SOME JUDGES BUSTED IT ALL UP, AN' THE ALIENS GOT LEFT IN A STORAGE FACILITY.

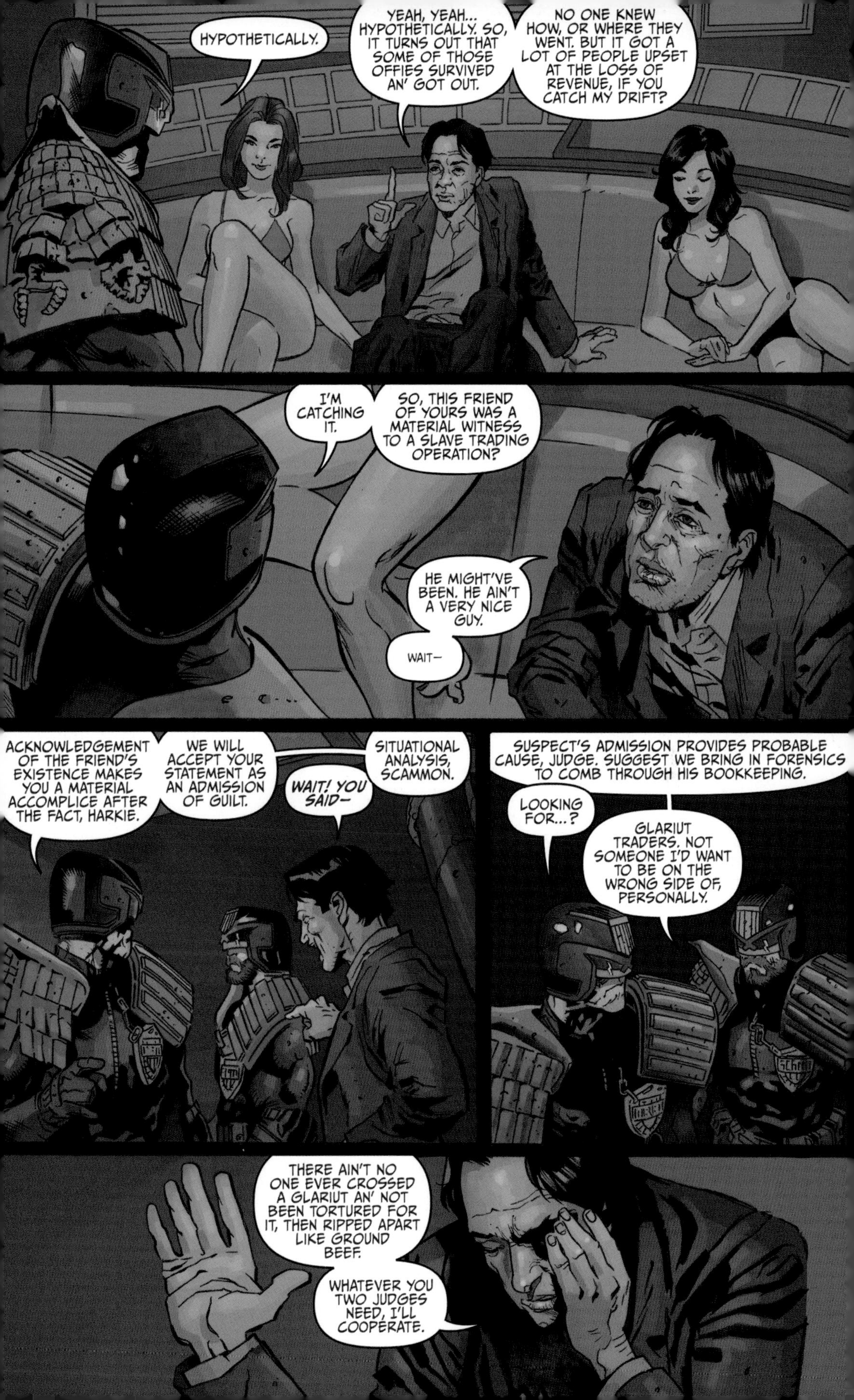
HYPOTHETICALLY.
YEAH, YEAH... HYPOTHETICALLY. SO, IT TURNS OUT THAT SOME OF THOSE OFFIES SURVIVED AN' GOT OUT.
NO ONE KNEW HOW, OR WHERE THEY WENT. BUT IT GOT A LOT OF PEOPLE UPSET AT THE LOSS OF REVENUE, IF YOU CATCH MY DRIFT?
I'M CATCHING IT.
SO, THIS FRIEND OF YOURS WAS A MATERIAL WITNESS TO A SLAVE TRADING OPERATION?
HE MIGHT'VE BEEN. HE AIN'T A VERY NICE GUY.
WAIT—
SITUATIONAL ANALYSIS, SCAMMON.
WE WILL ACCEPT YOUR STATEMENT AS AN ADMISSION OF GUILT.
ACKNOWLEDGEMENT OF THE FRIEND'S EXISTENCE MAKES YOU A MATERIAL ACCOMPLICE AFTER THE FACT, HARKIE.
WAIT! YOU SAID—
SUSPECT'S ADMISSION PROVIDES PROBABLE CAUSE, JUDGE. SUGGEST WE BRING IN FORENSICS TO COMB THROUGH HIS BOOKKEEPING.
LOOKING FOR...?
GLARIUT TRADERS. NOT SOMEONE I'D WANT TO BE ON THE WRONG SIDE OF, PERSONALLY.
THERE AIN'T NO ONE EVER CROSSED A GLARIUT AN' NOT BEEN TORTURED FOR IT, THEN RIPPED APART LIKE GROUND BEEF.
WHATEVER YOU TWO JUDGES NEED, I'LL COOPERATE.

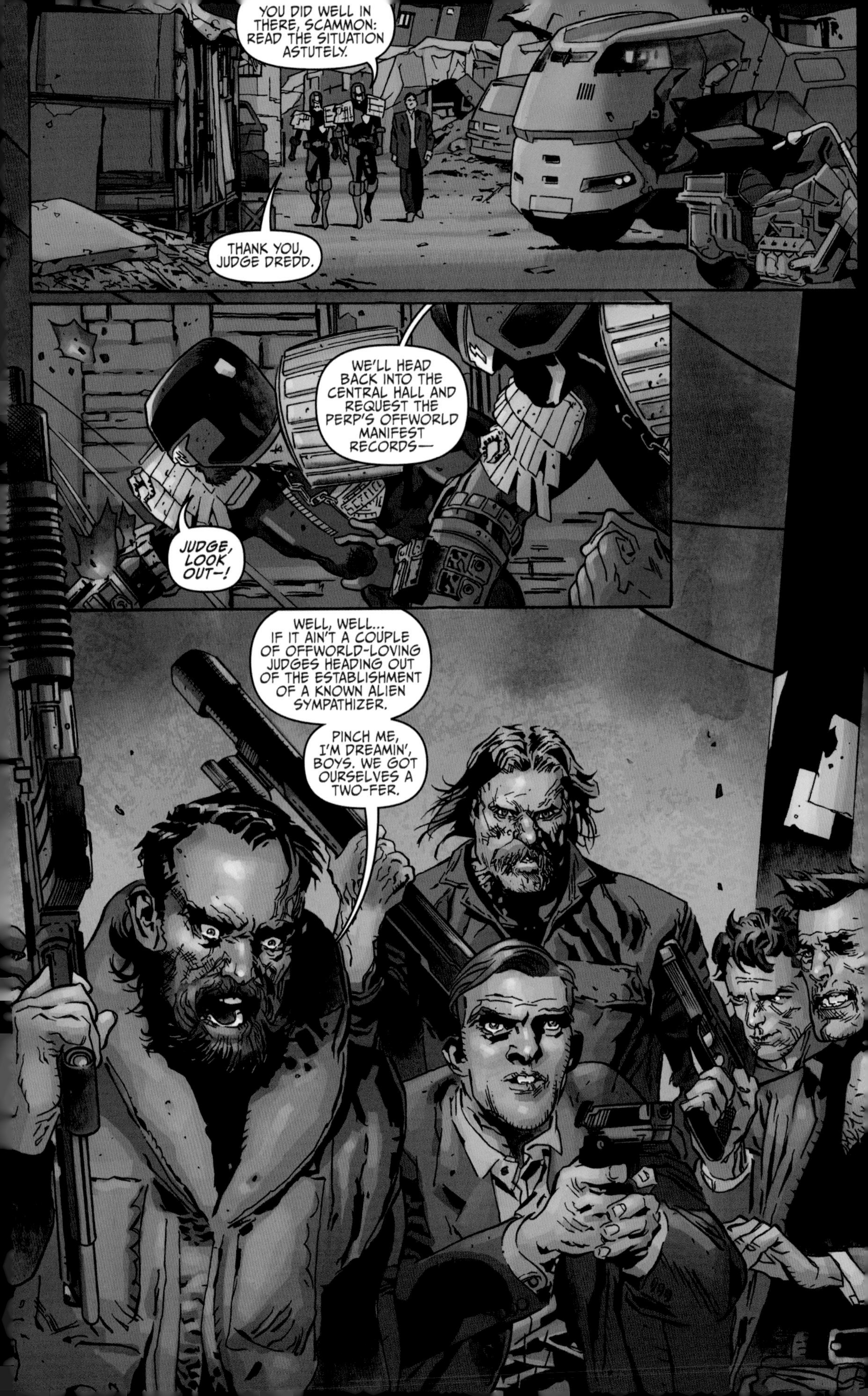
YOU DID WELL IN THERE, SCAMMON: READ THE SITUATION ASTUTELY.
THANK YOU, JUDGE DREDD.
WE'LL HEAD BACK INTO THE CENTRAL HALL AND REQUEST THE PERP'S OFFWORLD MANIFEST RECORDS—
JUDGE, LOOK OUT—!
WELL, WELL... IF IT AIN'T A COUPLE OF OFFWORLD-LOVING JUDGES HEADING OUT OF THE ESTABLISHMENT OF A KNOWN ALIEN SYMPATHIZER.
PINCH ME, I'M DREAMIN', BOYS. WE GOT OURSELVES A TWO-FER.

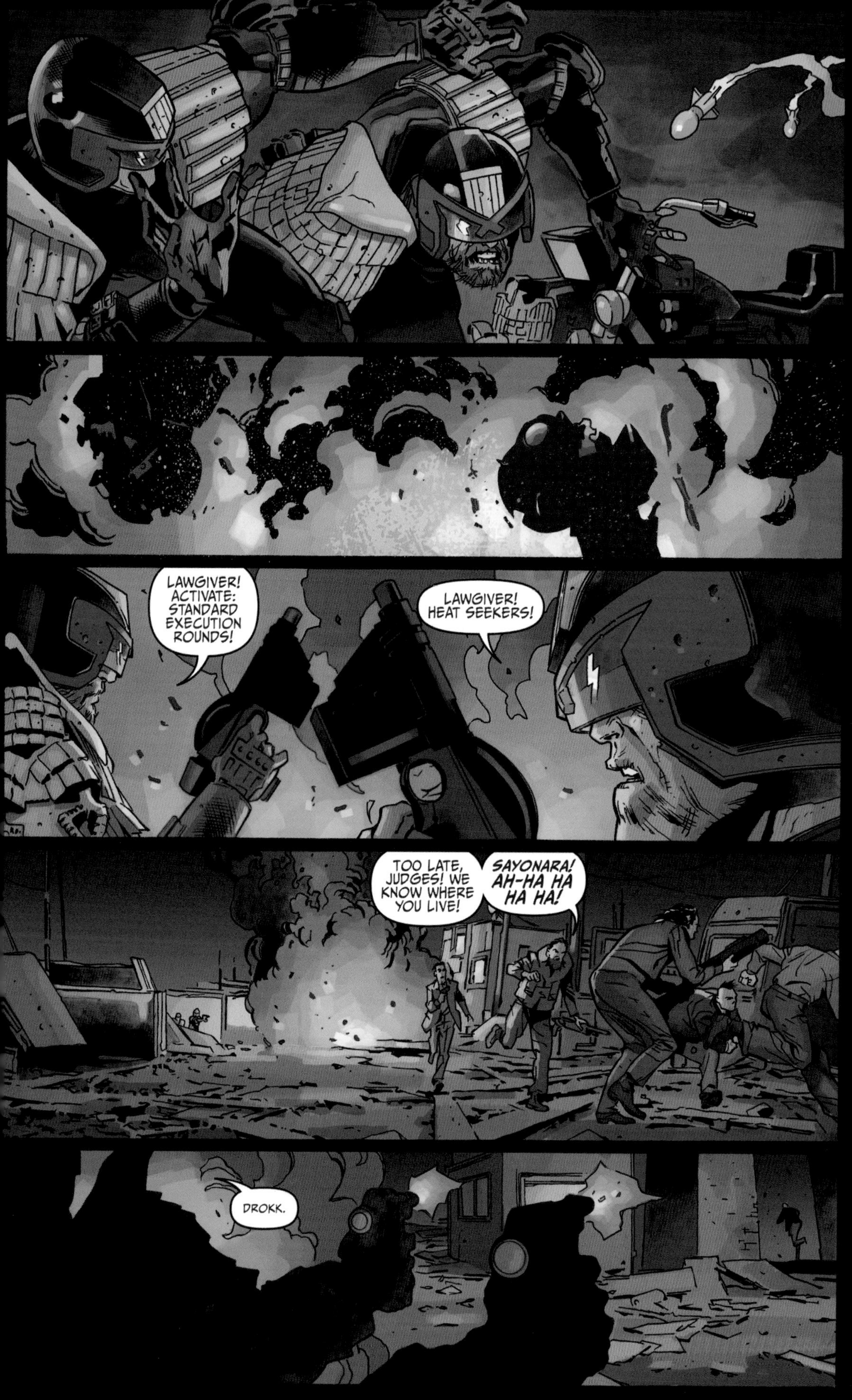

LAWGIVER! ACTIVATE: STANDARD EXECUTION ROUNDS!
LAWGIVER! HEAT SEEKERS!
TOO LATE, JUDGES! WE KNOW WHERE YOU LIVE!
SAYONARA! AH-HA HA HA HA!
DROKK.

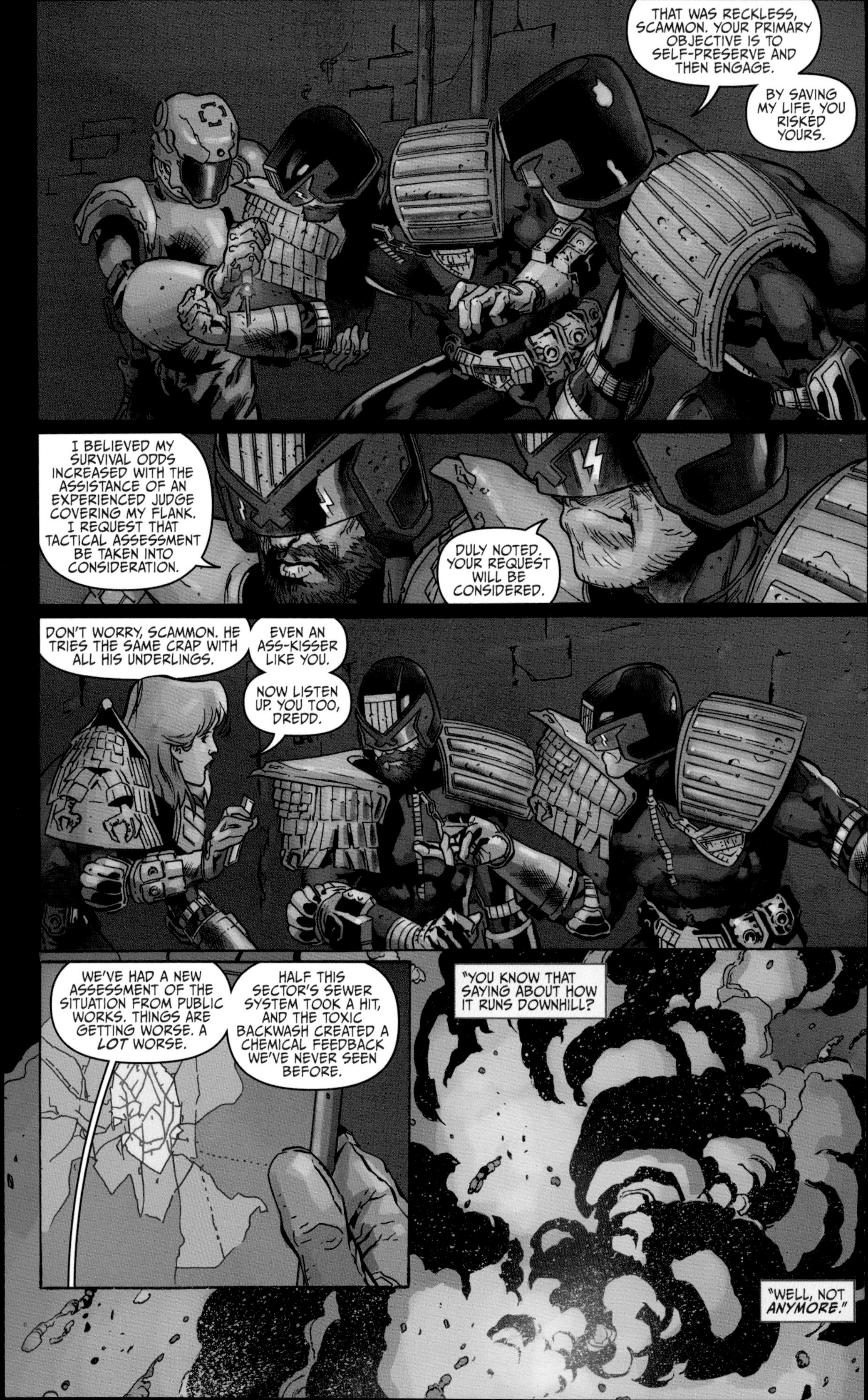
THAT WAS RECKLESS, SCAMMON. YOUR PRIMARY OBJECTIVE IS TO SELF-PRESERVE AND THEN ENGAGE.
BY SAVING MY LIFE, YOU RISKED YOURS.
I BELIEVED MY SURVIVAL ODDS INCREASED WITH THE ASSISTANCE OF AN EXPERIENCED JUDGE COVERING MY FLANK. I REQUEST THAT TACTICAL ASSESSMENT BE TAKEN INTO CONSIDERATION.
DULY NOTED. YOUR REQUEST WILL BE CONSIDERED.
DON'T WORRY, SCAMMON. HE TRIES THE SAME CRAP WITH ALL HIS UNDERLINGS.
EVEN AN ASS-KISSER LIKE YOU.
NOW LISTEN UP. YOU TOO, DREDD.
WE'VE HAD A NEW ASSESSMENT OF THE SITUATION FROM PUBLIC WORKS. THINGS ARE GETTING WORSE. A *LOT* WORSE.
HALF THIS SECTOR'S SEWER SYSTEM TOOK A HIT, AND THE TOXIC BACKWASH CREATED A CHEMICAL FEEDBACK WE'VE NEVER SEEN BEFORE.
"YOU KNOW THAT SAYING ABOUT HOW IT RUNS DOWNHILL?
"WELL, NOT *ANYMORE*."

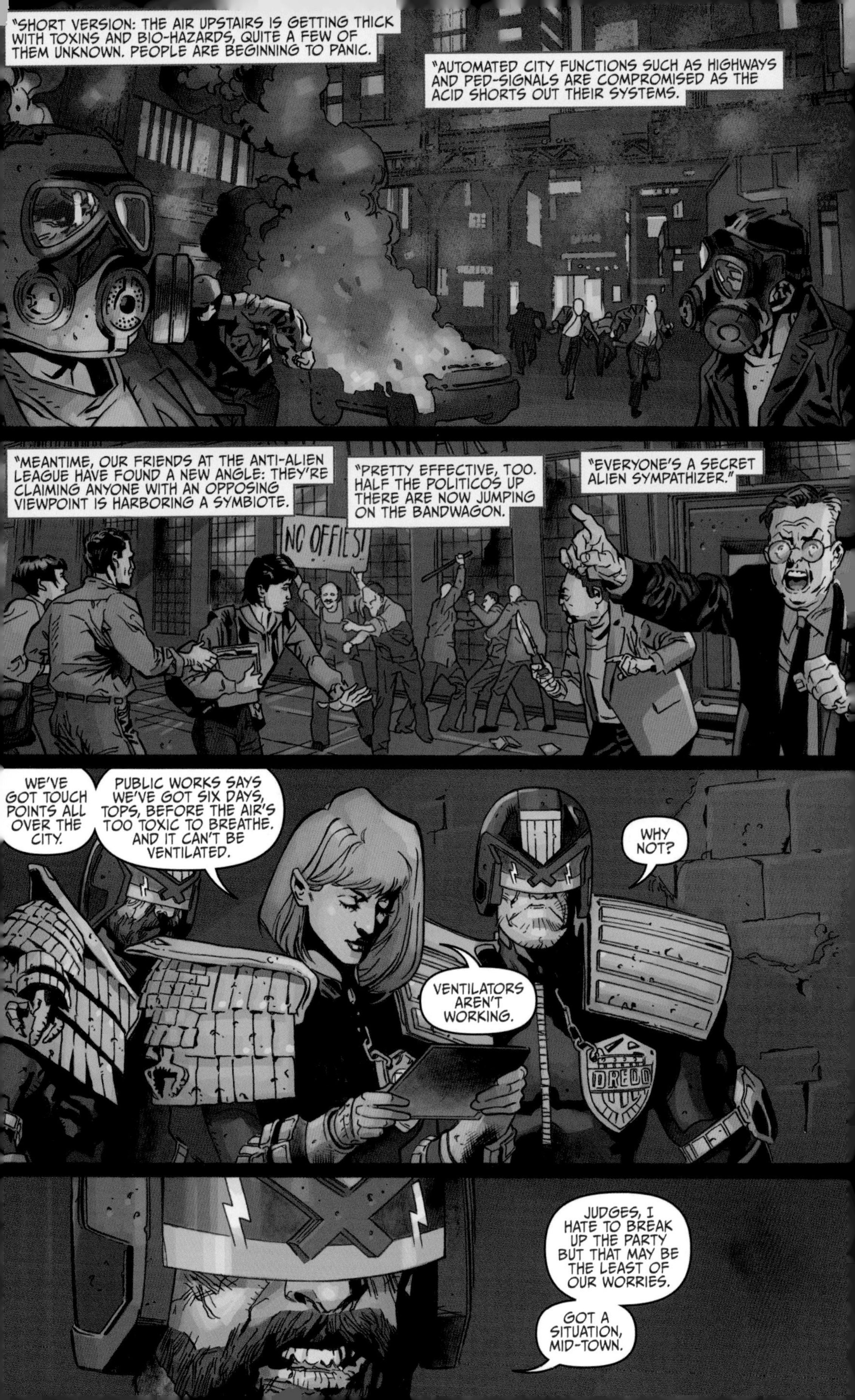
"SHORT VERSION: THE AIR UPSTAIRS IS GETTING THICK WITH TOXINS AND BIO-HAZARDS, QUITE A FEW OF THEM UNKNOWN. PEOPLE ARE BEGINNING TO PANIC.
"AUTOMATED CITY FUNCTIONS SUCH AS HIGHWAYS AND PED-SIGNALS ARE COMPROMISED AS THE ACID SHORTS OUT THEIR SYSTEMS.
"MEANTIME, OUR FRIENDS AT THE ANTI-ALIEN LEAGUE HAVE FOUND A NEW ANGLE: THEY'RE CLAIMING ANYONE WITH AN OPPOSING VIEWPOINT IS HARBORING A SYMBIOTE.
"PRETTY EFFECTIVE, TOO. HALF THE POLITICOS UP THERE ARE NOW JUMPING ON THE BANDWAGON.
"EVERYONE'S A SECRET ALIEN SYMPATHIZER."
NO OFFIES!
WE'VE GOT TOUCH POINTS ALL OVER THE CITY.
PUBLIC WORKS SAYS WE'VE GOT SIX DAYS, TOPS, BEFORE THE AIR'S TOO TOXIC TO BREATHE. AND IT CAN'T BE VENTILATED.
WHY NOT?
VENTILATORS AREN'T WORKING.
DREDD
JUDGES, I HATE TO BREAK UP THE PARTY BUT THAT MAY BE THE LEAST OF OUR WORRIES.
GOT A SITUATION, MID-TOWN.

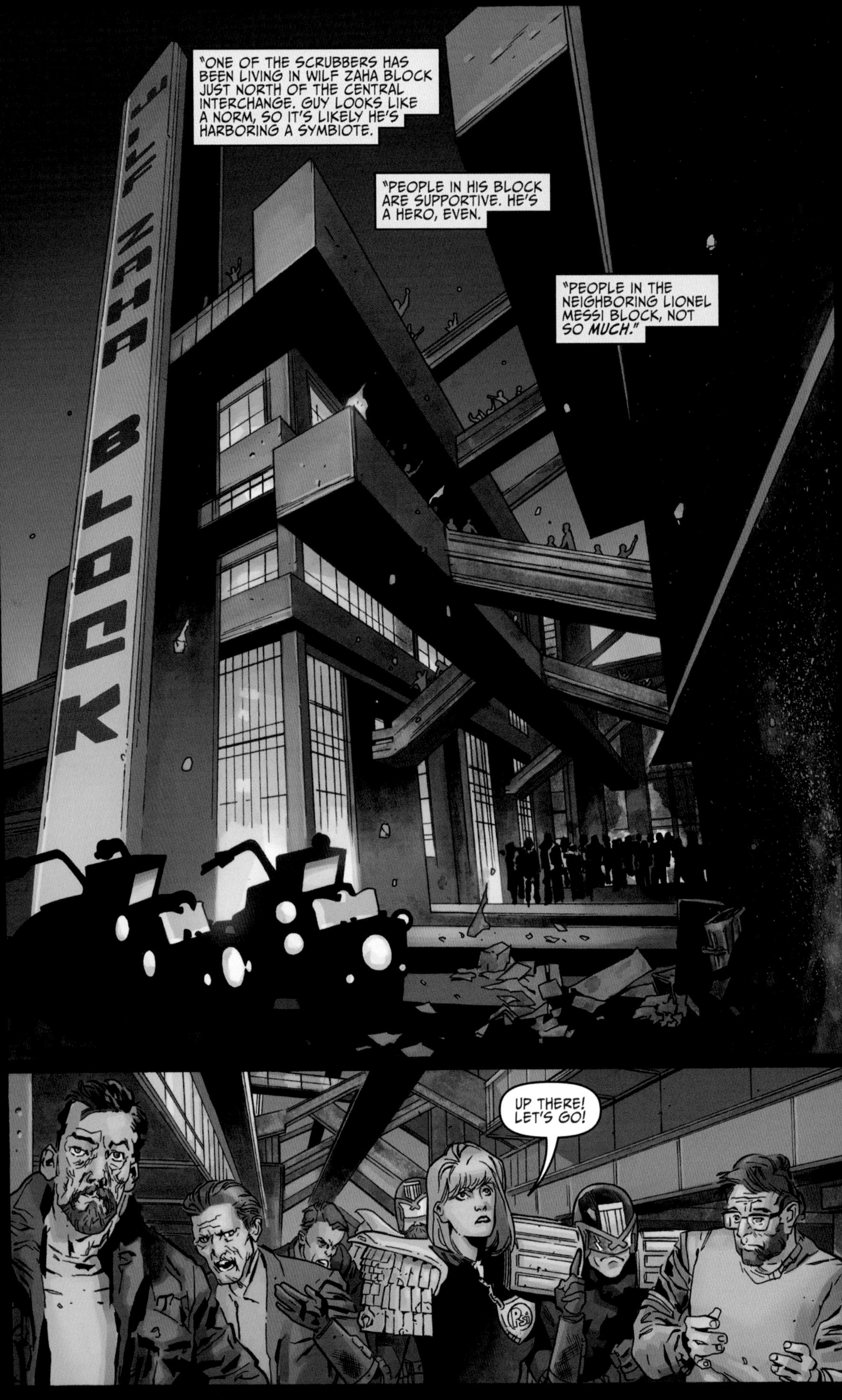

"ONE OF THE SCRUBBERS HAS BEEN LIVING IN WILF ZAHA BLOCK JUST NORTH OF THE CENTRAL INTERCHANGE. GUY LOOKS LIKE A NORM, SO IT'S LIKELY HE'S HARBORING A SYMBIOTE.
"PEOPLE IN HIS BLOCK ARE SUPPORTIVE. HE'S A HERO, EVEN.
"PEOPLE IN THE NEIGHBORING LIONEL MESSI BLOCK, NOT SO *MUCH*."
WILF ZAHA BLOCK
UP THERE! LET'S GO!

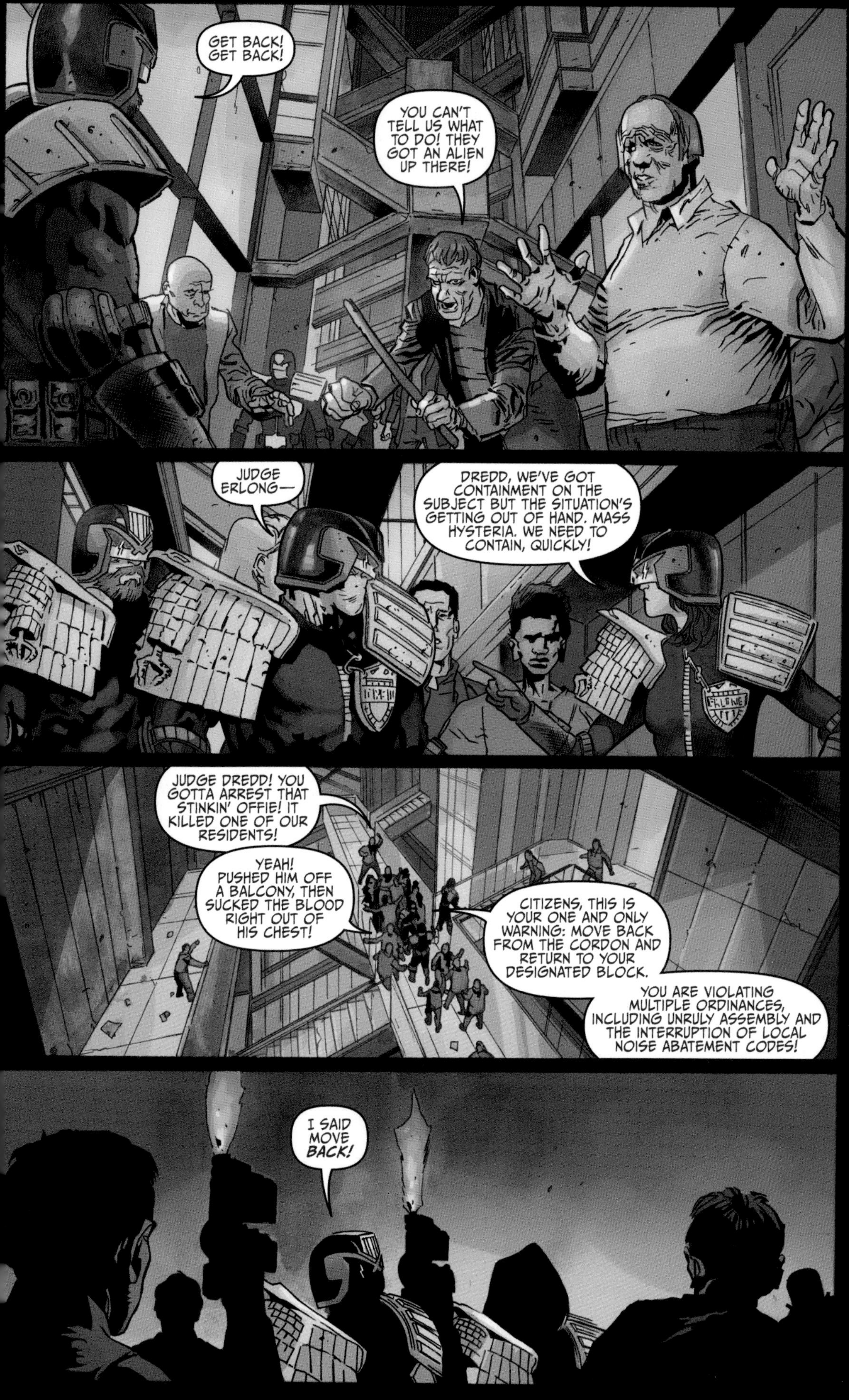
GET BACK! GET BACK!
YOU CAN'T TELL US WHAT TO DO! THEY GOT AN ALIEN UP THERE!
JUDGE ERLONG—
DREDD, WE'VE GOT CONTAINMENT ON THE SUBJECT BUT THE SITUATION'S GETTING OUT OF HAND. MASS HYSTERIA. WE NEED TO CONTAIN, QUICKLY!
JUDGE DREDD! YOU GOTTA ARREST THAT STINKIN' OFFIE! IT KILLED ONE OF OUR RESIDENTS!
YEAH! PUSHED HIM OFF A BALCONY, THEN SUCKED THE BLOOD RIGHT OUT OF HIS CHEST!
CITIZENS, THIS IS YOUR ONE AND ONLY WARNING: MOVE BACK FROM THE CORDON AND RETURN TO YOUR DESIGNATED BLOCK.
YOU ARE VIOLATING MULTIPLE ORDINANCES, INCLUDING UNRULY ASSEMBLY AND THE INTERRUPTION OF LOCAL NOISE ABATEMENT CODES!
I SAID MOVE BACK!

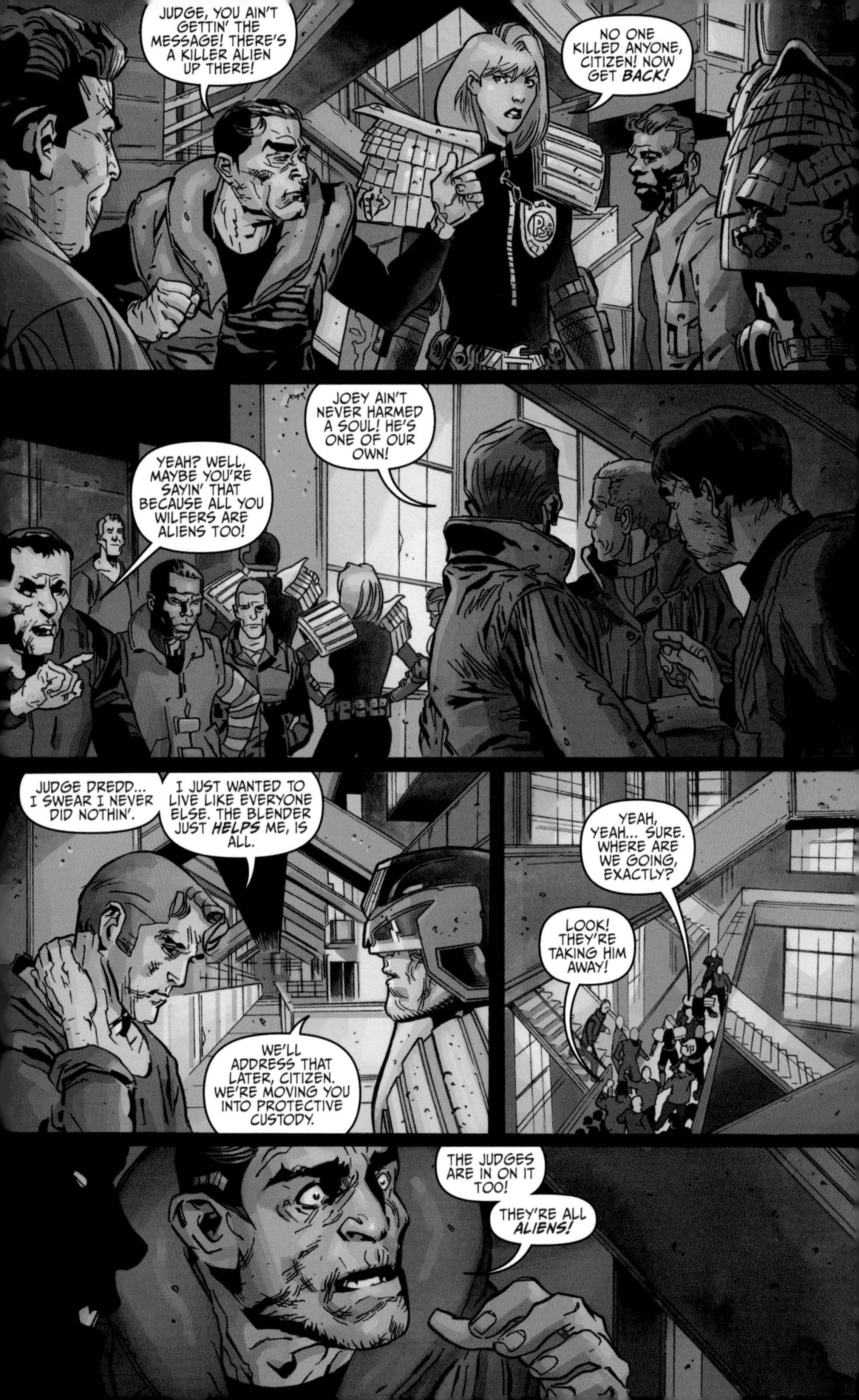
JUDGE, YOU AIN'T GETTIN' THE MESSAGE! THERE'S A KILLER ALIEN UP THERE!
NO ONE KILLED ANYONE, CITIZEN! NOW GET *BACK!*
JOEY AIN'T NEVER HARMED A SOUL! HE'S ONE OF OUR OWN!
YEAH? WELL, MAYBE YOU'RE SAYIN' THAT BECAUSE ALL YOU WILFERS ARE ALIENS TOO!
JUDGE DREDD... I SWEAR I NEVER DID NOTHIN'.
I JUST WANTED TO LIVE LIKE EVERYONE ELSE. THE BLENDER JUST *HELPS* ME, IS ALL.
WE'LL ADDRESS THAT LATER, CITIZEN. WE'RE MOVING YOU INTO PROTECTIVE CUSTODY.
YEAH, YEAH... SURE. WHERE ARE WE GOING, EXACTLY?
LOOK! THEY'RE TAKING HIM AWAY!
THE JUDGES ARE IN ON IT TOO!
THEY'RE ALL *ALIENS!*

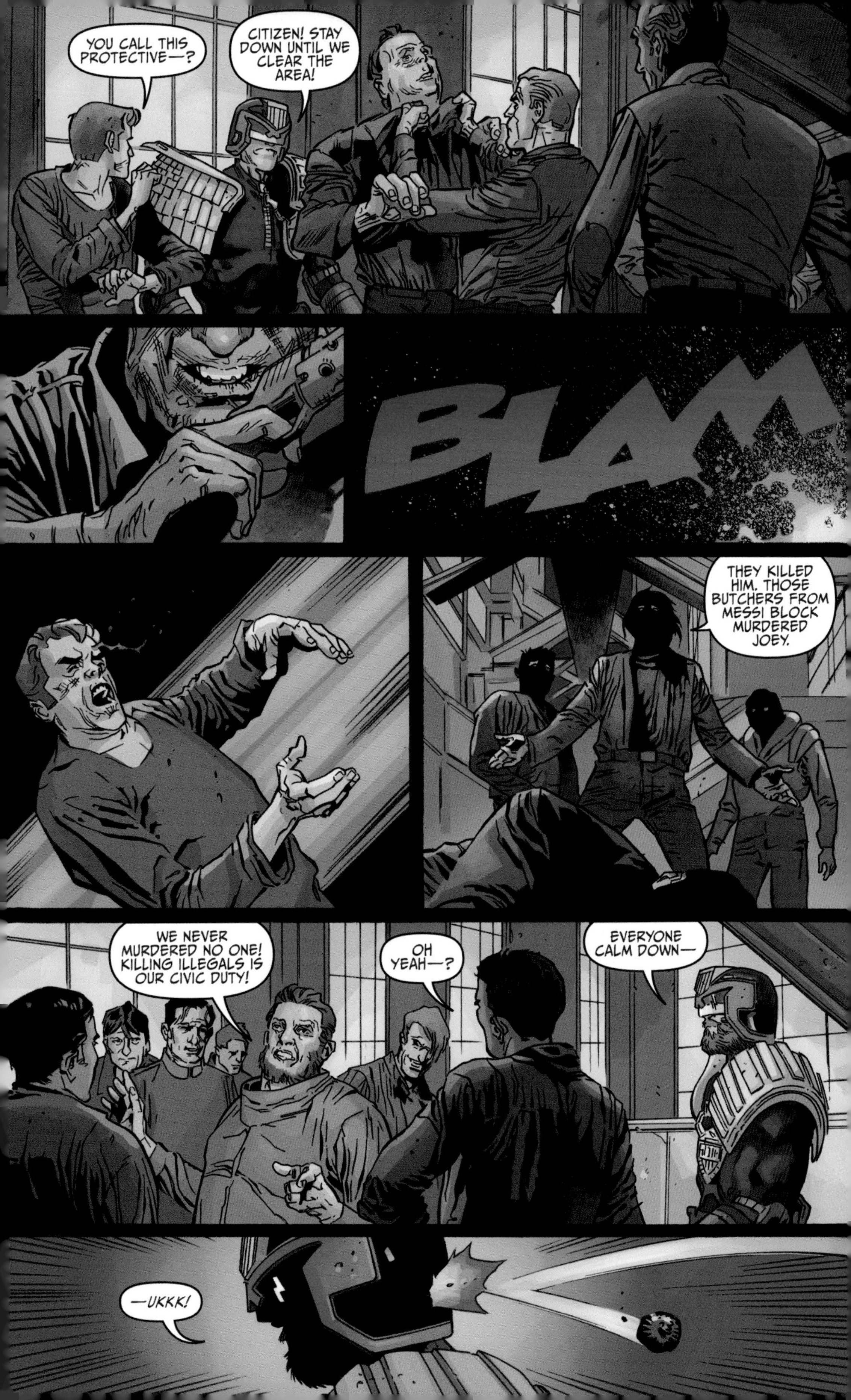
YOU CALL THIS PROTECTIVE—?
CITIZEN! STAY DOWN UNTIL WE CLEAR THE AREA!
BLAM
THEY KILLED HIM. THOSE BUTCHERS FROM MESSI BLOCK MURDERED JOEY.
WE NEVER MURDERED NO ONE! KILLING ILLEGALS IS OUR CIVIC DUTY!
OH YEAH—?
EVERYONE CALM DOWN—
—UKKK!

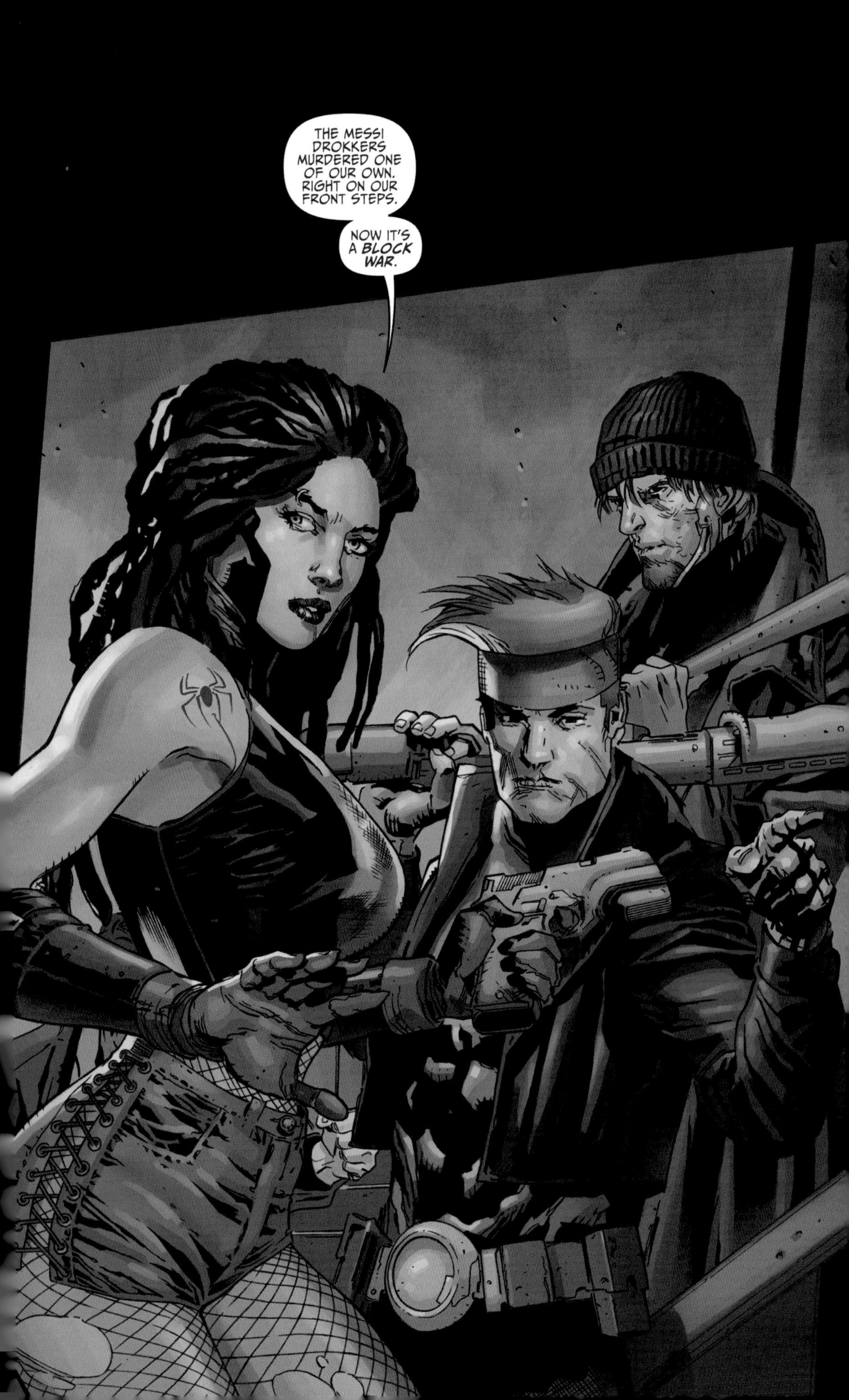
THE MESSI DROKKERS MURDERED ONE OF OUR OWN. RIGHT ON OUR FRONT STEPS.
NOW IT'S A *BLOCK WAR*.

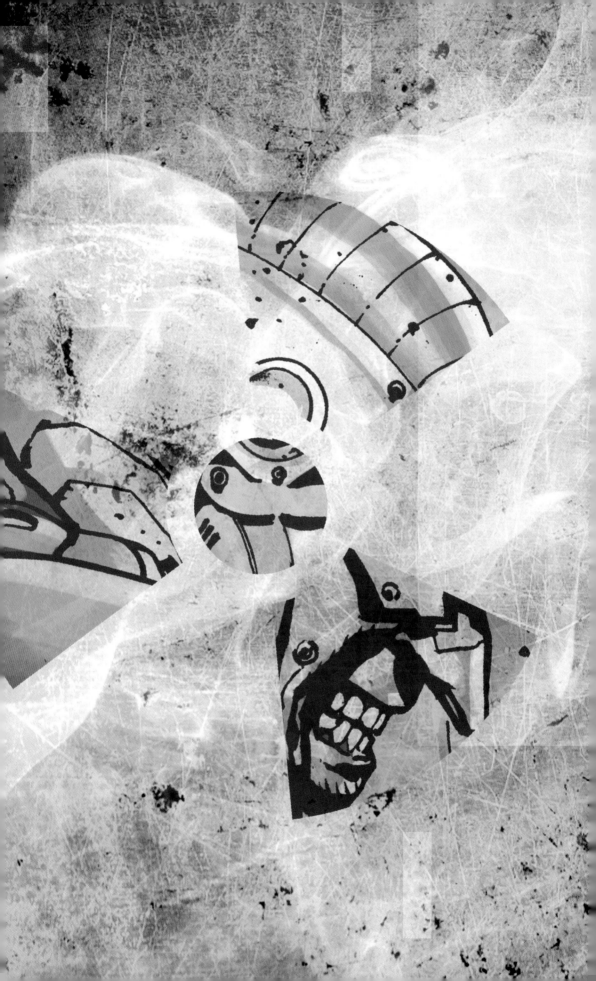

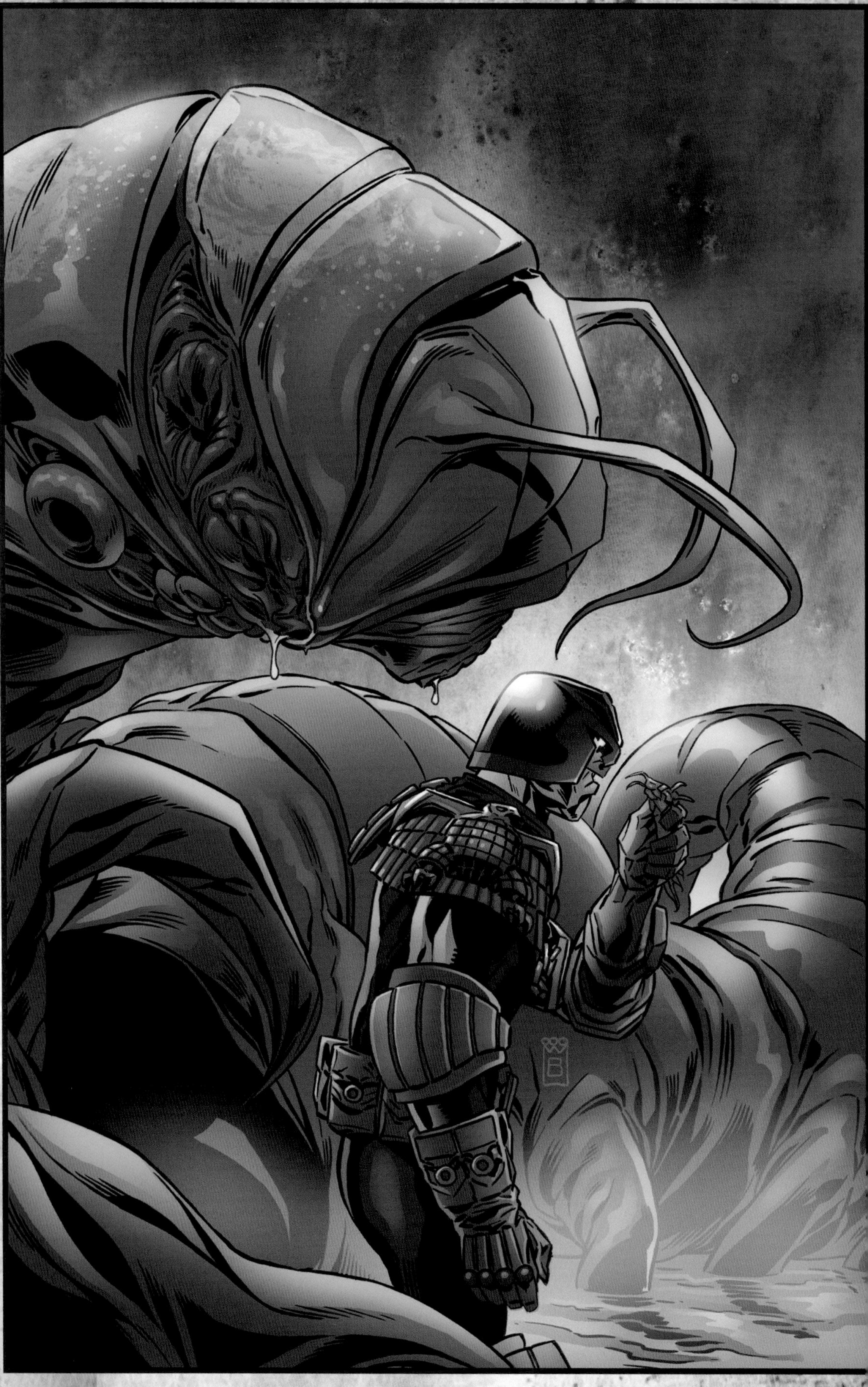

ART BY **MARK BUCKINGHAM** COLORS BY **CHRIS BLYTHE**

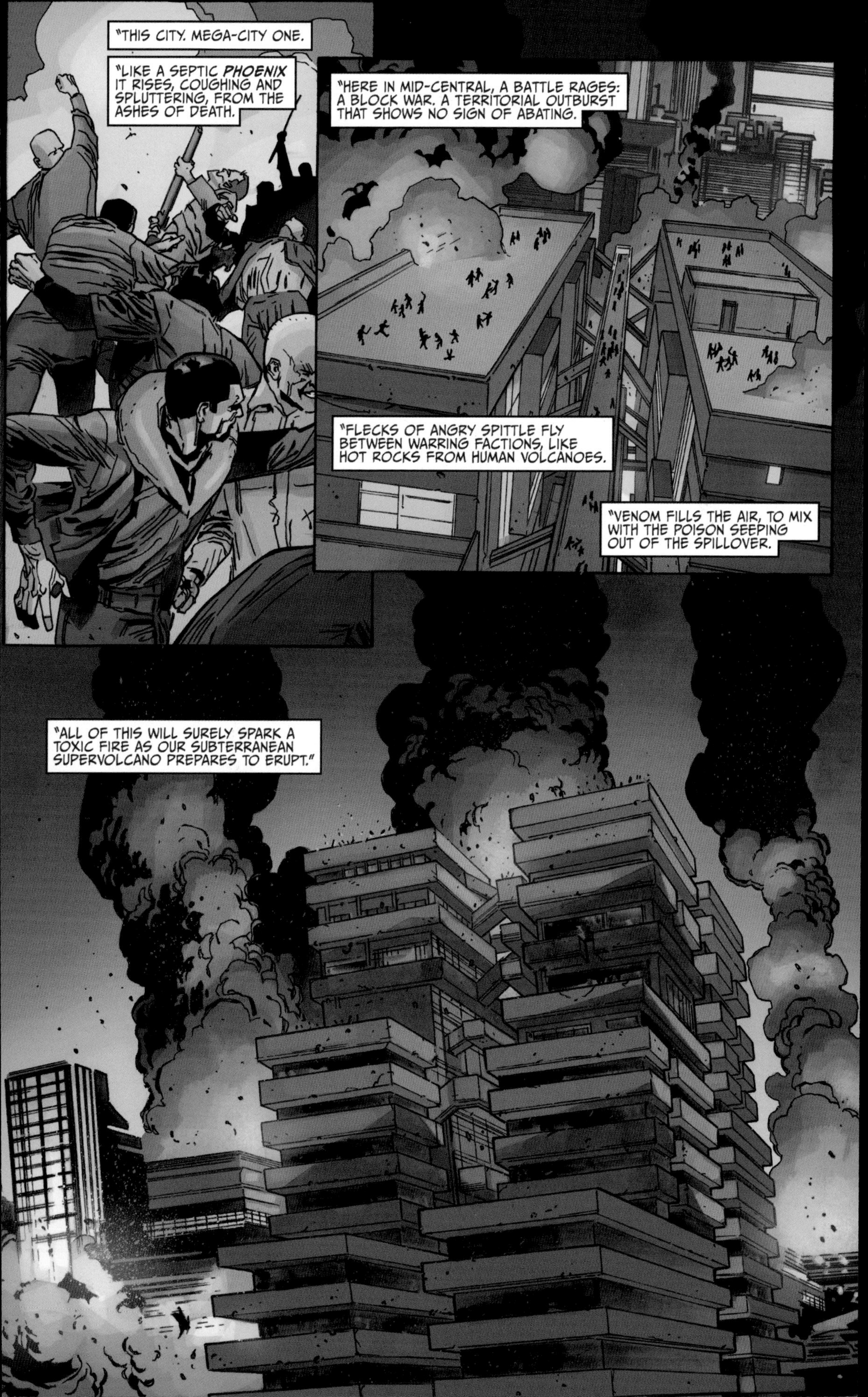
"THIS CITY. MEGA-CITY ONE.
"LIKE A SEPTIC PHOENIX IT RISES, COUGHING AND SPLUTTERING, FROM THE ASHES OF DEATH.
"HERE IN MID-CENTRAL, A BATTLE RAGES: A BLOCK WAR. A TERRITORIAL OUTBURST THAT SHOWS NO SIGN OF ABATING.
"FLECKS OF ANGRY SPITTLE FLY BETWEEN WARRING FACTIONS, LIKE HOT ROCKS FROM HUMAN VOLCANOES.
"VENOM FILLS THE AIR, TO MIX WITH THE POISON SEEPING OUT OF THE SPILLOVER.
"ALL OF THIS WILL SURELY SPARK A TOXIC FIRE AS OUR SUBTERRANEAN SUPERVOLCANO PREPARES TO ERUPT."

"THIS IS THE SCENE AT THE WILF ZAHA AND LIONEL MESSI BLOCKS—IN THE MID-CENTRAL TENANCY SECTOR—WHERE WARRING BLOCK FACTIONS ARE NOW FULLY ENGAGED.

"HOPING TO CONTAIN THE SITUATION, AN OVERMATCHED JUSTICE DEPARTMENT HAS CORDONED OFF ALL ENDS OF THE CONNECTING STREETS, LEAVING THE BATTLE TO RAGE, AND HOPEFULLY EXTINGUISH ITSELF.

"BUT THE FLAME OF ANTIPATHY BURNS MAGNESIUM-BRIGHT UNDER THE GLOOM OF THE DARKENING SKY. A *VOLCANIC WINTER* THREATENS.

"NEARBY, THE ZOOMTUBES AND BOOMWAYS LAY IDLE, SNARLED AND DAMAGED AS HEAVY MORTAR FIRE HAS MOVED INTO THE SURROUNDING NEIGHBORHOODS; A SUPERVOLCANO SPITTING PUMICE IN ALL DIRECTIONS.

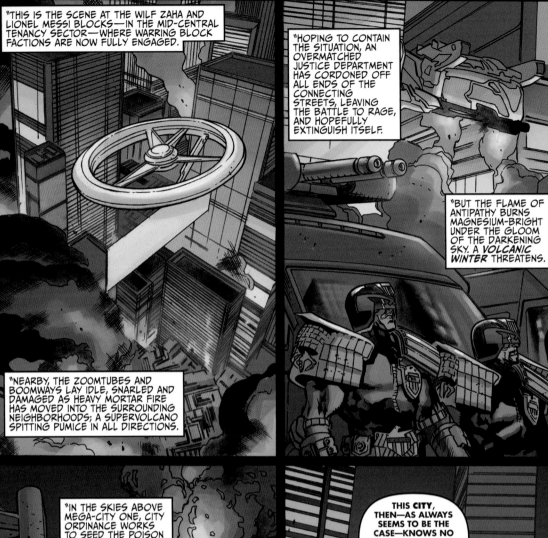

"IN THE SKIES ABOVE MEGA-CITY ONE, CITY ORDINANCE WORKS TO SEED THE POISON AIR, HOPING TO FLUSH THE ACID FROM THE ATMOSPHERE.

"FOR THE FIRST TIME IN CLIMATE-CONTROLLED MEMORY, RAIN WILL FALL AS FORECASTS CALL FOR HEAVY DOWNPOURS OF ACID RAIN AND BILE."

THIS **CITY**, THEN—AS ALWAYS SEEMS TO BE THE CASE—KNOWS NO CALM BEFORE THE STORM. INSTEAD, IT IS OVERWHELMED BY RAGING FIRES.

A PRECURSOR TO THE NEXT HUMAN **ERUPTION.**

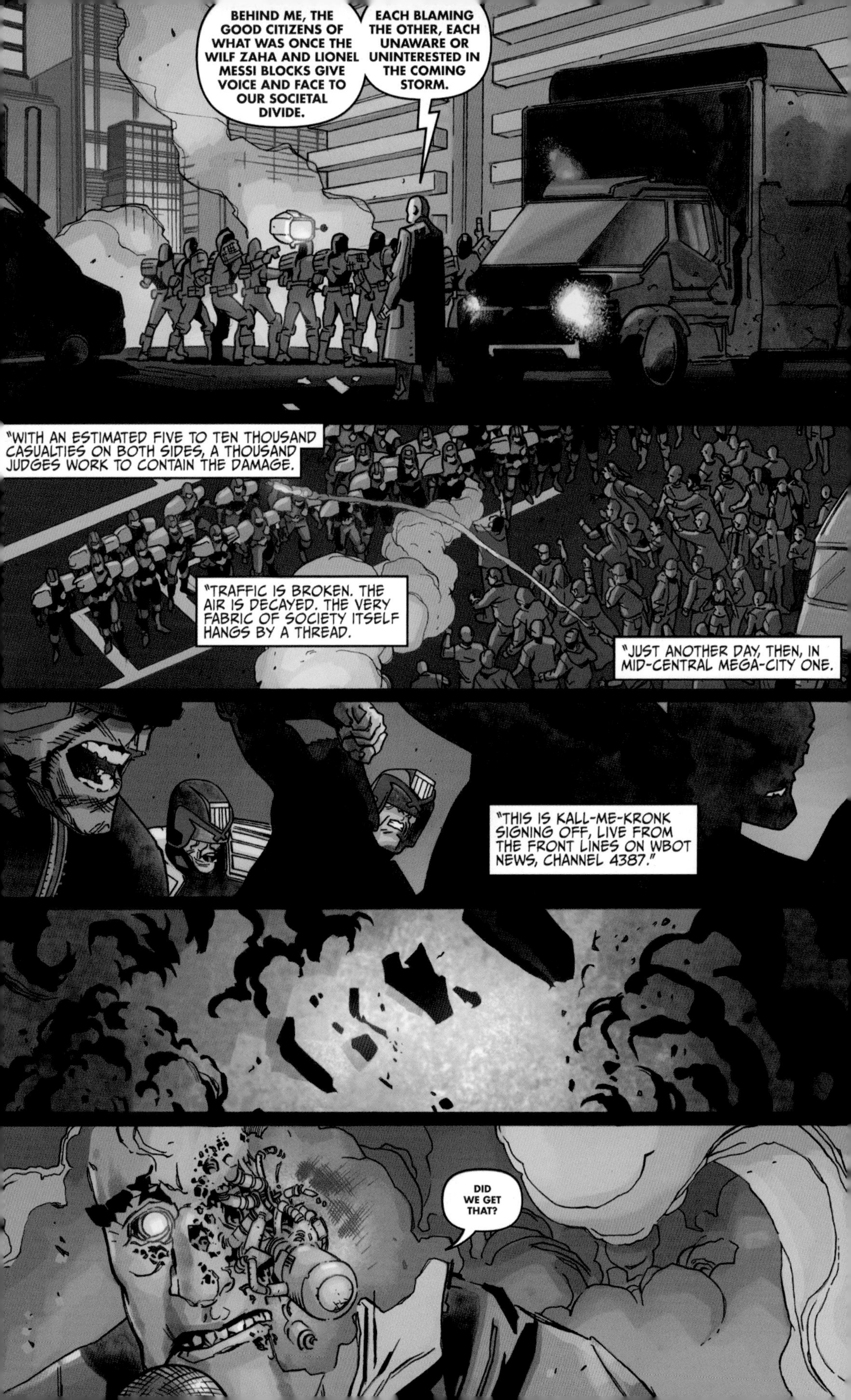
BEHIND ME, THE GOOD CITIZENS OF WHAT WAS ONCE THE WILF ZAHA AND LIONEL MESSI BLOCKS GIVE VOICE AND FACE TO OUR SOCIETAL DIVIDE.
EACH BLAMING THE OTHER, EACH UNAWARE OR UNINTERESTED IN THE COMING STORM.
"WITH AN ESTIMATED FIVE TO TEN THOUSAND CASUALTIES ON BOTH SIDES, A THOUSAND JUDGES WORK TO CONTAIN THE DAMAGE.
"TRAFFIC IS BROKEN. THE AIR IS DECAYED. THE VERY FABRIC OF SOCIETY ITSELF HANGS BY A THREAD.
"JUST ANOTHER DAY, THEN, IN MID-CENTRAL MEGA-CITY ONE.
"THIS IS KALL-ME-KRONK SIGNING OFF, LIVE FROM THE FRONT LINES ON WBOT NEWS, CHANNEL 4387."
DID WE GET THAT?

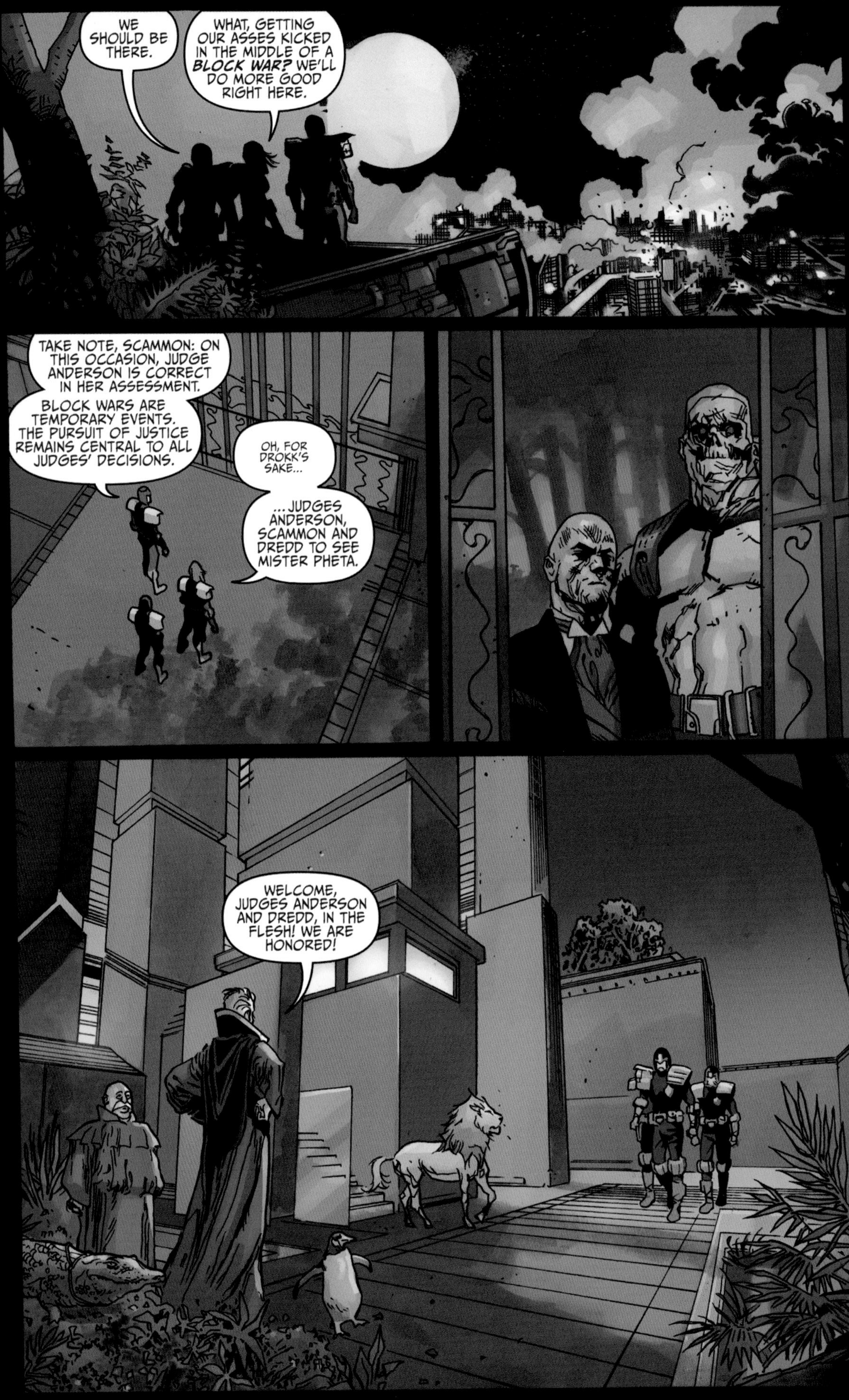
WE SHOULD BE THERE.
WHAT, GETTING OUR ASSES KICKED IN THE MIDDLE OF A BLOCK WAR? WE'LL DO MORE GOOD RIGHT HERE.
TAKE NOTE, SCAMMON: ON THIS OCCASION, JUDGE ANDERSON IS CORRECT IN HER ASSESSMENT.
BLOCK WARS ARE TEMPORARY EVENTS. THE PURSUIT OF JUSTICE REMAINS CENTRAL TO ALL JUDGES' DECISIONS.
OH, FOR DROKK'S SAKE...
...JUDGES ANDERSON, SCAMMON AND DREDD TO SEE MISTER PHETA.
WELCOME, JUDGES ANDERSON AND DREDD, IN THE FLESH! WE ARE HONORED!

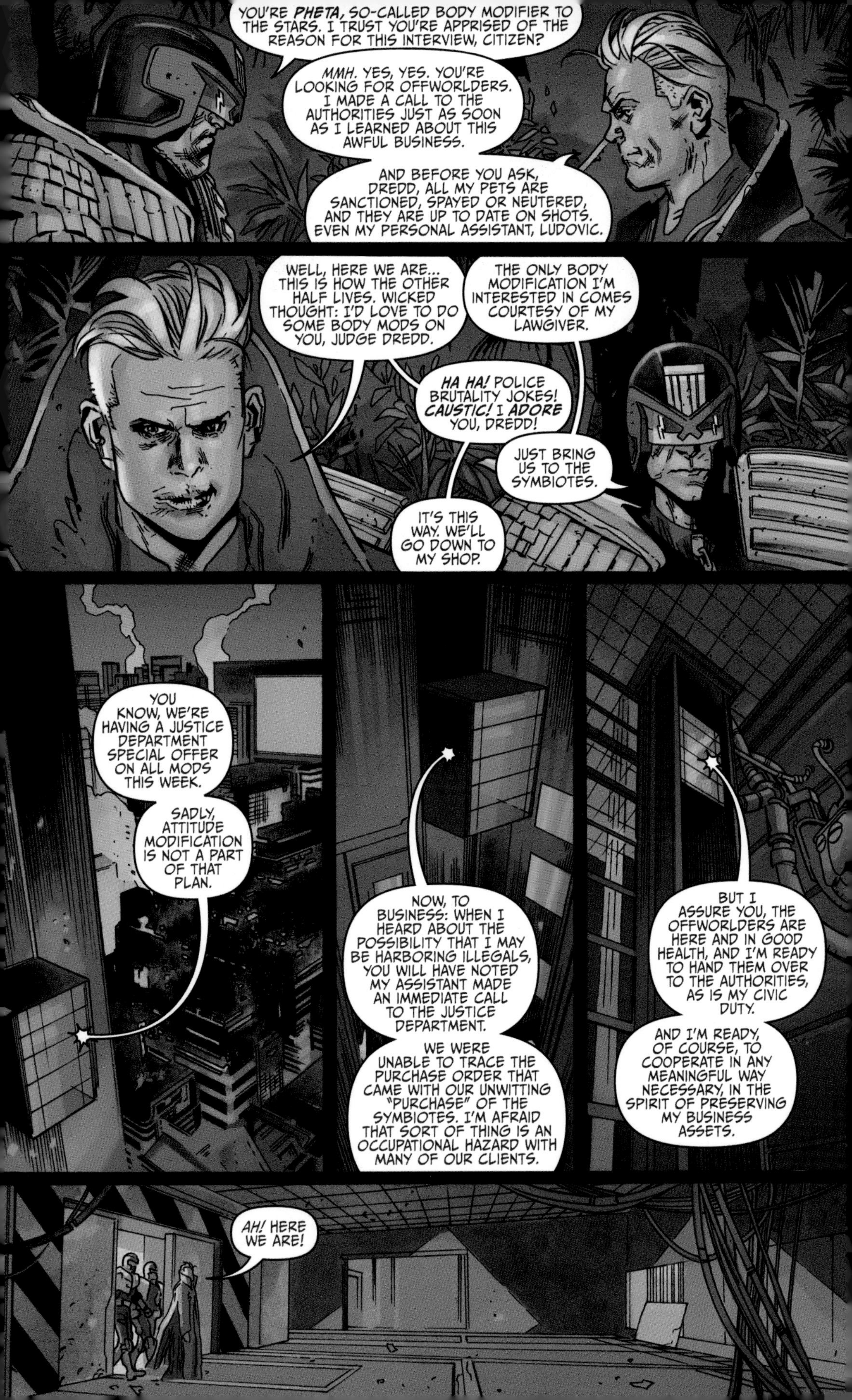
YOU'RE PHETA, SO-CALLED BODY MODIFIER TO THE STARS. I TRUST YOU'RE APPRISED OF THE REASON FOR THIS INTERVIEW, CITIZEN?
MMH. YES, YES. YOU'RE LOOKING FOR OFFWORLDERS. I MADE A CALL TO THE AUTHORITIES JUST AS SOON AS I LEARNED ABOUT THIS AWFUL BUSINESS.
AND BEFORE YOU ASK, DREDD, ALL MY PETS ARE SANCTIONED, SPAYED OR NEUTERED, AND THEY ARE UP TO DATE ON SHOTS. EVEN MY PERSONAL ASSISTANT, LUDOVIC.
WELL, HERE WE ARE... THIS IS HOW THE OTHER HALF LIVES. WICKED THOUGHT: I'D LOVE TO DO SOME BODY MODS ON YOU, JUDGE DREDD.
THE ONLY BODY MODIFICATION I'M INTERESTED IN COMES COURTESY OF MY LAWGIVER.
HA HA! POLICE BRUTALITY JOKES! CAUSTIC! I ADORE YOU, DREDD!
JUST BRING US TO THE SYMBIOTES.
IT'S THIS WAY. WE'LL GO DOWN TO MY SHOP.
YOU KNOW, WE'RE HAVING A JUSTICE DEPARTMENT SPECIAL OFFER ON ALL MODS THIS WEEK.
SADLY, ATTITUDE MODIFICATION IS NOT A PART OF THAT PLAN.
NOW, TO BUSINESS: WHEN I HEARD ABOUT THE POSSIBILITY THAT I MAY BE HARBORING ILLEGALS, YOU WILL HAVE NOTED MY ASSISTANT MADE AN IMMEDIATE CALL TO THE JUSTICE DEPARTMENT.
WE WERE UNABLE TO TRACE THE PURCHASE ORDER THAT CAME WITH OUR UNWITTING "PURCHASE" OF THE SYMBIOTES. I'M AFRAID THAT SORT OF THING IS AN OCCUPATIONAL HAZARD WITH MANY OF OUR CLIENTS.
BUT I ASSURE YOU, THE OFFWORLDERS ARE HERE AND IN GOOD HEALTH, AND I'M READY TO HAND THEM OVER TO THE AUTHORITIES, AS IS MY CIVIC DUTY.
AND I'M READY, OF COURSE, TO COOPERATE IN ANY MEANINGFUL WAY NECESSARY, IN THE SPIRIT OF PRESERVING MY BUSINESS ASSETS.
AH! HERE WE ARE!

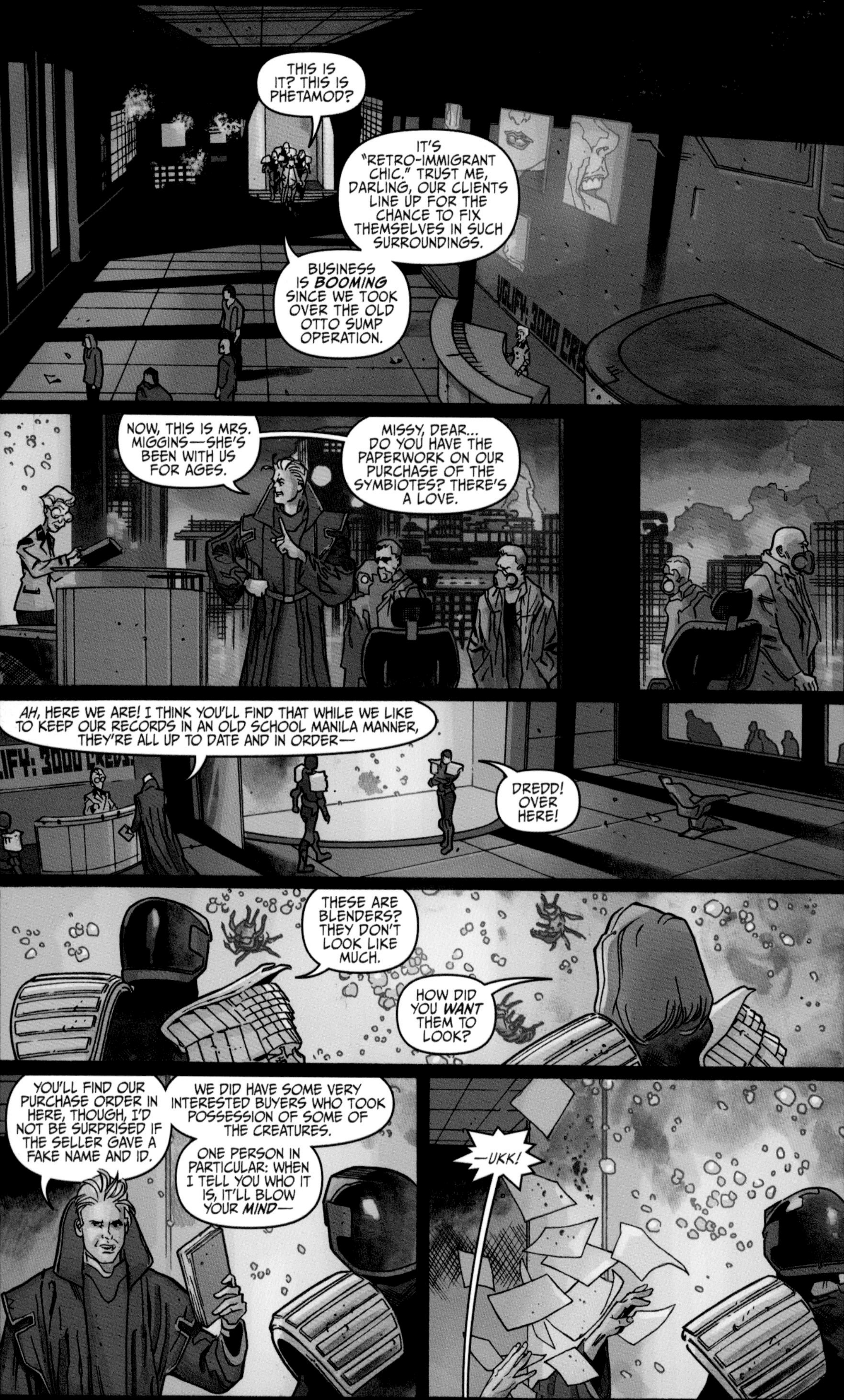
THIS IS IT? THIS IS PHETAMOD?
IT'S "RETRO-IMMIGRANT CHIC." TRUST ME, DARLING, OUR CLIENTS LINE UP FOR THE CHANCE TO FIX THEMSELVES IN SUCH SURROUNDINGS.
BUSINESS IS **BOOMING** SINCE WE TOOK OVER THE OLD OTTO SUMP OPERATION.
UGLIFY: 3000 CRE
NOW, THIS IS MRS. MIGGINS—SHE'S BEEN WITH US FOR AGES.
MISSY, DEAR... DO YOU HAVE THE PAPERWORK ON OUR PURCHASE OF THE SYMBIOTES? THERE'S A LOVE.
AH, HERE WE ARE! I THINK YOU'LL FIND THAT WHILE WE LIKE TO KEEP OUR RECORDS IN AN OLD SCHOOL MANILA MANNER, THEY'RE ALL UP TO DATE AND IN ORDER—
LIFY: 3000 CREDS!
DREDD! OVER HERE!
THESE ARE BLENDERS? THEY DON'T LOOK LIKE MUCH.
HOW DID YOU ***WANT*** THEM TO LOOK?
YOU'LL FIND OUR PURCHASE ORDER IN HERE, THOUGH, I'D NOT BE SURPRISED IF THE SELLER GAVE A FAKE NAME AND ID.
WE DID HAVE SOME VERY INTERESTED BUYERS WHO TOOK POSSESSION OF SOME OF THE CREATURES.
ONE PERSON IN PARTICULAR: WHEN I TELL YOU WHO IT IS, IT'LL BLOW YOUR ***MIND***—
—*UKK!*

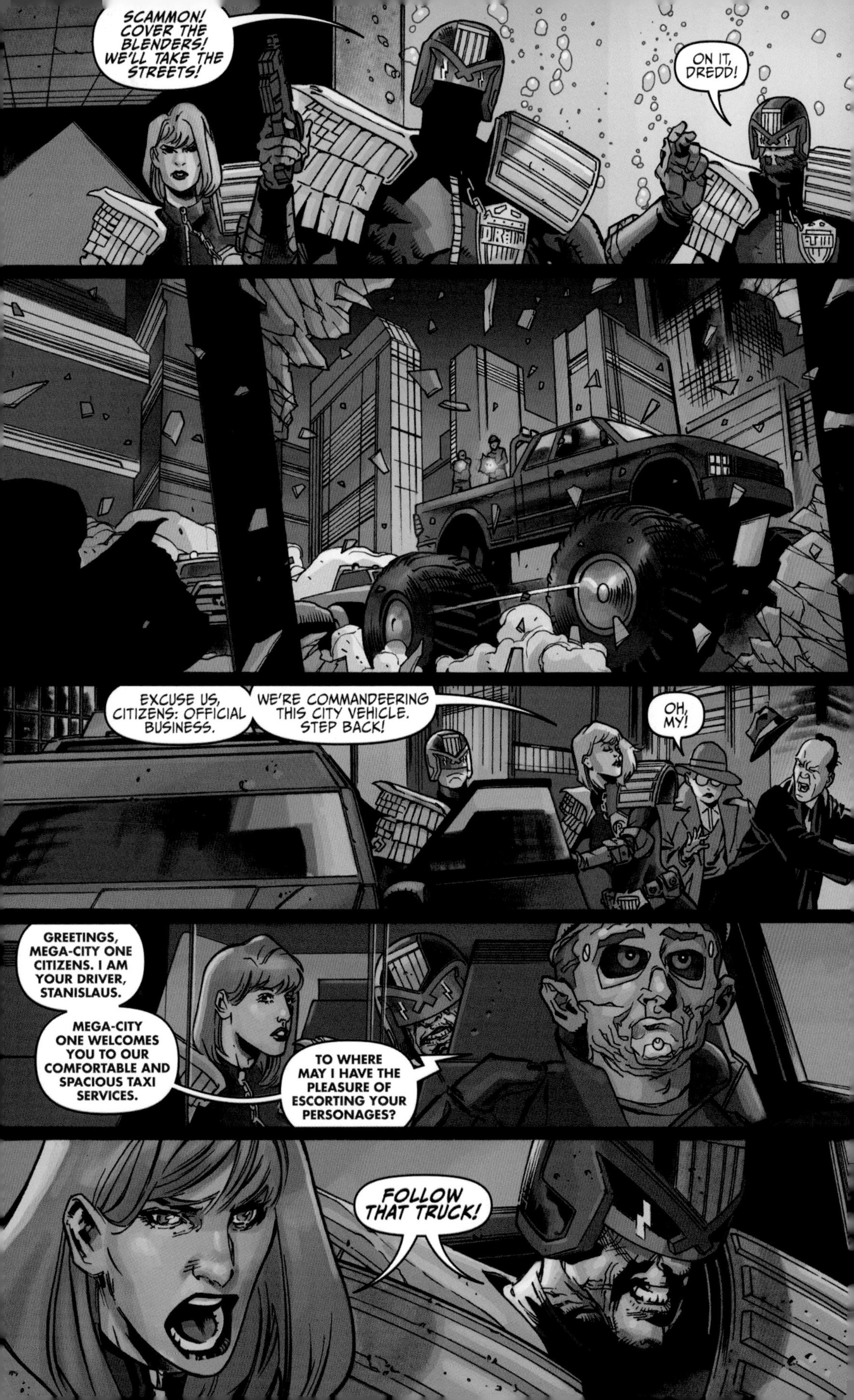
SCAMMON! COVER THE BLENDERS! WE'LL TAKE THE STREETS!
ON IT, DREDD!
EXCUSE US, CITIZENS: OFFICIAL BUSINESS.
WE'RE COMMANDEERING THIS CITY VEHICLE. STEP BACK!
OH, MY!
GREETINGS, MEGA-CITY ONE CITIZENS. I AM YOUR DRIVER, STANISLAUS.
MEGA-CITY ONE WELCOMES YOU TO OUR COMFORTABLE AND SPACIOUS TAXI SERVICES.
TO WHERE MAY I HAVE THE PLEASURE OF ESCORTING YOUR PERSONAGES?
FOLLOW THAT TRUCK!

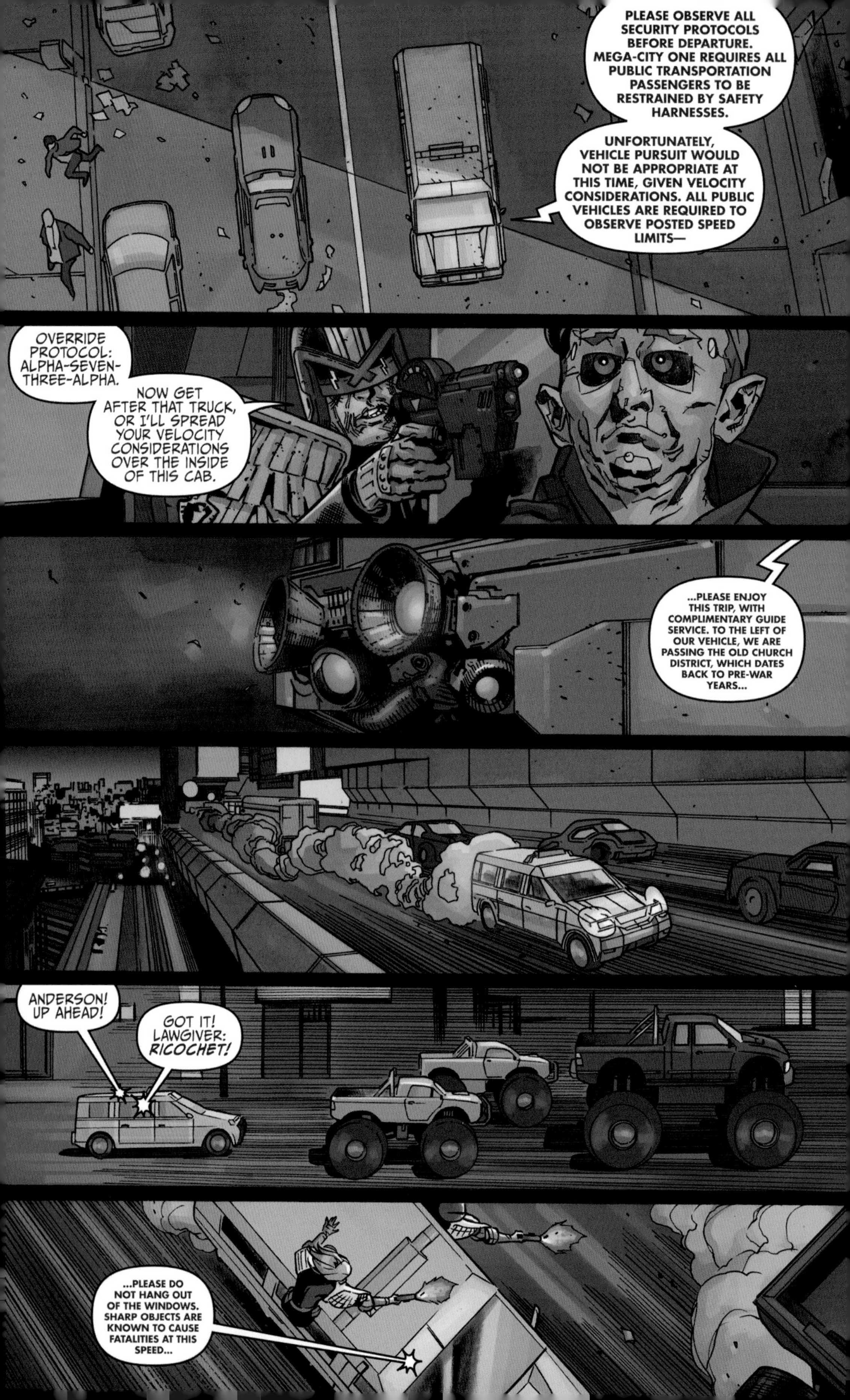
PLEASE OBSERVE ALL SECURITY PROTOCOLS BEFORE DEPARTURE. MEGA-CITY ONE REQUIRES ALL PUBLIC TRANSPORTATION PASSENGERS TO BE RESTRAINED BY SAFETY HARNESSES.
UNFORTUNATELY, VEHICLE PURSUIT WOULD NOT BE APPROPRIATE AT THIS TIME, GIVEN VELOCITY CONSIDERATIONS. ALL PUBLIC VEHICLES ARE REQUIRED TO OBSERVE POSTED SPEED LIMITS—
OVERRIDE PROTOCOL: ALPHA-SEVEN-THREE-ALPHA.
NOW GET AFTER THAT TRUCK, OR I'LL SPREAD YOUR VELOCITY CONSIDERATIONS OVER THE INSIDE OF THIS CAB.
...PLEASE ENJOY THIS TRIP, WITH COMPLIMENTARY GUIDE SERVICE. TO THE LEFT OF OUR VEHICLE, WE ARE PASSING THE OLD CHURCH DISTRICT, WHICH DATES BACK TO PRE-WAR YEARS...
ANDERSON! UP AHEAD!
GOT IT! LAWGIVER: *RICOCHET!*
...PLEASE DO NOT HANG OUT OF THE WINDOWS. SHARP OBJECTS ARE KNOWN TO CAUSE FATALITIES AT THIS SPEED...

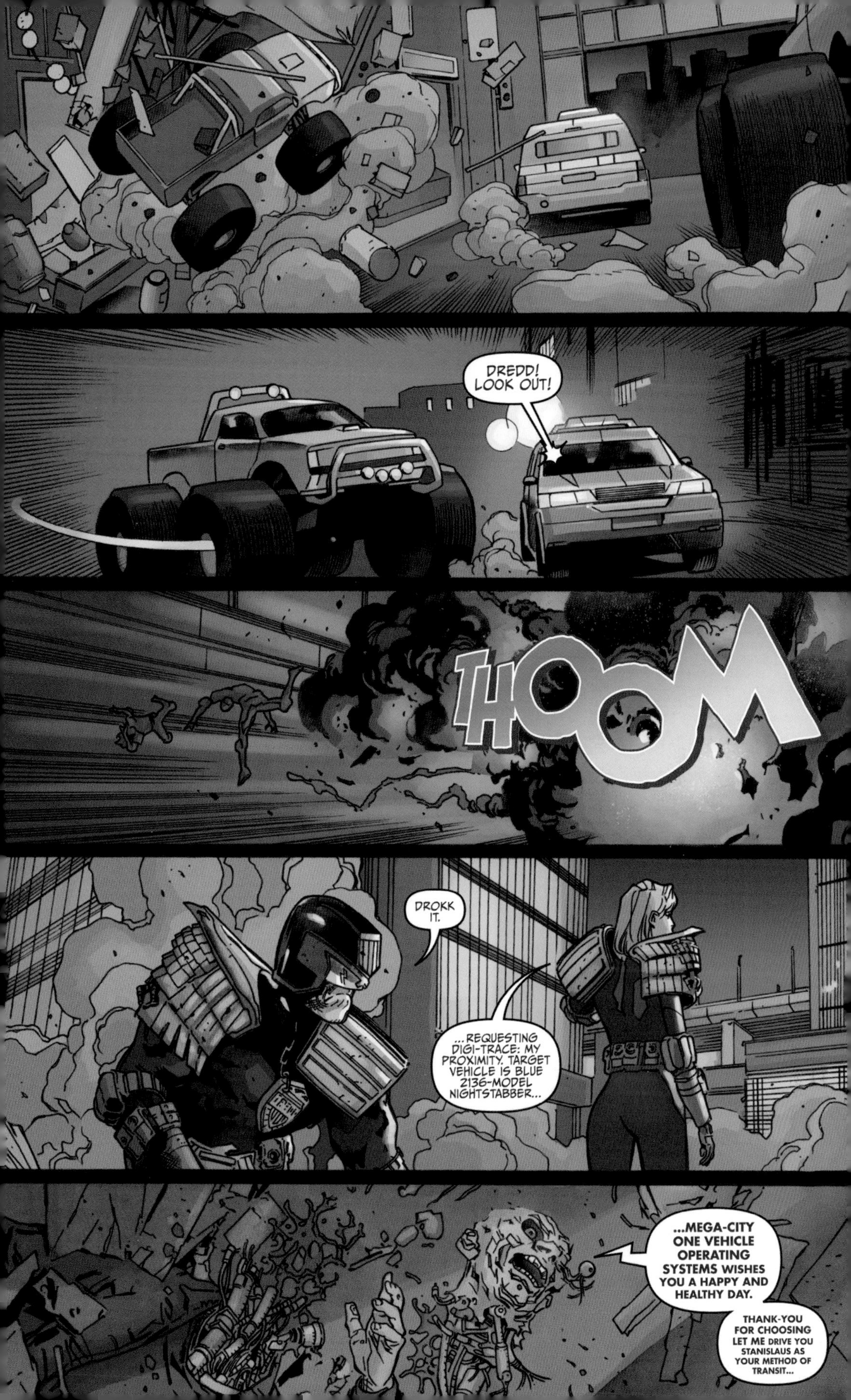
DREDD! LOOK OUT!
THOOM
DROKK IT.
...REQUESTING DIGI-TRACE: MY PROXIMITY. TARGET VEHICLE IS BLUE 2136-MODEL NIGHTSTABBER...
...MEGA-CITY ONE VEHICLE OPERATING SYSTEMS WISHES YOU A HAPPY AND HEALTHY DAY.
THANK-YOU FOR CHOOSING LET ME DRIVE YOU STANISLAUS AS YOUR METHOD OF TRANSIT...

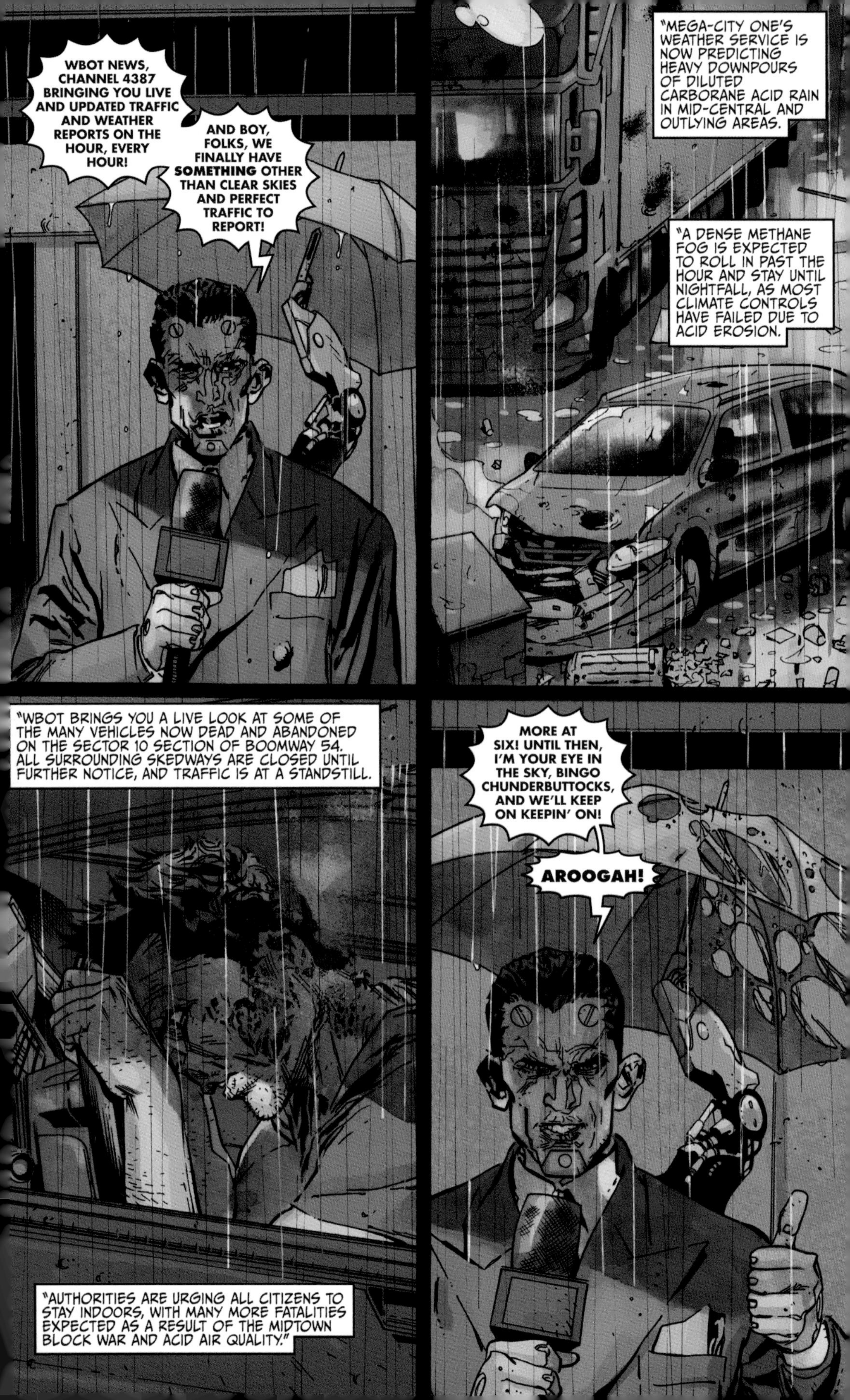

WBOT NEWS, CHANNEL 4387 BRINGING YOU LIVE AND UPDATED TRAFFIC AND WEATHER REPORTS ON THE HOUR, EVERY HOUR!
AND BOY, FOLKS, WE FINALLY HAVE SOMETHING OTHER THAN CLEAR SKIES AND PERFECT TRAFFIC TO REPORT!
"MEGA-CITY ONE'S WEATHER SERVICE IS NOW PREDICTING HEAVY DOWNPOURS OF DILUTED CARBORANE ACID RAIN IN MID-CENTRAL AND OUTLYING AREAS.
"A DENSE METHANE FOG IS EXPECTED TO ROLL IN PAST THE HOUR AND STAY UNTIL NIGHTFALL, AS MOST CLIMATE CONTROLS HAVE FAILED DUE TO ACID EROSION.
"WBOT BRINGS YOU A LIVE LOOK AT SOME OF THE MANY VEHICLES NOW DEAD AND ABANDONED ON THE SECTOR 10 SECTION OF BOOMWAY 54. ALL SURROUNDING SKEDWAYS ARE CLOSED UNTIL FURTHER NOTICE, AND TRAFFIC IS AT A STANDSTILL.
"AUTHORITIES ARE URGING ALL CITIZENS TO STAY INDOORS, WITH MANY MORE FATALITIES EXPECTED AS A RESULT OF THE MIDTOWN BLOCK WAR AND ACID AIR QUALITY."
MORE AT SIX! UNTIL THEN, I'M YOUR EYE IN THE SKY, BINGO CHUNDERBUTTOCKS, AND WE'LL KEEP ON KEEPIN' ON!
AROOGAH!

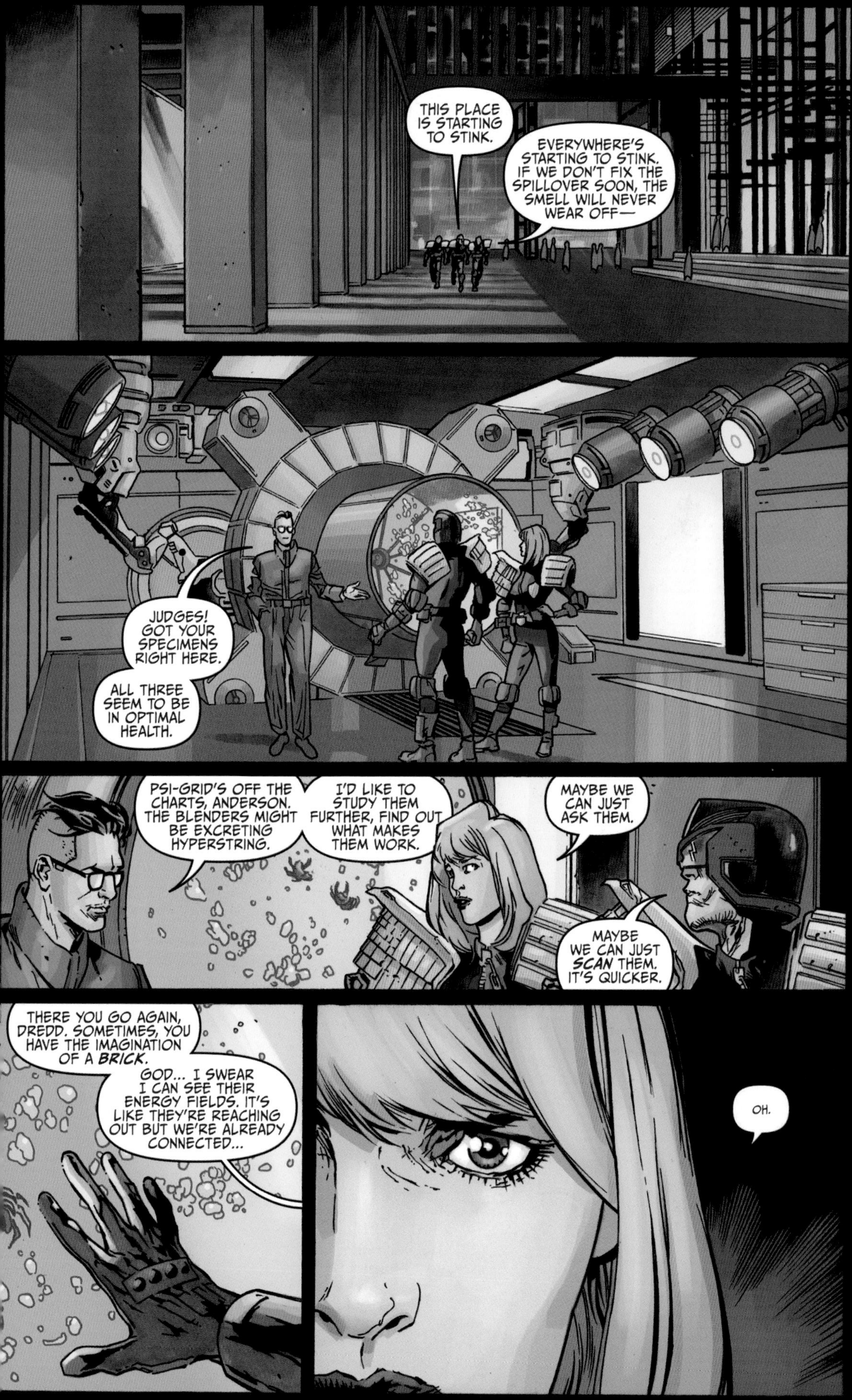
THIS PLACE IS STARTING TO STINK.
EVERYWHERE'S STARTING TO STINK. IF WE DON'T FIX THE SPILLOVER SOON, THE SMELL WILL NEVER WEAR OFF—
JUDGES! GOT YOUR SPECIMENS RIGHT HERE.
ALL THREE SEEM TO BE IN OPTIMAL HEALTH.
PSI-GRID'S OFF THE CHARTS, ANDERSON. THE BLENDERS MIGHT BE EXCRETING HYPERSTRING.
I'D LIKE TO STUDY THEM FURTHER, FIND OUT WHAT MAKES THEM WORK.
MAYBE WE CAN JUST ASK THEM.
MAYBE WE CAN JUST *SCAN* THEM. IT'S QUICKER.
THERE YOU GO AGAIN, DREDD. SOMETIMES, YOU HAVE THE IMAGINATION OF A *BRICK*.
GOD... I SWEAR I CAN SEE THEIR ENERGY FIELDS. IT'S LIKE THEY'RE REACHING OUT BUT WE'RE ALREADY CONNECTED...
OH.

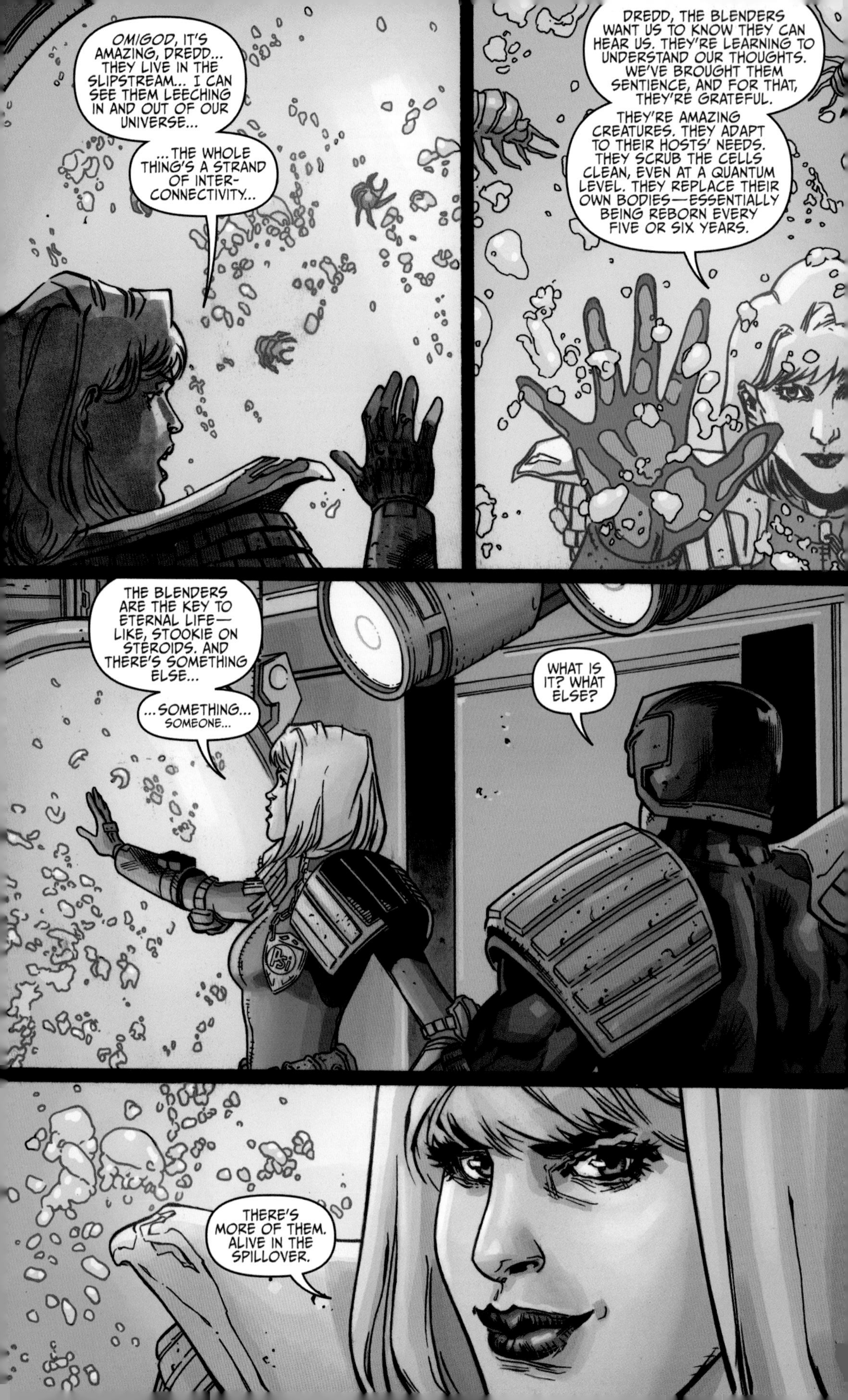
OMIGOD, IT'S AMAZING, DREDD... THEY LIVE IN THE SLIPSTREAM... I CAN SEE THEM LEECHING IN AND OUT OF OUR UNIVERSE...
...THE WHOLE THING'S A STRAND OF INTER-CONNECTIVITY...
DREDD, THE BLENDERS WANT US TO KNOW THEY CAN HEAR US. THEY'RE LEARNING TO UNDERSTAND OUR THOUGHTS. WE'VE BROUGHT THEM SENTIENCE, AND FOR THAT, THEY'RE GRATEFUL.
THEY'RE AMAZING CREATURES. THEY ADAPT TO THEIR HOSTS' NEEDS. THEY SCRUB THE CELLS CLEAN, EVEN AT A QUANTUM LEVEL. THEY REPLACE THEIR OWN BODIES—ESSENTIALLY BEING REBORN EVERY FIVE OR SIX YEARS.
THE BLENDERS ARE THE KEY TO ETERNAL LIFE—LIKE, STOOKIE ON STEROIDS. AND THERE'S SOMETHING ELSE...
...SOMETHING... SOMEONE...
WHAT IS IT? WHAT ELSE?
THERE'S MORE OF THEM. ALIVE IN THE SPILLOVER.

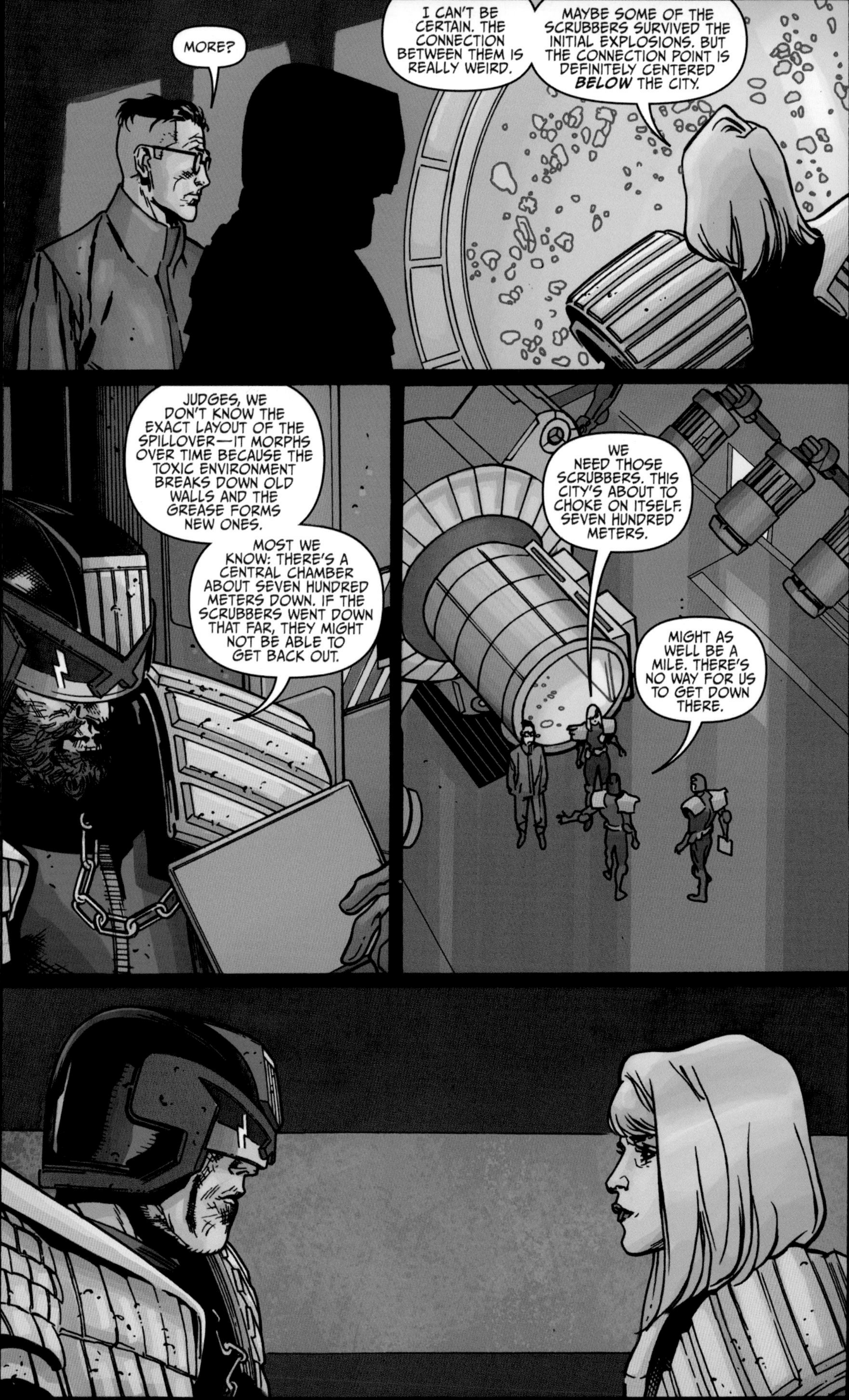
MORE?
I CAN'T BE CERTAIN. THE CONNECTION BETWEEN THEM IS REALLY WEIRD.
MAYBE SOME OF THE SCRUBBERS SURVIVED THE INITIAL EXPLOSIONS. BUT THE CONNECTION POINT IS DEFINITELY CENTERED *BELOW* THE CITY.
JUDGES, WE DON'T KNOW THE EXACT LAYOUT OF THE SPILLOVER—IT MORPHS OVER TIME BECAUSE THE TOXIC ENVIRONMENT BREAKS DOWN OLD WALLS AND THE GREASE FORMS NEW ONES.
MOST WE KNOW: THERE'S A CENTRAL CHAMBER ABOUT SEVEN HUNDRED METERS DOWN. IF THE SCRUBBERS WENT DOWN THAT FAR, THEY MIGHT NOT BE ABLE TO GET BACK OUT.
WE NEED THOSE SCRUBBERS. THIS CITY'S ABOUT TO CHOKE ON ITSELF. SEVEN HUNDRED METERS.
MIGHT AS WELL BE A MILE. THERE'S NO WAY FOR US TO GET DOWN THERE.

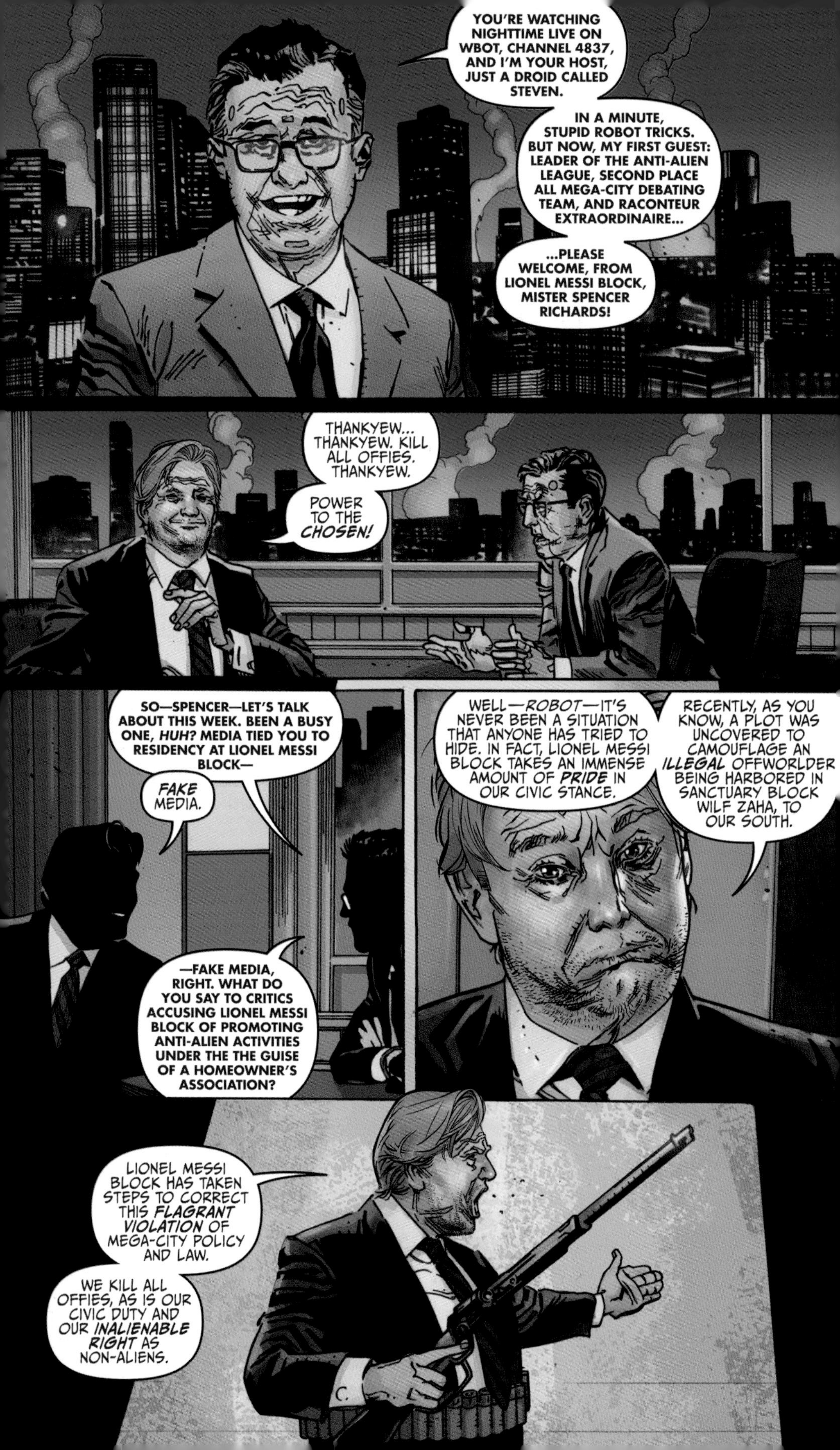
YOU'RE WATCHING NIGHTTIME LIVE ON WBOT, CHANNEL 4837, AND I'M YOUR HOST, JUST A DROID CALLED STEVEN.
IN A MINUTE, STUPID ROBOT TRICKS. BUT NOW, MY FIRST GUEST: LEADER OF THE ANTI-ALIEN LEAGUE, SECOND PLACE ALL MEGA-CITY DEBATING TEAM, AND RACONTEUR EXTRAORDINAIRE...
...PLEASE WELCOME, FROM LIONEL MESSI BLOCK, MISTER SPENCER RICHARDS!
THANKYEW... THANKYEW. KILL ALL OFFIES. THANKYEW.
POWER TO THE *CHOSEN!*
SO—SPENCER—LET'S TALK ABOUT THIS WEEK. BEEN A BUSY ONE, *HUH?* MEDIA TIED YOU TO RESIDENCY AT LIONEL MESSI BLOCK—
FAKE MEDIA.
—FAKE MEDIA, RIGHT. WHAT DO YOU SAY TO CRITICS ACCUSING LIONEL MESSI BLOCK OF PROMOTING ANTI-ALIEN ACTIVITIES UNDER THE THE GUISE OF A HOMEOWNER'S ASSOCIATION?
WELL—*ROBOT*—IT'S NEVER BEEN A SITUATION THAT ANYONE HAS TRIED TO HIDE. IN FACT, LIONEL MESSI BLOCK TAKES AN IMMENSE AMOUNT OF *PRIDE* IN OUR CIVIC STANCE.
RECENTLY, AS YOU KNOW, A PLOT WAS UNCOVERED TO CAMOUFLAGE AN *ILLEGAL* OFFWORLDER BEING HARBORED IN SANCTUARY BLOCK WILF ZAHA, TO OUR SOUTH.
LIONEL MESSI BLOCK HAS TAKEN STEPS TO CORRECT THIS *FLAGRANT VIOLATION* OF MEGA-CITY POLICY AND LAW.
WE KILL ALL OFFIES, AS IS OUR CIVIC DUTY AND OUR *INALIENABLE RIGHT* AS NON-ALIENS.

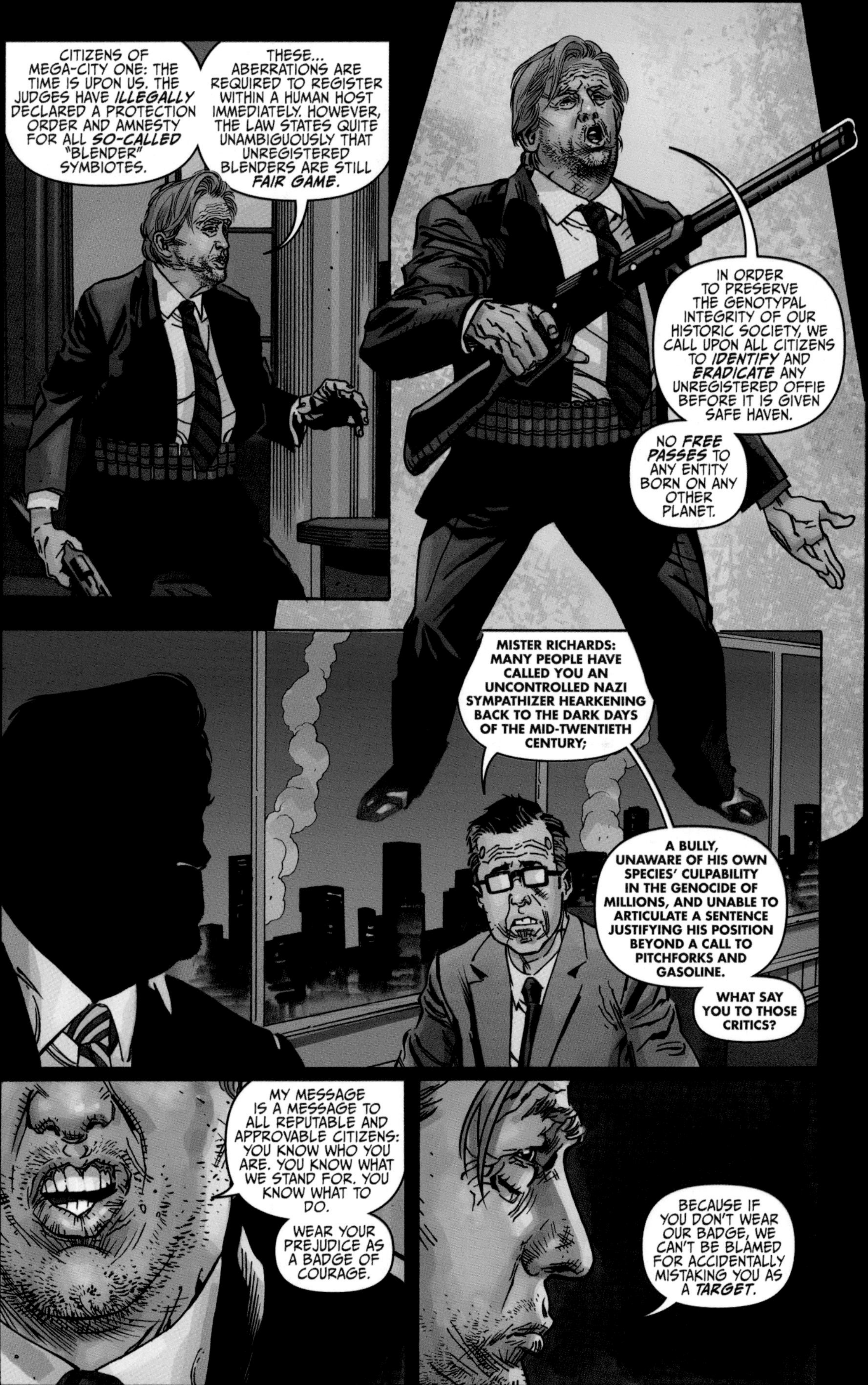
CITIZENS OF MEGA-CITY ONE: THE TIME IS UPON US. THE JUDGES HAVE ILLEGALLY DECLARED A PROTECTION ORDER AND AMNESTY FOR ALL SO-CALLED "BLENDER" SYMBIOTES.
THESE... ABERRATIONS ARE REQUIRED TO REGISTER WITHIN A HUMAN HOST IMMEDIATELY. HOWEVER, THE LAW STATES QUITE UNAMBIGUOUSLY THAT UNREGISTERED BLENDERS ARE STILL FAIR GAME.
IN ORDER TO PRESERVE THE GENOTYPAL INTEGRITY OF OUR HISTORIC SOCIETY, WE CALL UPON ALL CITIZENS TO IDENTIFY AND ERADICATE ANY UNREGISTERED OFFIE BEFORE IT IS GIVEN SAFE HAVEN.
NO FREE PASSES TO ANY ENTITY BORN ON ANY OTHER PLANET.
MISTER RICHARDS: MANY PEOPLE HAVE CALLED YOU AN UNCONTROLLED NAZI SYMPATHIZER HEARKENING BACK TO THE DARK DAYS OF THE MID-TWENTIETH CENTURY;
A BULLY, UNAWARE OF HIS OWN SPECIES' CULPABILITY IN THE GENOCIDE OF MILLIONS, AND UNABLE TO ARTICULATE A SENTENCE JUSTIFYING HIS POSITION BEYOND A CALL TO PITCHFORKS AND GASOLINE.
WHAT SAY YOU TO THOSE CRITICS?
MY MESSAGE IS A MESSAGE TO ALL REPUTABLE AND APPROVABLE CITIZENS: YOU KNOW WHO YOU ARE. YOU KNOW WHAT WE STAND FOR. YOU KNOW WHAT TO DO.
WEAR YOUR PREJUDICE AS A BADGE OF COURAGE.
BECAUSE IF YOU DON'T WEAR OUR BADGE, WE CAN'T BE BLAMED FOR ACCIDENTALLY MISTAKING YOU AS A TARGET.

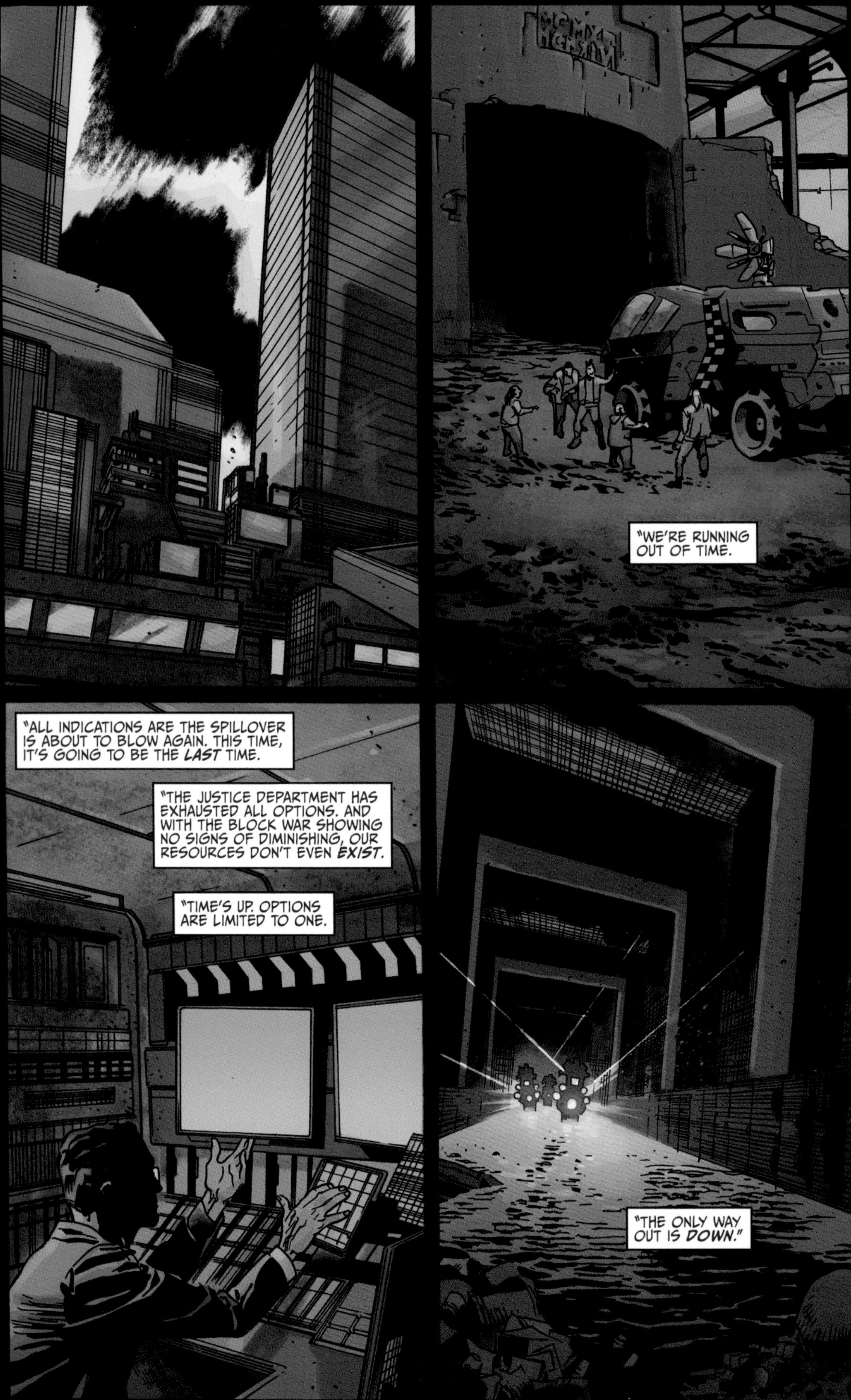
"WE'RE RUNNING OUT OF TIME.
"ALL INDICATIONS ARE THE SPILLOVER IS ABOUT TO BLOW AGAIN. THIS TIME, IT'S GOING TO BE THE *LAST* TIME.
"THE JUSTICE DEPARTMENT HAS EXHAUSTED ALL OPTIONS. AND WITH THE BLOCK WAR SHOWING NO SIGNS OF DIMINISHING, OUR RESOURCES DON'T EVEN *EXIST*.
"TIME'S UP. OPTIONS ARE LIMITED TO ONE.
"THE ONLY WAY OUT IS *DOWN*."

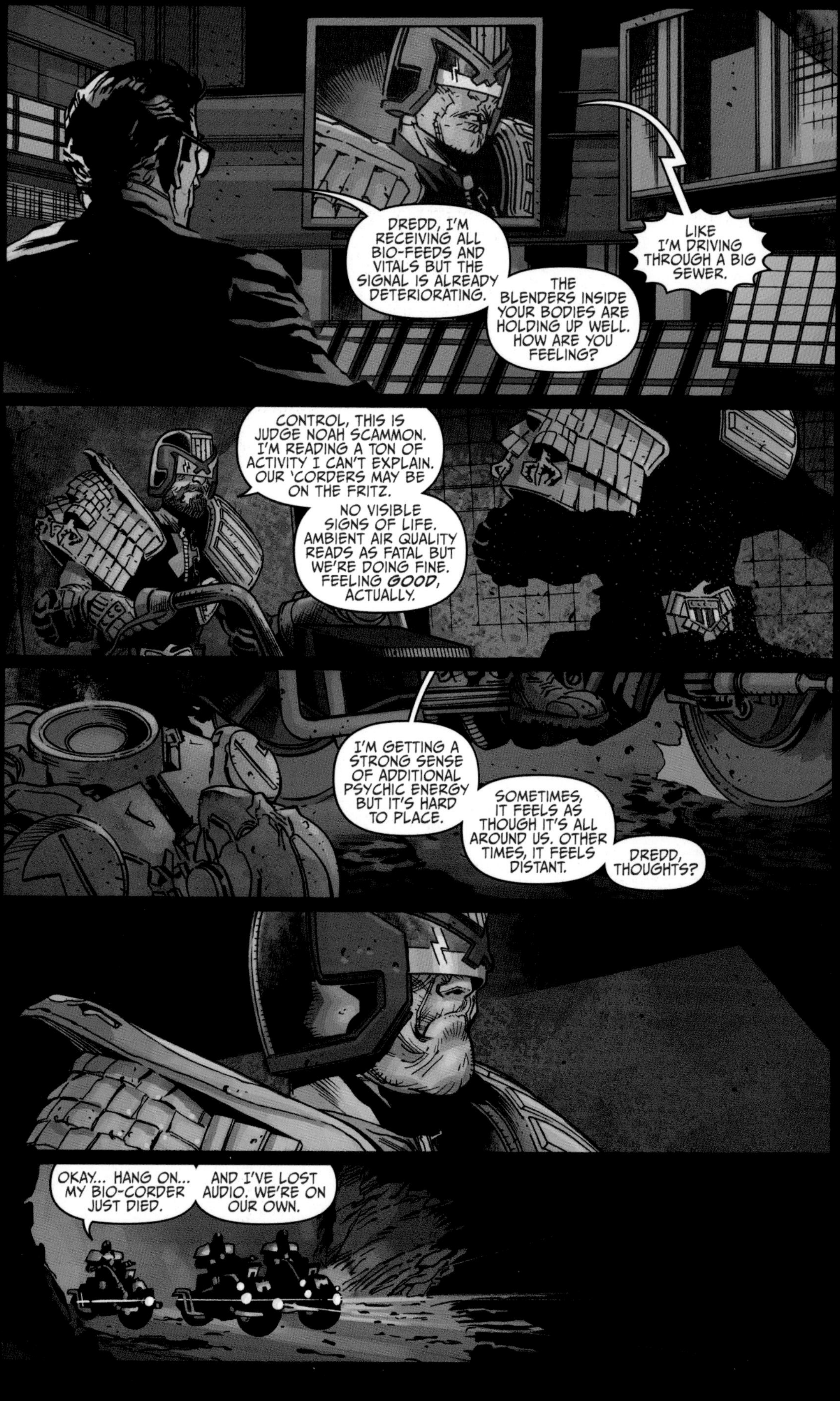
DREDD, I'M RECEIVING ALL BIO-FEEDS AND VITALS BUT THE SIGNAL IS ALREADY DETERIORATING.
THE BLENDERS INSIDE YOUR BODIES ARE HOLDING UP WELL. HOW ARE YOU FEELING?
LIKE I'M DRIVING THROUGH A BIG SEWER.
CONTROL, THIS IS JUDGE NOAH SCAMMON. I'M READING A TON OF ACTIVITY I CAN'T EXPLAIN. OUR 'CORDERS MAY BE ON THE FRITZ.
NO VISIBLE SIGNS OF LIFE. AMBIENT AIR QUALITY READS AS FATAL BUT WE'RE DOING FINE. FEELING *GOOD*, ACTUALLY.
I'M GETTING A STRONG SENSE OF ADDITIONAL PSYCHIC ENERGY BUT IT'S HARD TO PLACE.
SOMETIMES, IT FEELS AS THOUGH IT'S ALL AROUND US. OTHER TIMES, IT FEELS DISTANT.
DREDD, THOUGHTS?
OKAY... HANG ON... MY BIO-CORDER JUST DIED.
AND I'VE LOST AUDIO. WE'RE ON OUR OWN.

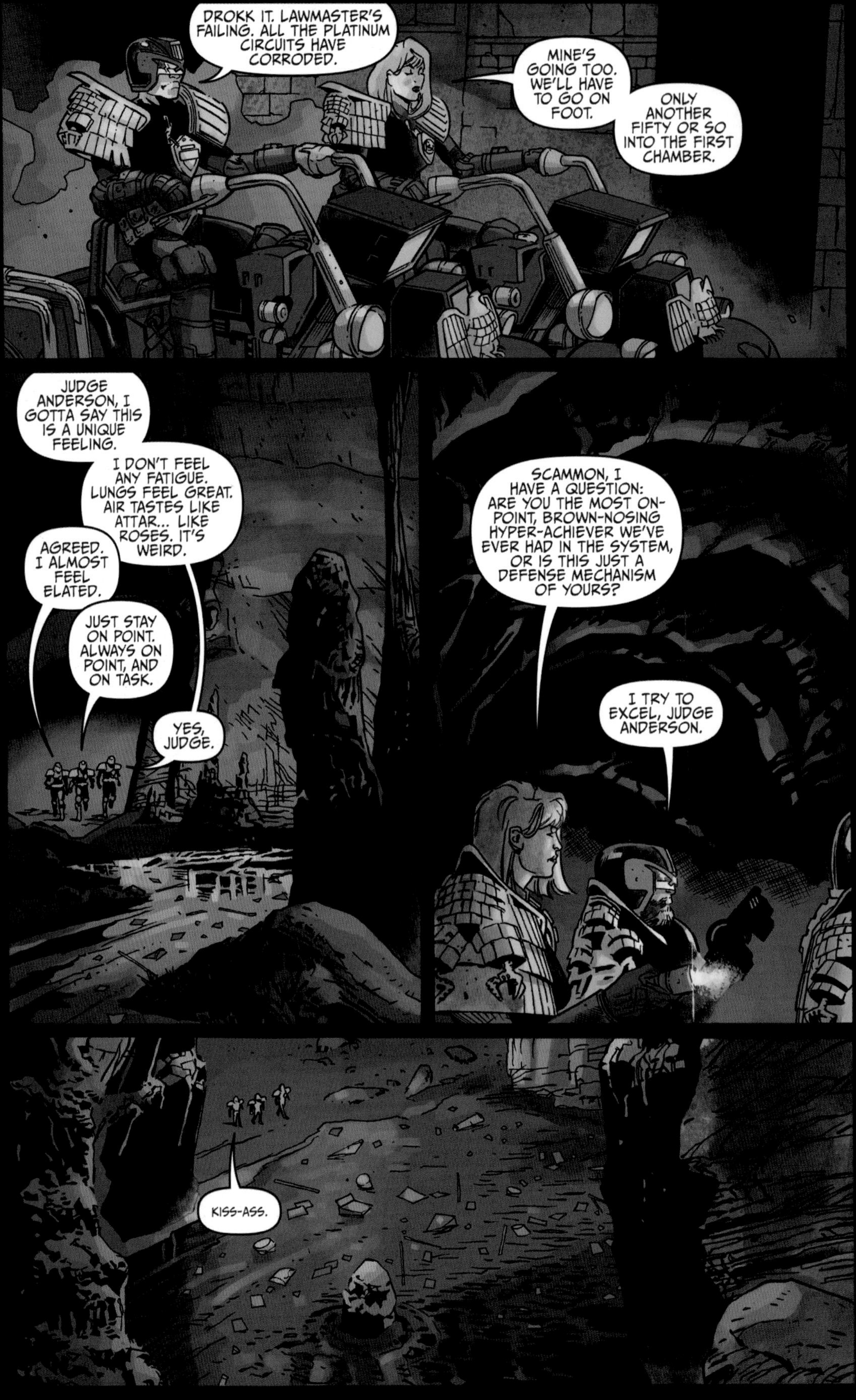
DROKK IT. LAWMASTER'S FAILING. ALL THE PLATINUM CIRCUITS HAVE CORRODED.
MINE'S GOING TOO. WE'LL HAVE TO GO ON FOOT.
ONLY ANOTHER FIFTY OR SO INTO THE FIRST CHAMBER.
JUDGE ANDERSON, I GOTTA SAY THIS IS A UNIQUE FEELING.
I DON'T FEEL ANY FATIGUE. LUNGS FEEL GREAT. AIR TASTES LIKE ATTAR... LIKE ROSES. IT'S WEIRD.
AGREED. I ALMOST FEEL ELATED.
JUST STAY ON POINT. ALWAYS ON POINT, AND ON TASK.
YES, JUDGE.
SCAMMON, I HAVE A QUESTION: ARE YOU THE MOST ON-POINT, BROWN-NOSING HYPER-ACHIEVER WE'VE EVER HAD IN THE SYSTEM, OR IS THIS JUST A DEFENSE MECHANISM OF YOURS?
I TRY TO EXCEL, JUDGE ANDERSON.
KISS-ASS.

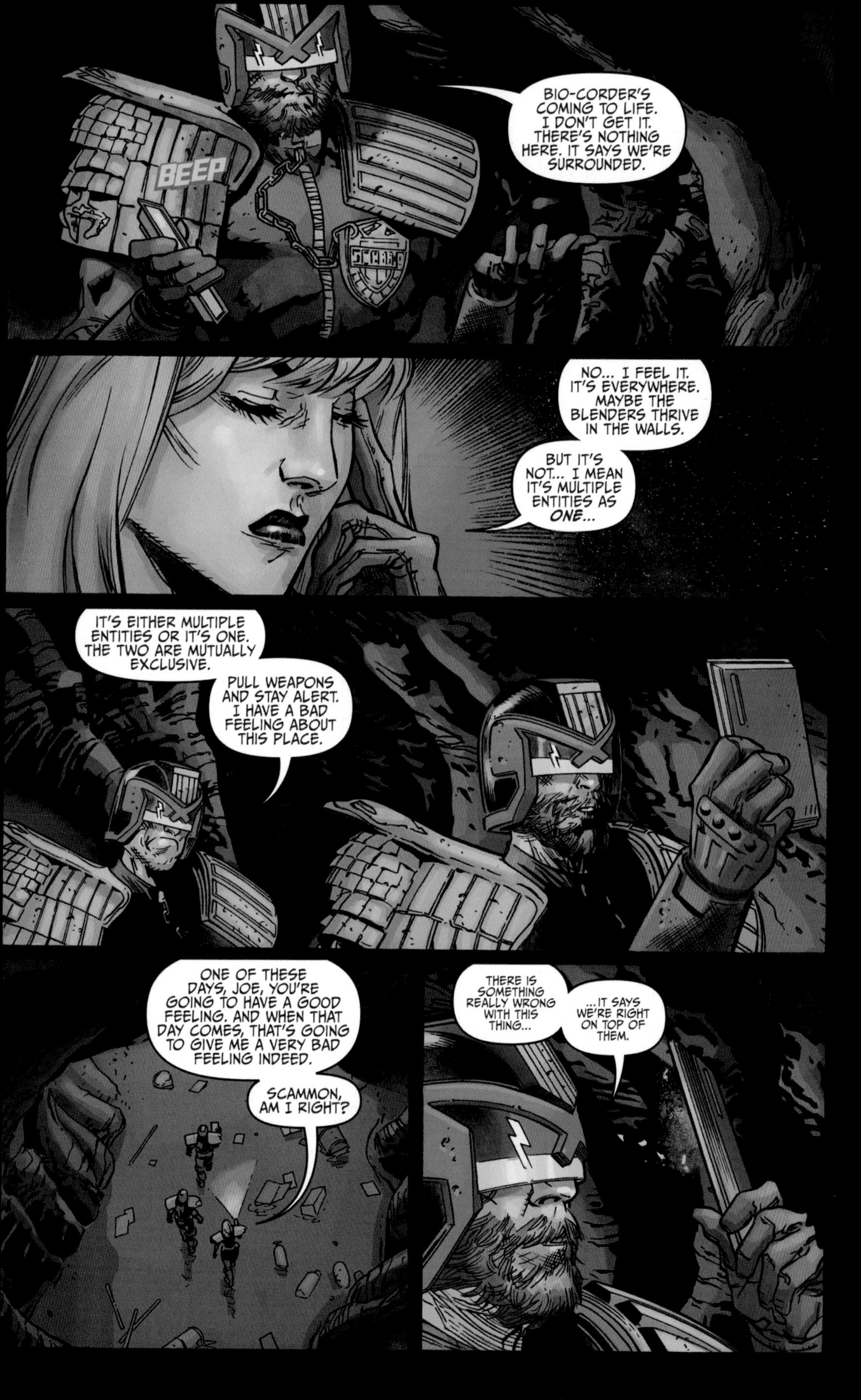
BEEP
BIO-CORDER'S COMING TO LIFE. I DON'T GET IT. THERE'S NOTHING HERE. IT SAYS WE'RE SURROUNDED.
NO... I FEEL IT. IT'S EVERYWHERE. MAYBE THE BLENDERS THRIVE IN THE WALLS.
BUT IT'S NOT... I MEAN IT'S MULTIPLE ENTITIES AS ONE...
IT'S EITHER MULTIPLE ENTITIES OR IT'S ONE. THE TWO ARE MUTUALLY EXCLUSIVE.
PULL WEAPONS AND STAY ALERT. I HAVE A BAD FEELING ABOUT THIS PLACE.
ONE OF THESE DAYS, JOE, YOU'RE GOING TO HAVE A GOOD FEELING. AND WHEN THAT DAY COMES, THAT'S GOING TO GIVE ME A VERY BAD FEELING INDEED.
SCAMMON, AM I RIGHT?
THERE IS SOMETHING REALLY WRONG WITH THIS THING...
...IT SAYS WE'RE RIGHT ON TOP OF THEM.

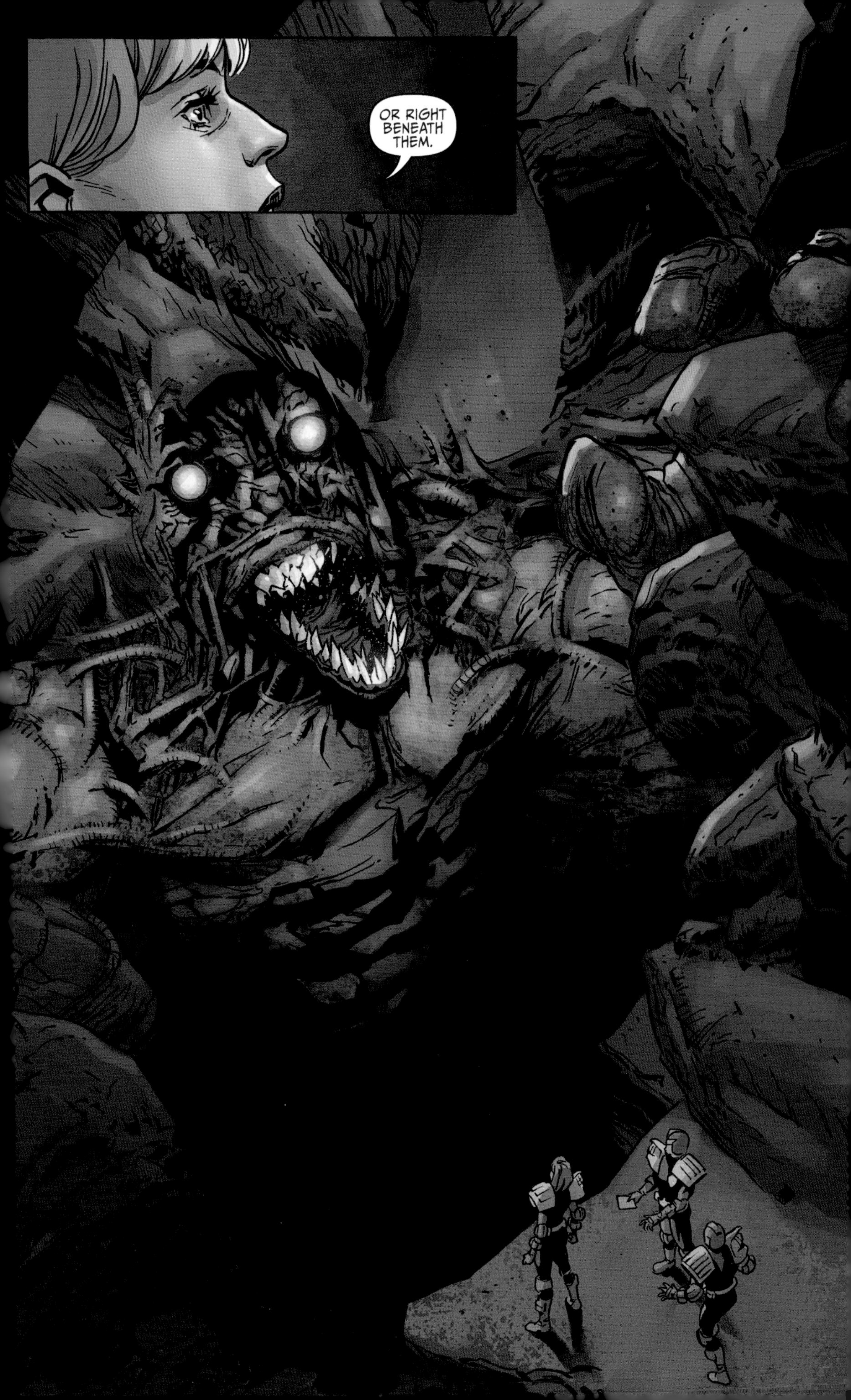
OR RIGHT BENEATH THEM.

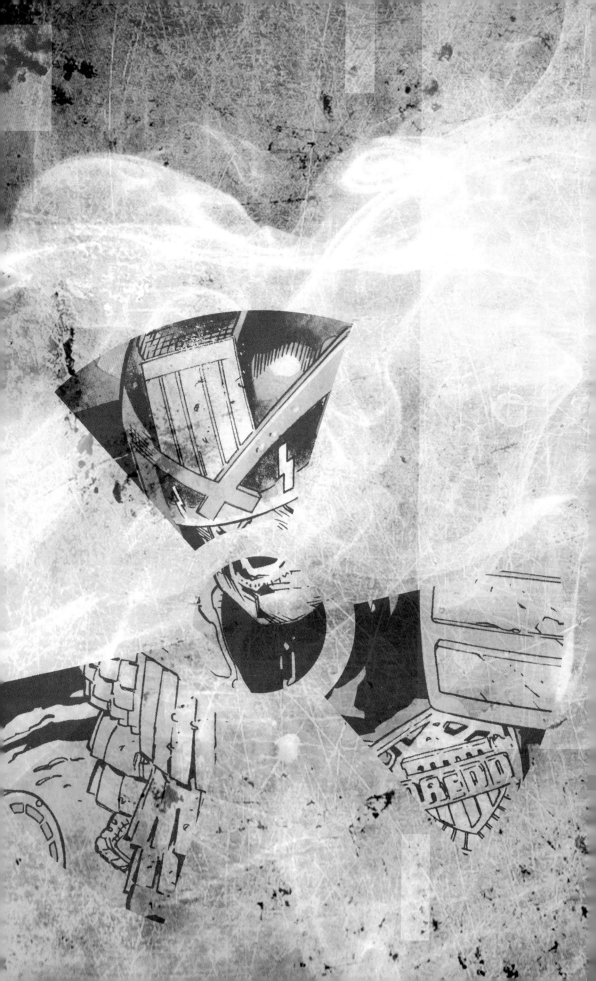

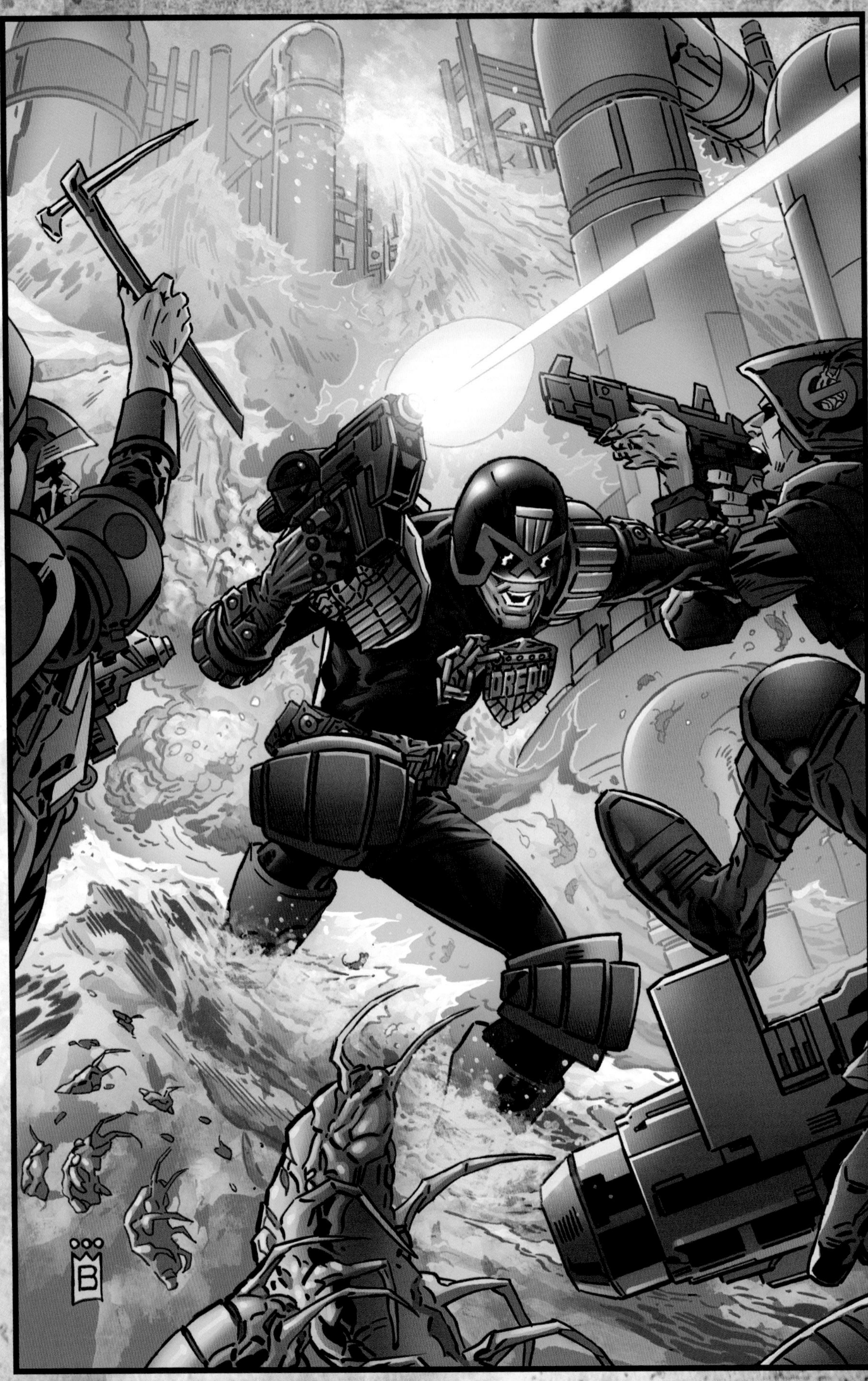
DREDD

ART BY **MARK BUCKINGHAM** COLORS BY **CHRIS BLYTHE**

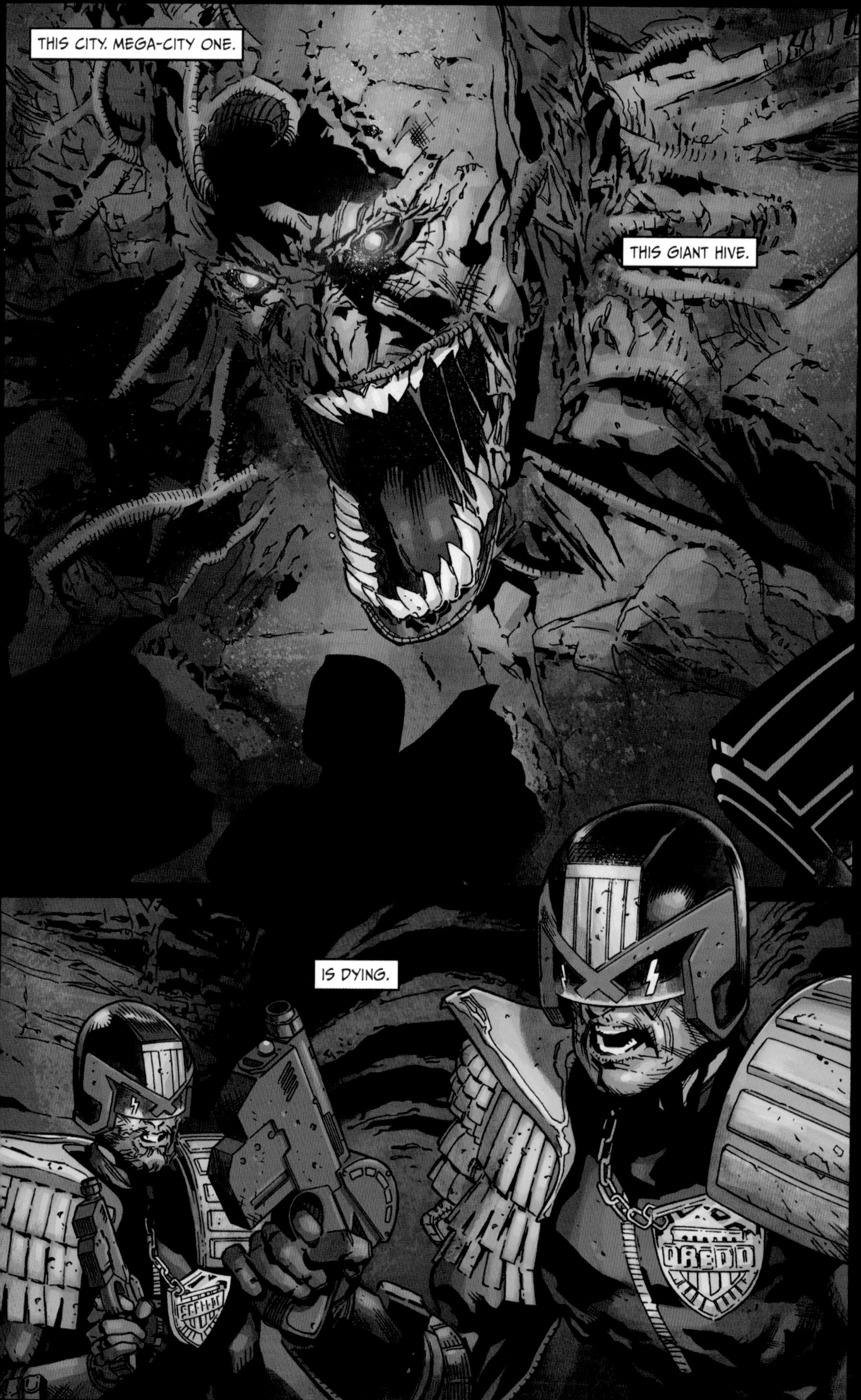
THIS CITY. MEGA-CITY ONE.
THIS GIANT HIVE.
IS DYING.

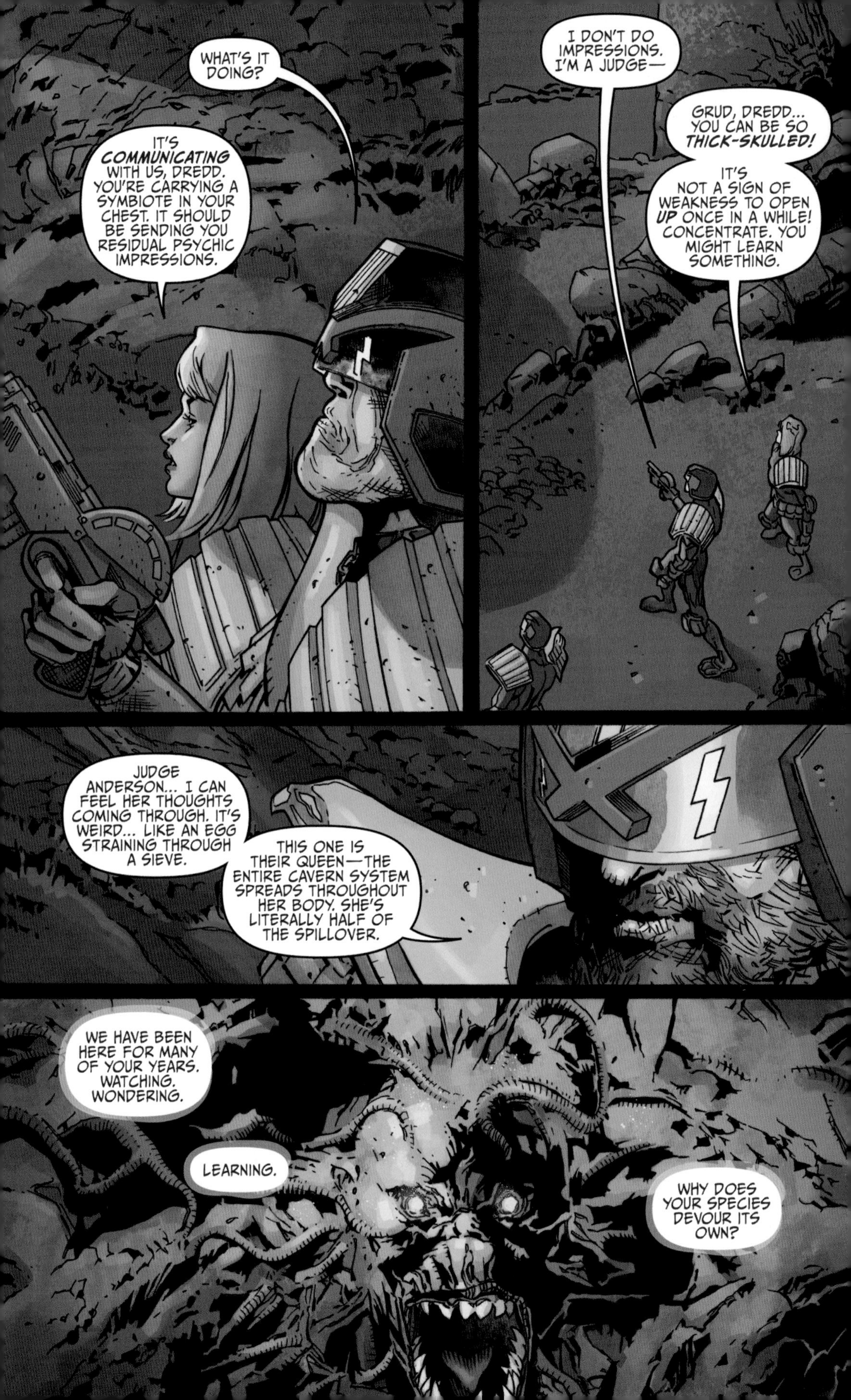
WHAT'S IT DOING?
IT'S COMMUNICATING WITH US, DREDD. YOU'RE CARRYING A SYMBIOTE IN YOUR CHEST. IT SHOULD BE SENDING YOU RESIDUAL PSYCHIC IMPRESSIONS.
I DON'T DO IMPRESSIONS. I'M A JUDGE—
GRUD, DREDD... YOU CAN BE SO THICK-SKULLED!
IT'S NOT A SIGN OF WEAKNESS TO OPEN UP ONCE IN A WHILE! CONCENTRATE. YOU MIGHT LEARN SOMETHING.
JUDGE ANDERSON... I CAN FEEL HER THOUGHTS COMING THROUGH. IT'S WEIRD... LIKE AN EGG STRAINING THROUGH A SIEVE.
THIS ONE IS THEIR QUEEN—THE ENTIRE CAVERN SYSTEM SPREADS THROUGHOUT HER BODY. SHE'S LITERALLY HALF OF THE SPILLOVER.
WE HAVE BEEN HERE FOR MANY OF YOUR YEARS. WATCHING. WONDERING.
LEARNING.
WHY DOES YOUR SPECIES DEVOUR ITS OWN?

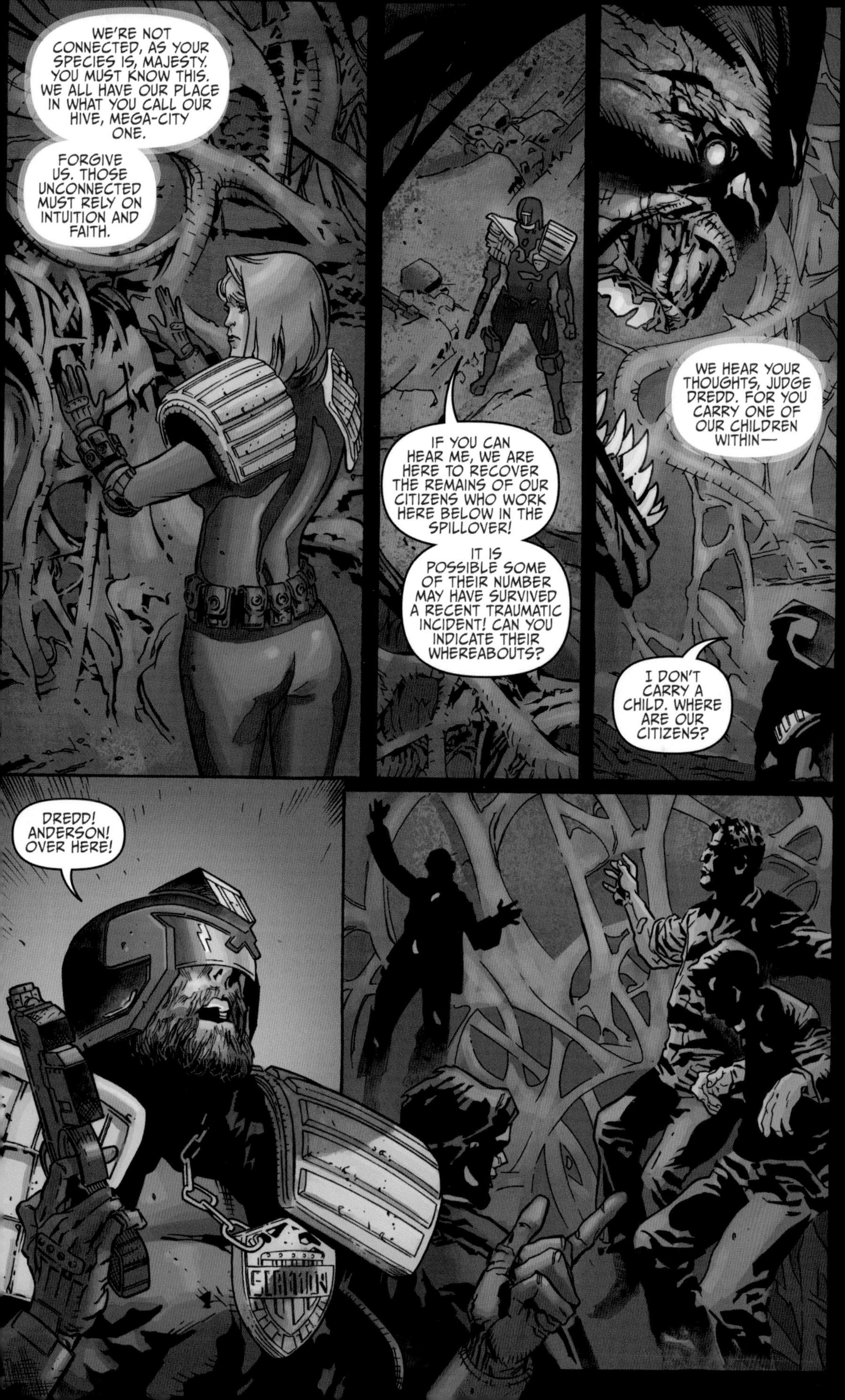
WE'RE NOT CONNECTED, AS YOUR SPECIES IS, MAJESTY. YOU MUST KNOW THIS. WE ALL HAVE OUR PLACE IN WHAT YOU CALL OUR HIVE, MEGA-CITY ONE.
FORGIVE US. THOSE UNCONNECTED MUST RELY ON INTUITION AND FAITH.
IF YOU CAN HEAR ME, WE ARE HERE TO RECOVER THE REMAINS OF OUR CITIZENS WHO WORK HERE BELOW IN THE SPILLOVER!
IT IS POSSIBLE SOME OF THEIR NUMBER MAY HAVE SURVIVED A RECENT TRAUMATIC INCIDENT! CAN YOU INDICATE THEIR WHEREABOUTS?
WE HEAR YOUR THOUGHTS, JUDGE DREDD. FOR YOU CARRY ONE OF OUR CHILDREN WITHIN—
I DON'T CARRY A CHILD. WHERE ARE OUR CITIZENS?
DREDD! ANDERSON! OVER HERE!

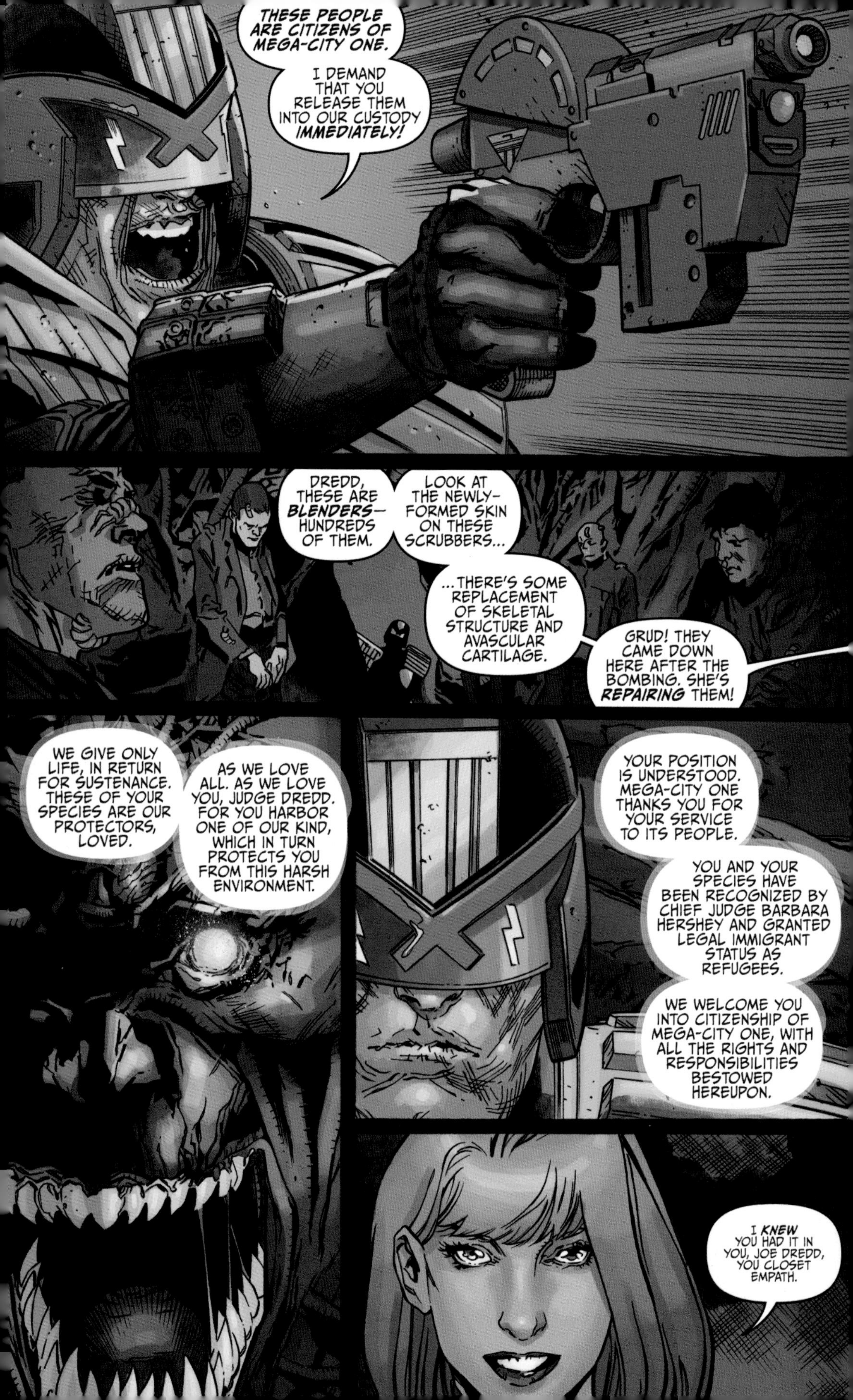
THESE PEOPLE ARE CITIZENS OF MEGA-CITY ONE.
I DEMAND THAT YOU RELEASE THEM INTO OUR CUSTODY IMMEDIATELY!
DREDD, THESE ARE BLENDERS— HUNDREDS OF THEM.
LOOK AT THE NEWLY-FORMED SKIN ON THESE SCRUBBERS...
...THERE'S SOME REPLACEMENT OF SKELETAL STRUCTURE AND AVASCULAR CARTILAGE.
GRUD! THEY CAME DOWN HERE AFTER THE BOMBING. SHE'S REPAIRING THEM!
WE GIVE ONLY LIFE, IN RETURN FOR SUSTENANCE. THESE OF YOUR SPECIES ARE OUR PROTECTORS, LOVED.
AS WE LOVE ALL. AS WE LOVE YOU, JUDGE DREDD. FOR YOU HARBOR ONE OF OUR KIND, WHICH IN TURN PROTECTS YOU FROM THIS HARSH ENVIRONMENT.
YOUR POSITION IS UNDERSTOOD. MEGA-CITY ONE THANKS YOU FOR YOUR SERVICE TO ITS PEOPLE.
YOU AND YOUR SPECIES HAVE BEEN RECOGNIZED BY CHIEF JUDGE BARBARA HERSHEY AND GRANTED LEGAL IMMIGRANT STATUS AS REFUGEES.
WE WELCOME YOU INTO CITIZENSHIP OF MEGA-CITY ONE, WITH ALL THE RIGHTS AND RESPONSIBILITIES BESTOWED HEREUPON.
I KNEW YOU HAD IT IN YOU, JOE DREDD, YOU CLOSET EMPATH.

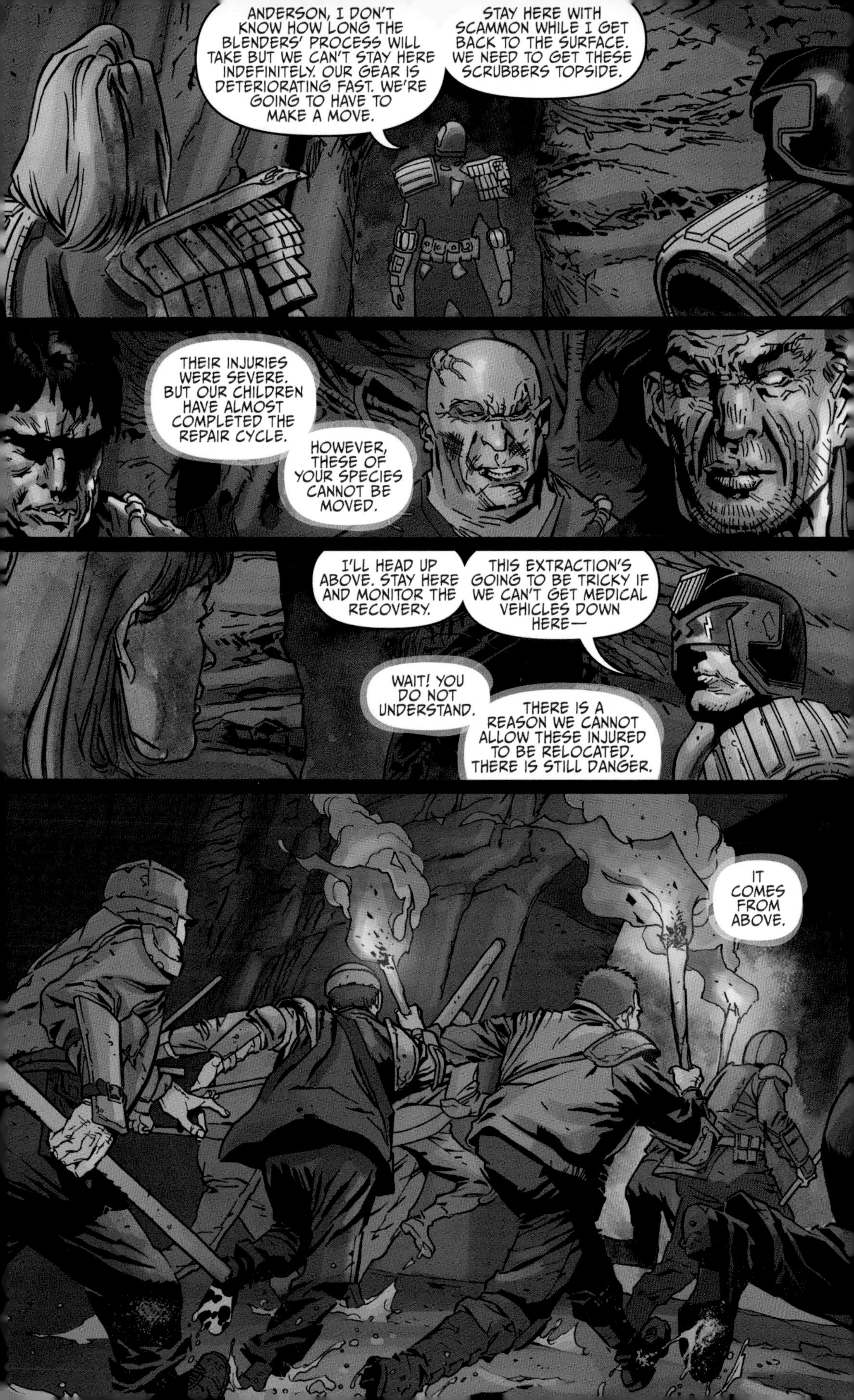
ANDERSON, I DON'T KNOW HOW LONG THE BLENDERS' PROCESS WILL TAKE BUT WE CAN'T STAY HERE INDEFINITELY. OUR GEAR IS DETERIORATING FAST. WE'RE GOING TO HAVE TO MAKE A MOVE.
STAY HERE WITH SCAMMON WHILE I GET BACK TO THE SURFACE. WE NEED TO GET THESE SCRUBBERS TOPSIDE.
THEIR INJURIES WERE SEVERE. BUT OUR CHILDREN HAVE ALMOST COMPLETED THE REPAIR CYCLE.
HOWEVER, THESE OF YOUR SPECIES CANNOT BE MOVED.
I'LL HEAD UP ABOVE. STAY HERE AND MONITOR THE RECOVERY.
THIS EXTRACTION'S GOING TO BE TRICKY IF WE CAN'T GET MEDICAL VEHICLES DOWN HERE—
WAIT! YOU DO NOT UNDERSTAND.
THERE IS A REASON WE CANNOT ALLOW THESE INJURED TO BE RELOCATED. THERE IS STILL DANGER.
IT COMES FROM ABOVE.

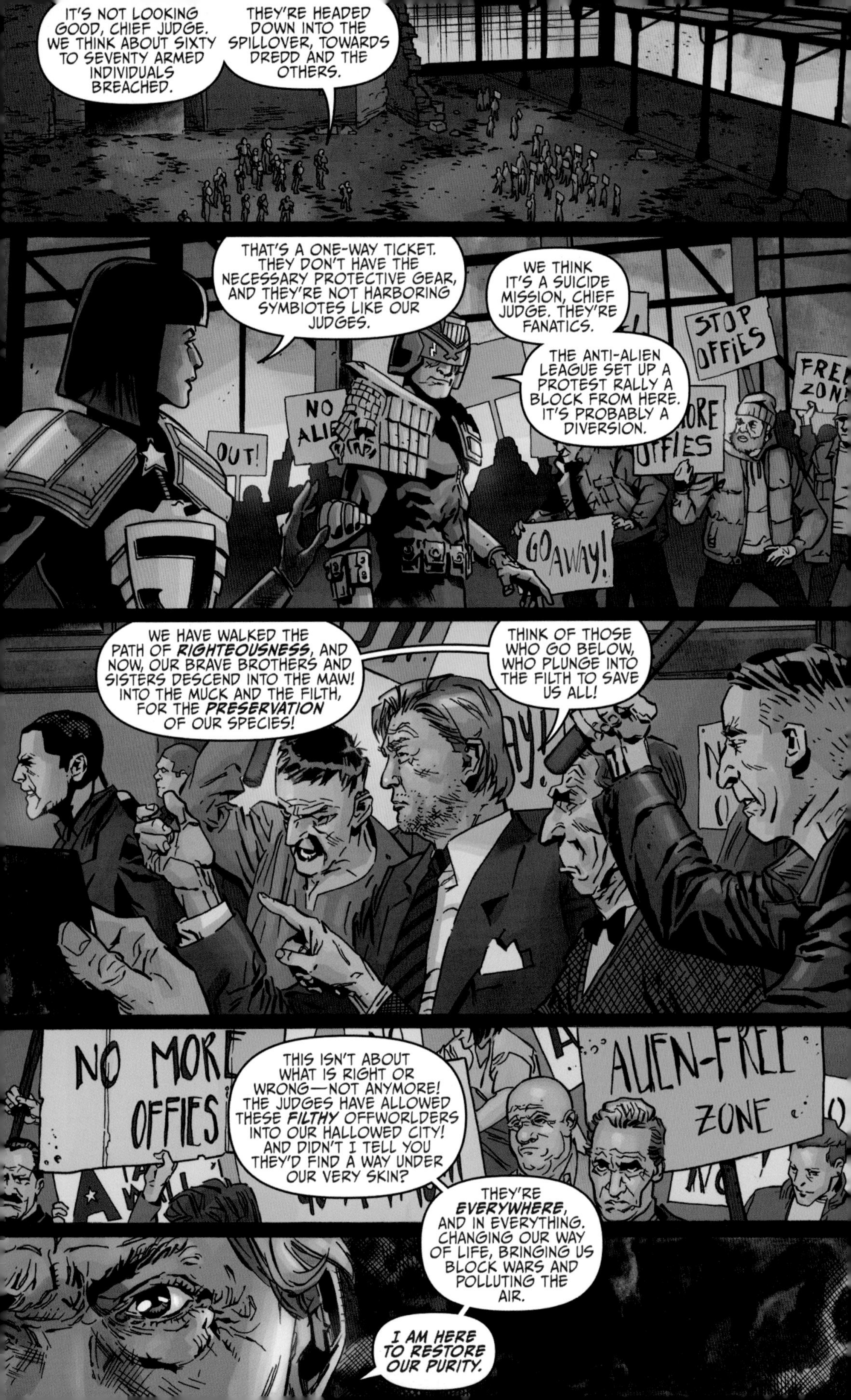
IT'S NOT LOOKING GOOD, CHIEF JUDGE. WE THINK ABOUT SIXTY TO SEVENTY ARMED INDIVIDUALS BREACHED.
THEY'RE HEADED DOWN INTO THE SPILLOVER, TOWARDS DREDD AND THE OTHERS.
THAT'S A ONE-WAY TICKET. THEY DON'T HAVE THE NECESSARY PROTECTIVE GEAR, AND THEY'RE NOT HARBORING SYMBIOTES LIKE OUR JUDGES.
WE THINK IT'S A SUICIDE MISSION, CHIEF JUDGE. THEY'RE FANATICS.
THE ANTI-ALIEN LEAGUE SET UP A PROTEST RALLY A BLOCK FROM HERE. IT'S PROBABLY A DIVERSION.
STOP OFFIES
OUT!
GO AWAY!
WE HAVE WALKED THE PATH OF RIGHTEOUSNESS, AND NOW, OUR BRAVE BROTHERS AND SISTERS DESCEND INTO THE MAW! INTO THE MUCK AND THE FILTH, FOR THE PRESERVATION OF OUR SPECIES!
THINK OF THOSE WHO GO BELOW, WHO PLUNGE INTO THE FILTH TO SAVE US ALL!
NO MORE OFFIES
ALIEN-FREE ZONE
THIS ISN'T ABOUT WHAT IS RIGHT OR WRONG—NOT ANYMORE! THE JUDGES HAVE ALLOWED THESE FILTHY OFFWORLDERS INTO OUR HALLOWED CITY! AND DIDN'T I TELL YOU THEY'D FIND A WAY UNDER OUR VERY SKIN?
THEY'RE EVERYWHERE, AND IN EVERYTHING. CHANGING OUR WAY OF LIFE, BRINGING US BLOCK WARS AND POLLUTING THE AIR.
I AM HERE TO RESTORE OUR PURITY.

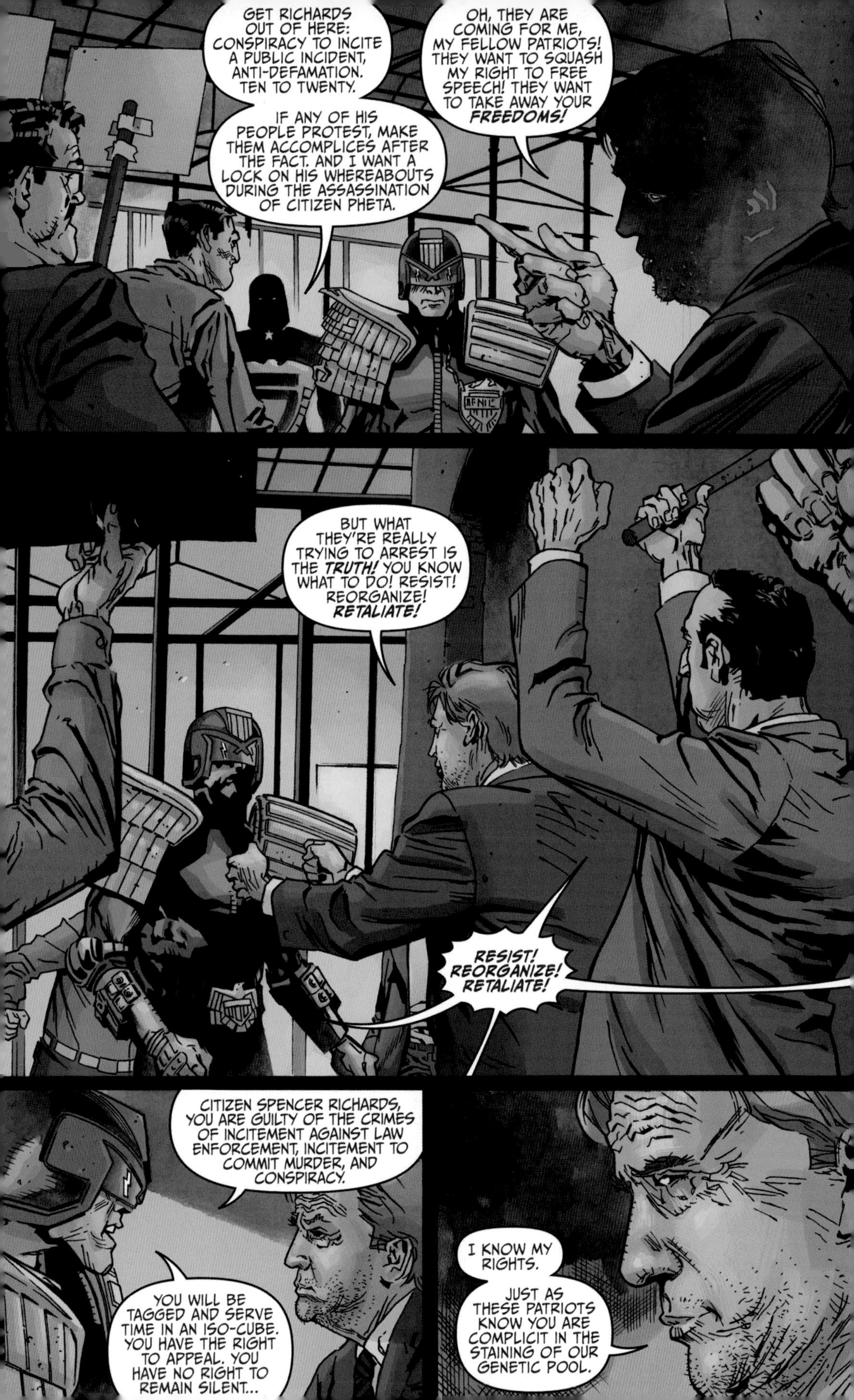
GET RICHARDS OUT OF HERE: CONSPIRACY TO INCITE A PUBLIC INCIDENT, ANTI-DEFAMATION. TEN TO TWENTY.
IF ANY OF HIS PEOPLE PROTEST, MAKE THEM ACCOMPLICES AFTER THE FACT. AND I WANT A LOCK ON HIS WHEREABOUTS DURING THE ASSASSINATION OF CITIZEN PHETA.
OH, THEY ARE COMING FOR ME, MY FELLOW PATRIOTS! THEY WANT TO SQUASH MY RIGHT TO FREE SPEECH! THEY WANT TO TAKE AWAY YOUR ***FREEDOMS!***
BUT WHAT THEY'RE REALLY TRYING TO ARREST IS THE ***TRUTH!*** YOU KNOW WHAT TO DO! RESIST! REORGANIZE! ***RETALIATE!***
RESIST! REORGANIZE! RETALIATE!
CITIZEN SPENCER RICHARDS, YOU ARE GUILTY OF THE CRIMES OF INCITEMENT AGAINST LAW ENFORCEMENT, INCITEMENT TO COMMIT MURDER, AND CONSPIRACY.
YOU WILL BE TAGGED AND SERVE TIME IN AN ISO-CUBE. YOU HAVE THE RIGHT TO APPEAL. YOU HAVE NO RIGHT TO REMAIN SILENT...
I KNOW MY RIGHTS.
JUST AS THESE PATRIOTS KNOW YOU ARE COMPLICIT IN THE STAINING OF OUR GENETIC POOL.

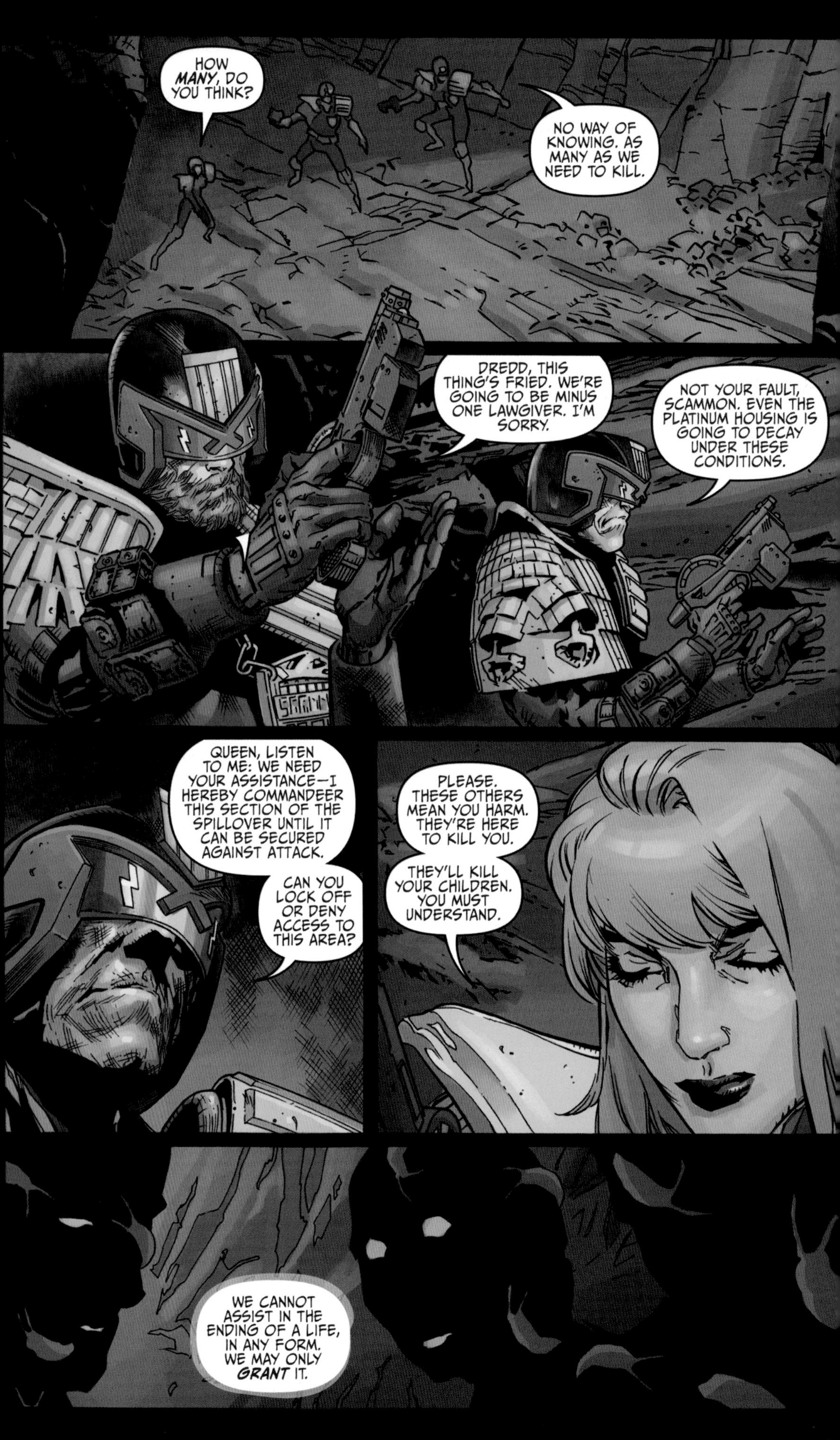
HOW *MANY*, DO YOU THINK?
NO WAY OF KNOWING. AS MANY AS WE NEED TO KILL.
DREDD, THIS THING'S FRIED. WE'RE GOING TO BE MINUS ONE LAWGIVER. I'M SORRY.
NOT YOUR FAULT, SCAMMON. EVEN THE PLATINUM HOUSING IS GOING TO DECAY UNDER THESE CONDITIONS.
QUEEN, LISTEN TO ME: WE NEED YOUR ASSISTANCE—I HEREBY COMMANDEER THIS SECTION OF THE SPILLOVER UNTIL IT CAN BE SECURED AGAINST ATTACK.
CAN YOU LOCK OFF OR DENY ACCESS TO THIS AREA?
PLEASE. THESE OTHERS MEAN YOU HARM. THEY'RE HERE TO KILL YOU.
THEY'LL KILL YOUR CHILDREN. YOU MUST UNDERSTAND.
WE CANNOT ASSIST IN THE ENDING OF A LIFE, IN ANY FORM. WE MAY ONLY *GRANT* IT.

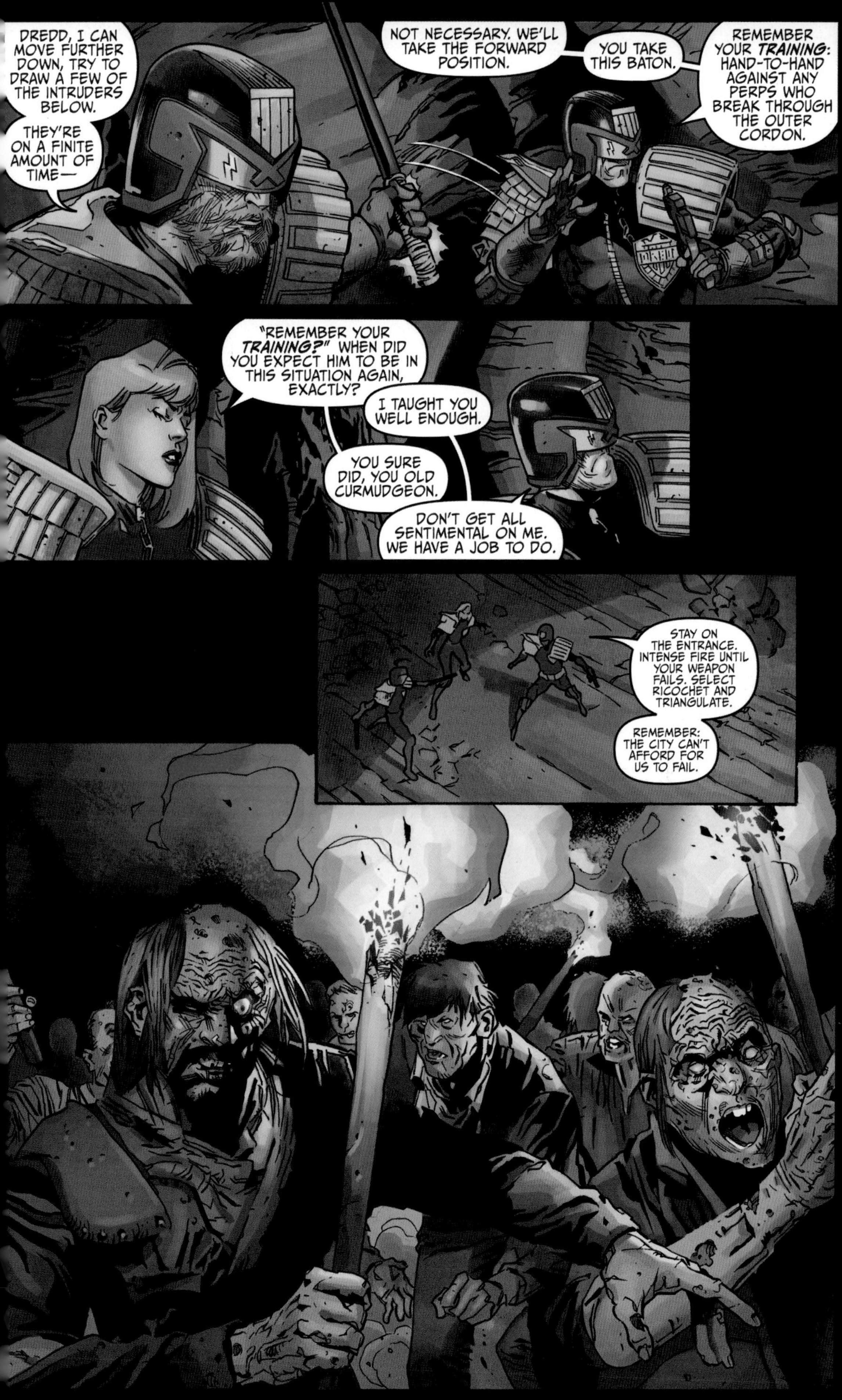
DREDD, I CAN MOVE FURTHER DOWN, TRY TO DRAW A FEW OF THE INTRUDERS BELOW.
THEY'RE ON A FINITE AMOUNT OF TIME—
NOT NECESSARY. WE'LL TAKE THE FORWARD POSITION.
YOU TAKE THIS BATON.
REMEMBER YOUR TRAINING: HAND-TO-HAND AGAINST ANY PERPS WHO BREAK THROUGH THE OUTER CORDON.
"REMEMBER YOUR TRAINING?" WHEN DID YOU EXPECT HIM TO BE IN THIS SITUATION AGAIN, EXACTLY?
I TAUGHT YOU WELL ENOUGH.
YOU SURE DID, YOU OLD CURMUDGEON.
DON'T GET ALL SENTIMENTAL ON ME. WE HAVE A JOB TO DO.
STAY ON THE ENTRANCE. INTENSE FIRE UNTIL YOUR WEAPON FAILS. SELECT RICOCHET AND TRIANGULATE.
REMEMBER: THE CITY CAN'T AFFORD FOR US TO FAIL.

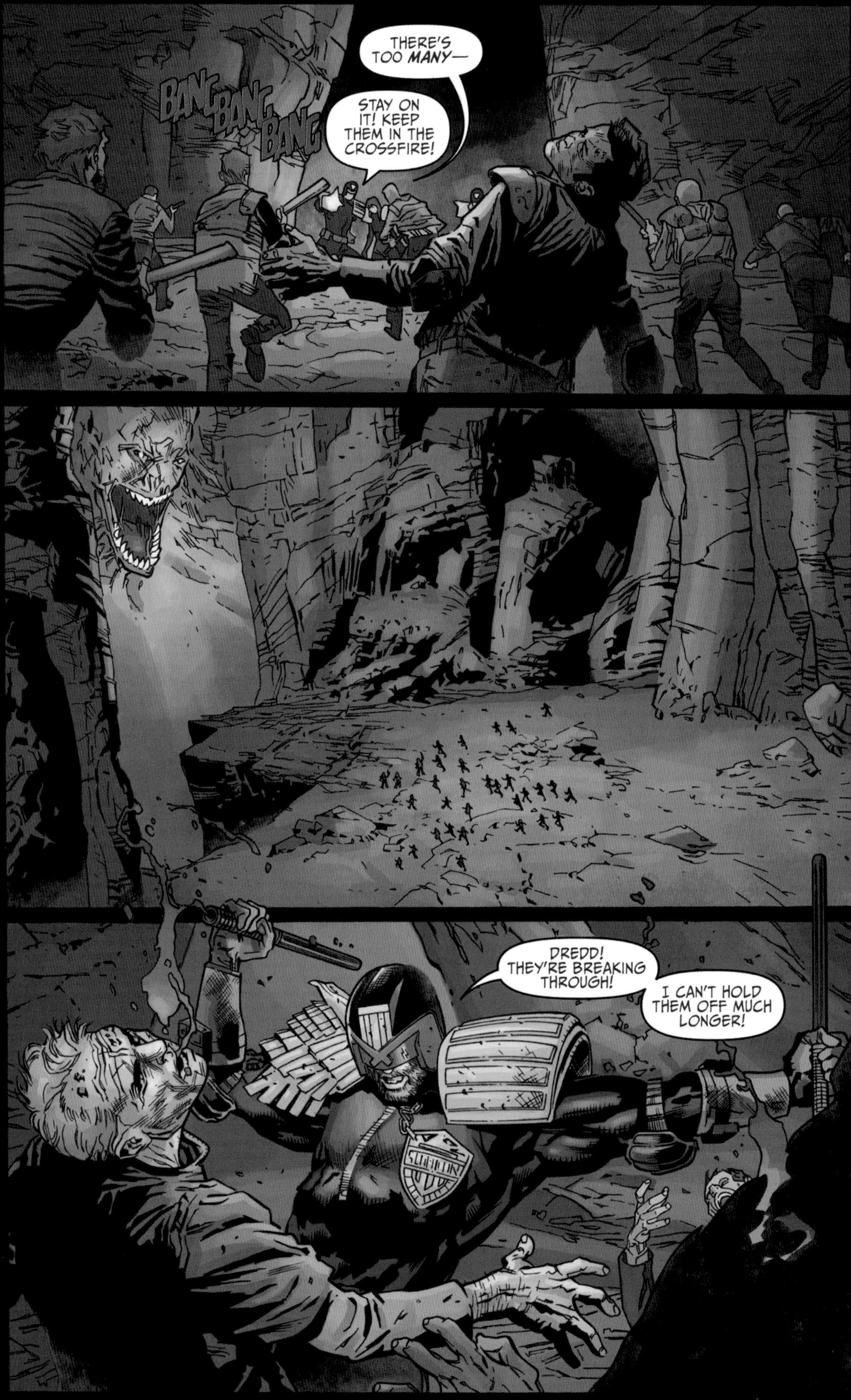
BANG BANG BANG
THERE'S TOO MANY—
STAY ON IT! KEEP THEM IN THE CROSSFIRE!
DREDD! THEY'RE BREAKING THROUGH!
I CAN'T HOLD THEM OFF MUCH LONGER!

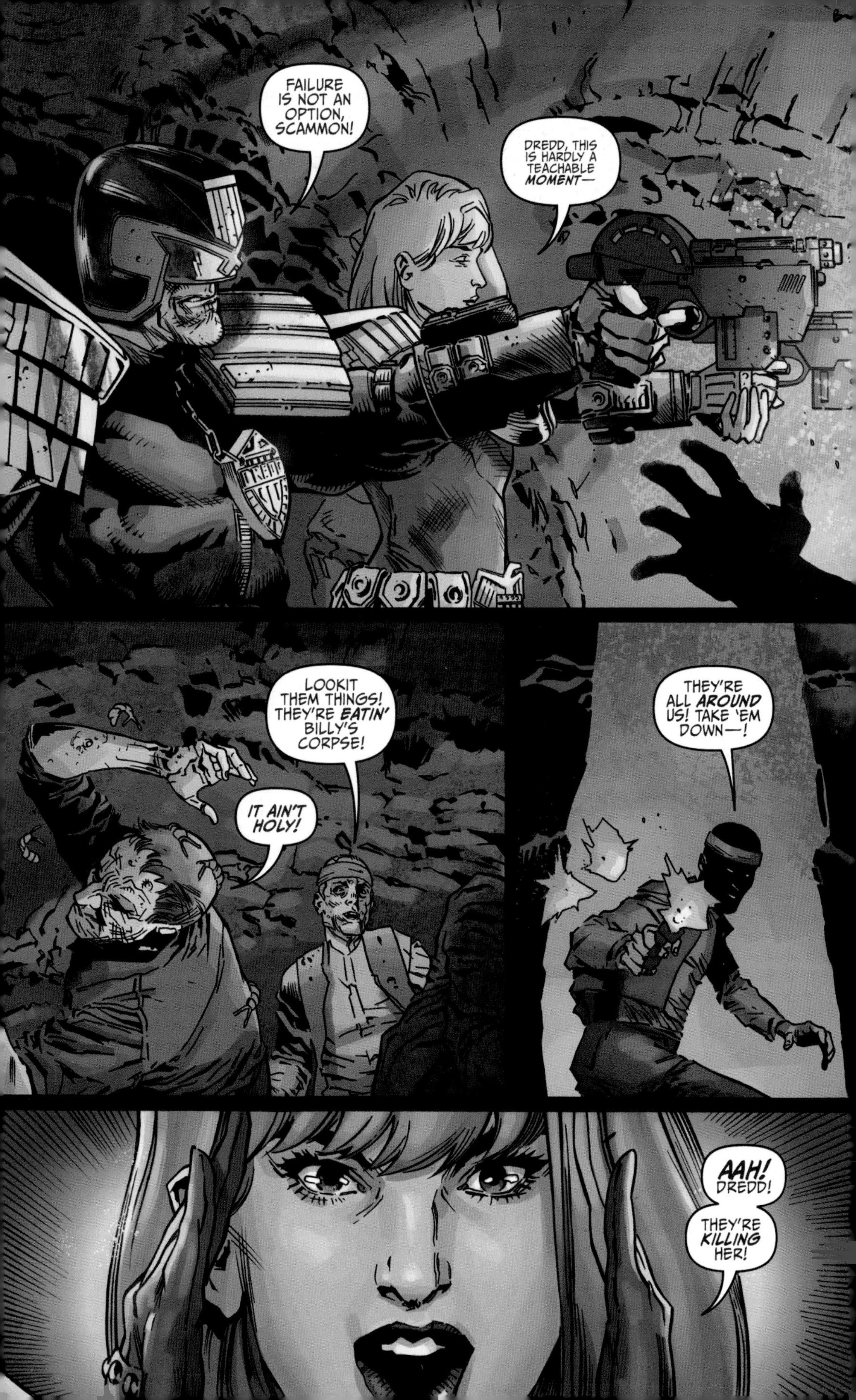
FAILURE IS NOT AN OPTION, SCAMMON!
DREDD, THIS IS HARDLY A TEACHABLE MOMENT—
LOOKIT THEM THINGS! THEY'RE EATIN' BILLY'S CORPSE!
IT AIN'T HOLY!
THEY'RE ALL AROUND US! TAKE 'EM DOWN—!
AAH! DREDD!
THEY'RE KILLING HER!

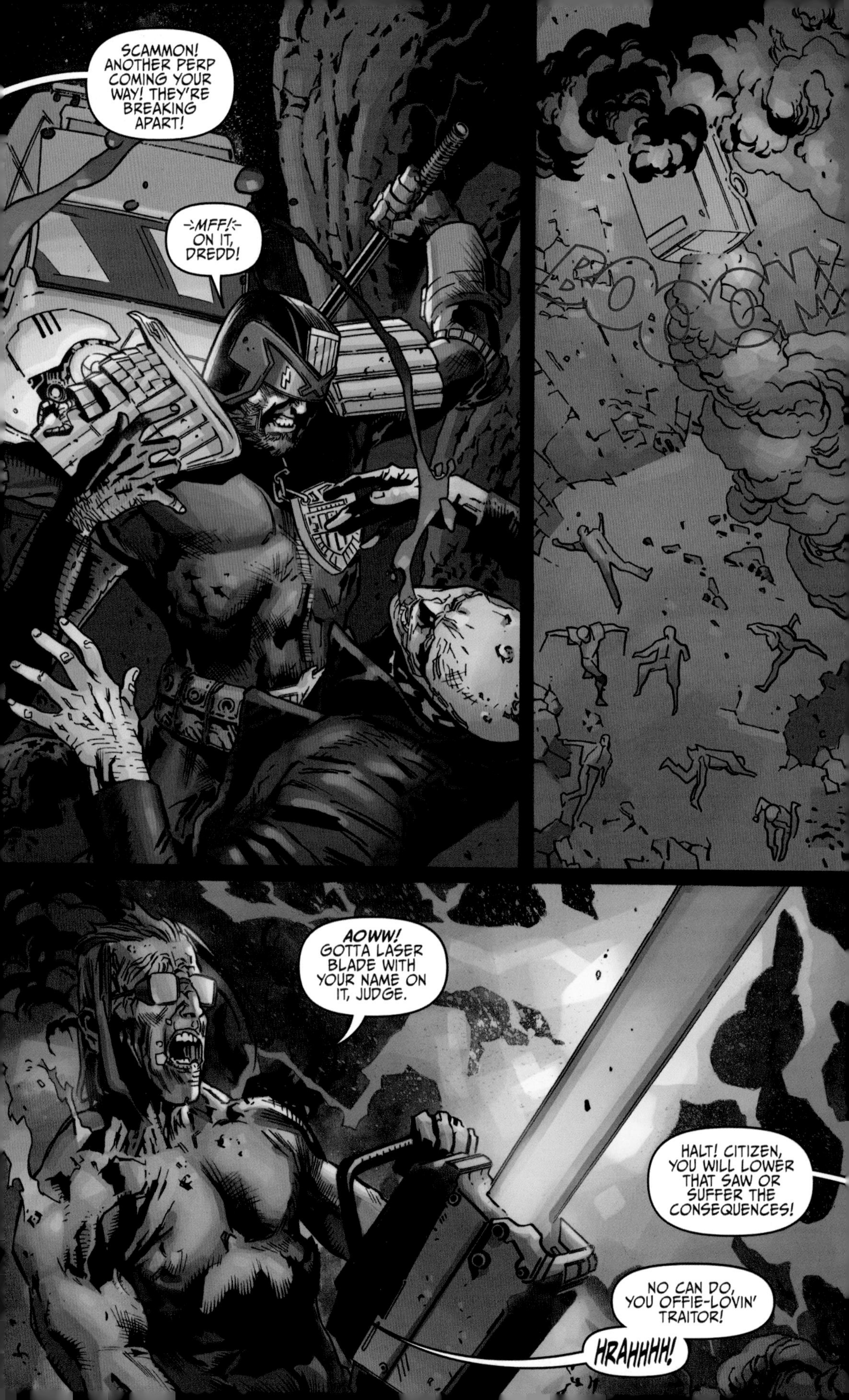
SCAMMON! ANOTHER PERP COMING YOUR WAY! THEY'RE BREAKING APART!
-MFF!- ON IT, DREDD!
BOOOOM
AOWW! GOTTA LASER BLADE WITH YOUR NAME ON IT, JUDGE.
HALT! CITIZEN, YOU WILL LOWER THAT SAW OR SUFFER THE CONSEQUENCES!
NO CAN DO, YOU OFFIE-LOVIN' TRAITOR!
HRAHHHH!

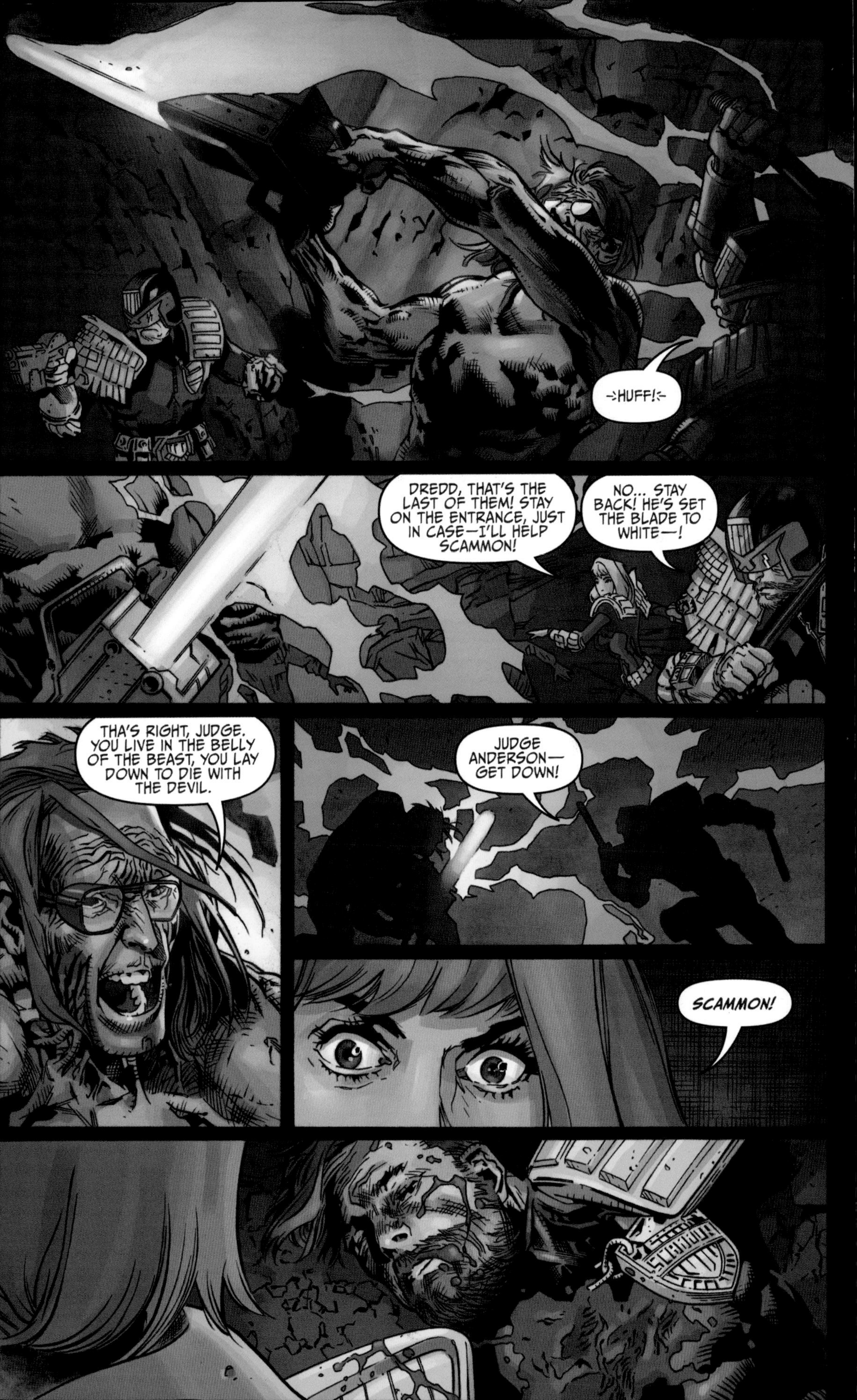
-HUFF!-
DREDD, THAT'S THE LAST OF THEM! STAY ON THE ENTRANCE, JUST IN CASE—I'LL HELP SCAMMON!
NO... STAY BACK! HE'S SET THE BLADE TO WHITE—!
THA'S RIGHT, JUDGE. YOU LIVE IN THE BELLY OF THE BEAST, YOU LAY DOWN TO DIE WITH THE DEVIL.
JUDGE ANDERSON—GET DOWN!
SCAMMON!

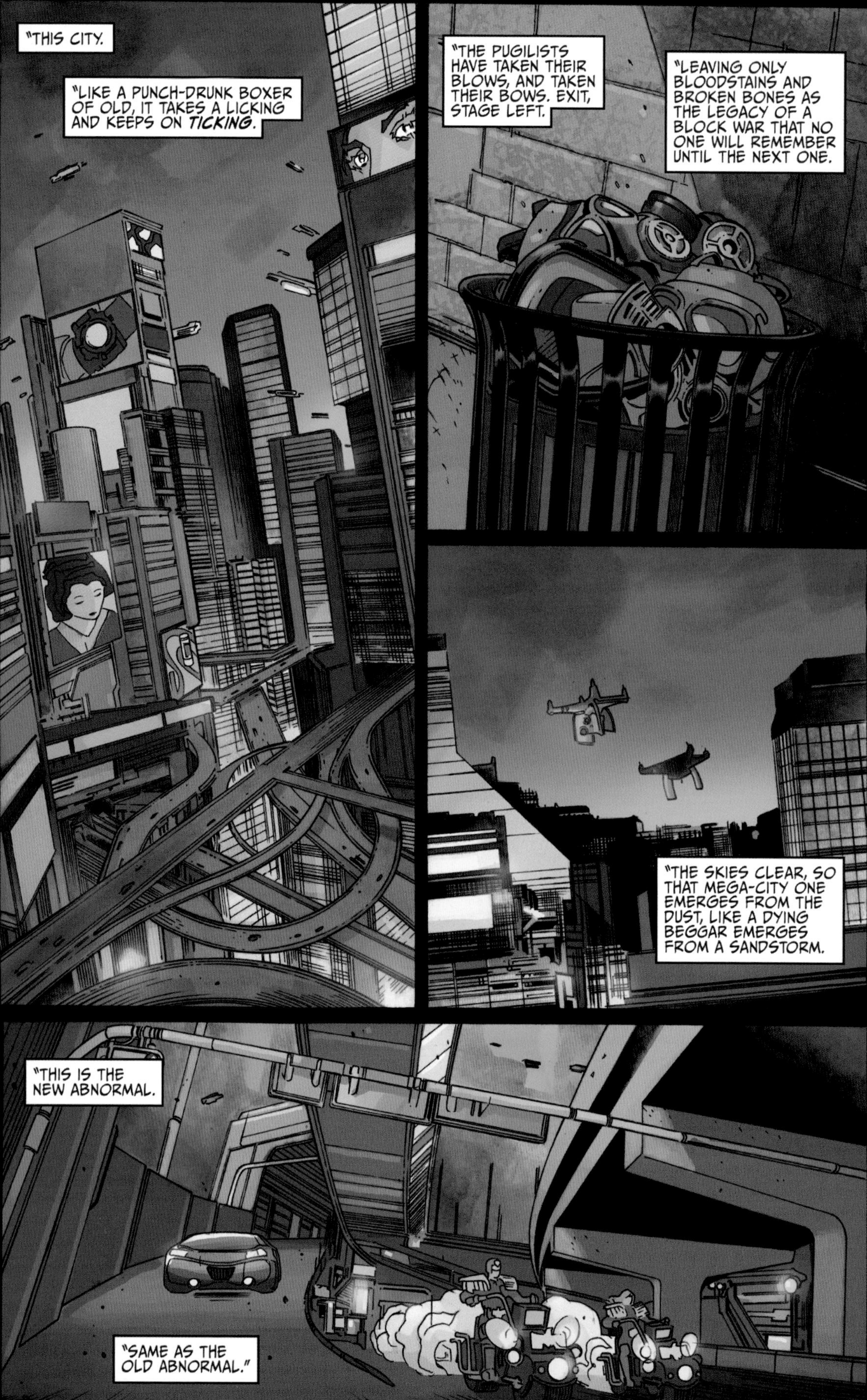
"THIS CITY.
"LIKE A PUNCH-DRUNK BOXER OF OLD, IT TAKES A LICKING AND KEEPS ON *TICKING*.
"THE PUGILISTS HAVE TAKEN THEIR BLOWS, AND TAKEN THEIR BOWS. EXIT, STAGE LEFT.
"LEAVING ONLY BLOODSTAINS AND BROKEN BONES AS THE LEGACY OF A BLOCK WAR THAT NO ONE WILL REMEMBER UNTIL THE NEXT ONE.
"THE SKIES CLEAR, SO THAT MEGA-CITY ONE EMERGES FROM THE DUST, LIKE A DYING BEGGAR EMERGES FROM A SANDSTORM.
"THIS IS THE NEW ABNORMAL.
"SAME AS THE OLD ABNORMAL."

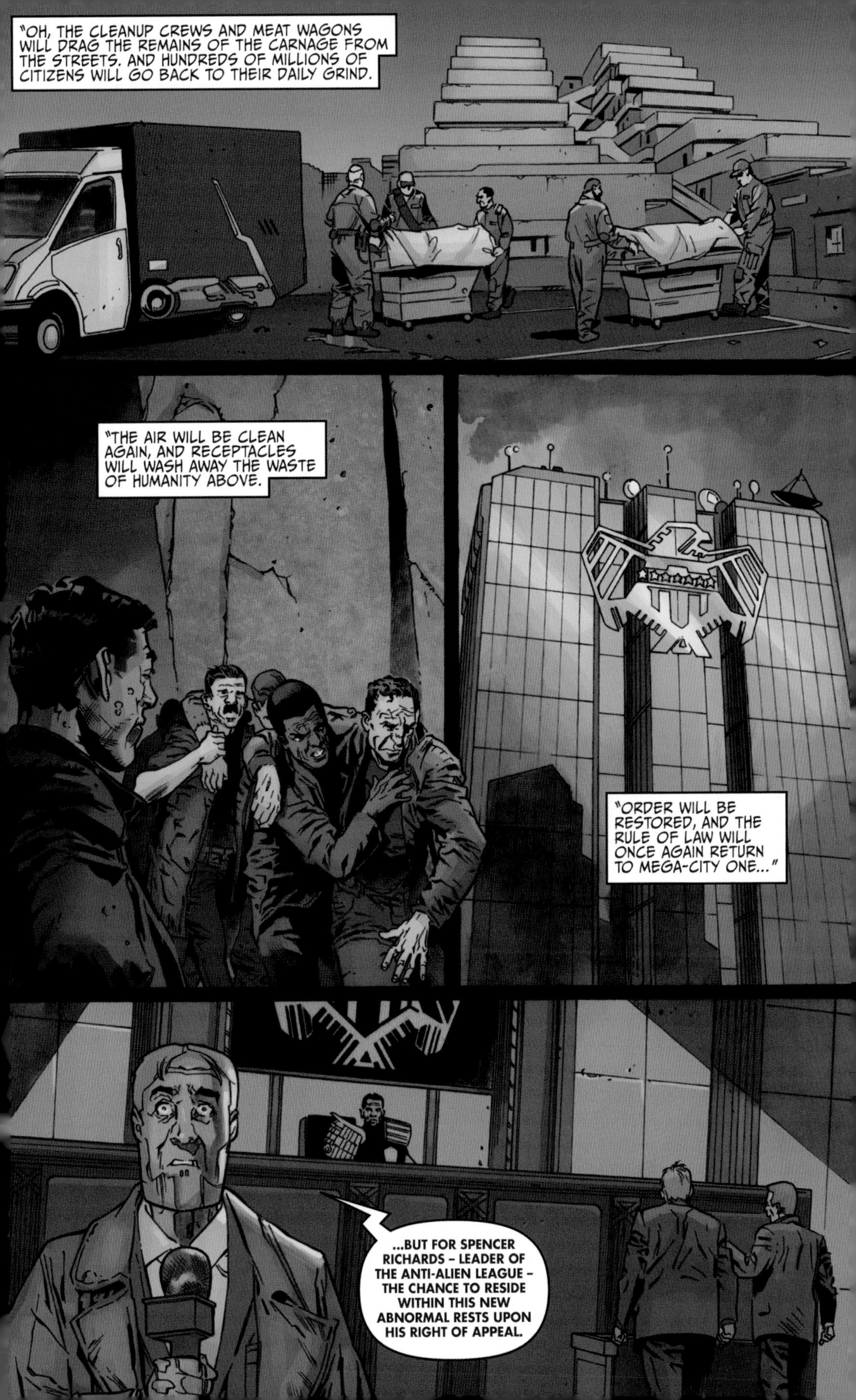
"OH, THE CLEANUP CREWS AND MEAT WAGONS WILL DRAG THE REMAINS OF THE CARNAGE FROM THE STREETS. AND HUNDREDS OF MILLIONS OF CITIZENS WILL GO BACK TO THEIR DAILY GRIND.
"THE AIR WILL BE CLEAN AGAIN, AND RECEPTACLES WILL WASH AWAY THE WASTE OF HUMANITY ABOVE.
"ORDER WILL BE RESTORED, AND THE RULE OF LAW WILL ONCE AGAIN RETURN TO MEGA-CITY ONE..."
...BUT FOR SPENCER RICHARDS – LEADER OF THE ANTI-ALIEN LEAGUE – THE CHANCE TO RESIDE WITHIN THIS NEW ABNORMAL RESTS UPON HIS RIGHT OF APPEAL.

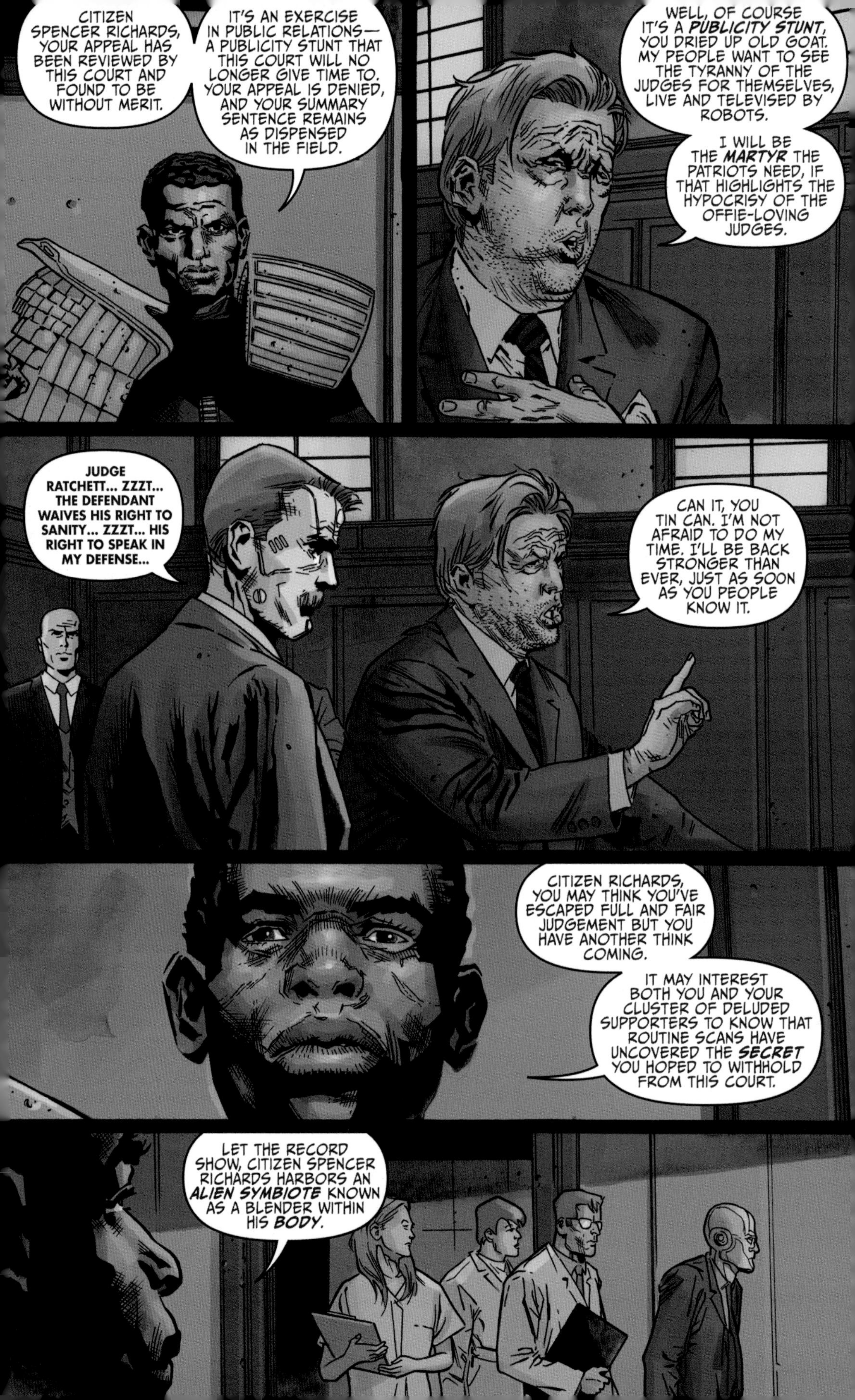
CITIZEN SPENCER RICHARDS, YOUR APPEAL HAS BEEN REVIEWED BY THIS COURT AND FOUND TO BE WITHOUT MERIT.
IT'S AN EXERCISE IN PUBLIC RELATIONS— A PUBLICITY STUNT THAT THIS COURT WILL NO LONGER GIVE TIME TO. YOUR APPEAL IS DENIED, AND YOUR SUMMARY SENTENCE REMAINS AS DISPENSED IN THE FIELD.
WELL, OF COURSE IT'S A ***PUBLICITY STUNT***, YOU DRIED UP OLD GOAT. MY PEOPLE WANT TO SEE THE TYRANNY OF THE JUDGES FOR THEMSELVES, LIVE AND TELEVISED BY ROBOTS.
I WILL BE THE ***MARTYR*** THE PATRIOTS NEED, IF THAT HIGHLIGHTS THE HYPOCRISY OF THE OFFIE-LOVING JUDGES.
JUDGE RATCHETT... ZZZT... THE DEFENDANT WAIVES HIS RIGHT TO SANITY... ZZZT... HIS RIGHT TO SPEAK IN MY DEFENSE...
CAN IT, YOU TIN CAN. I'M NOT AFRAID TO DO MY TIME. I'LL BE BACK STRONGER THAN EVER, JUST AS SOON AS YOU PEOPLE KNOW IT.
CITIZEN RICHARDS, YOU MAY THINK YOU'VE ESCAPED FULL AND FAIR JUDGEMENT BUT YOU HAVE ANOTHER THINK COMING.
IT MAY INTEREST BOTH YOU AND YOUR CLUSTER OF DELUDED SUPPORTERS TO KNOW THAT ROUTINE SCANS HAVE UNCOVERED THE ***SECRET*** YOU HOPED TO WITHHOLD FROM THIS COURT.
LET THE RECORD SHOW, CITIZEN SPENCER RICHARDS HARBORS AN ***ALIEN SYMBIOTE*** KNOWN AS A BLENDER WITHIN HIS ***BODY***.

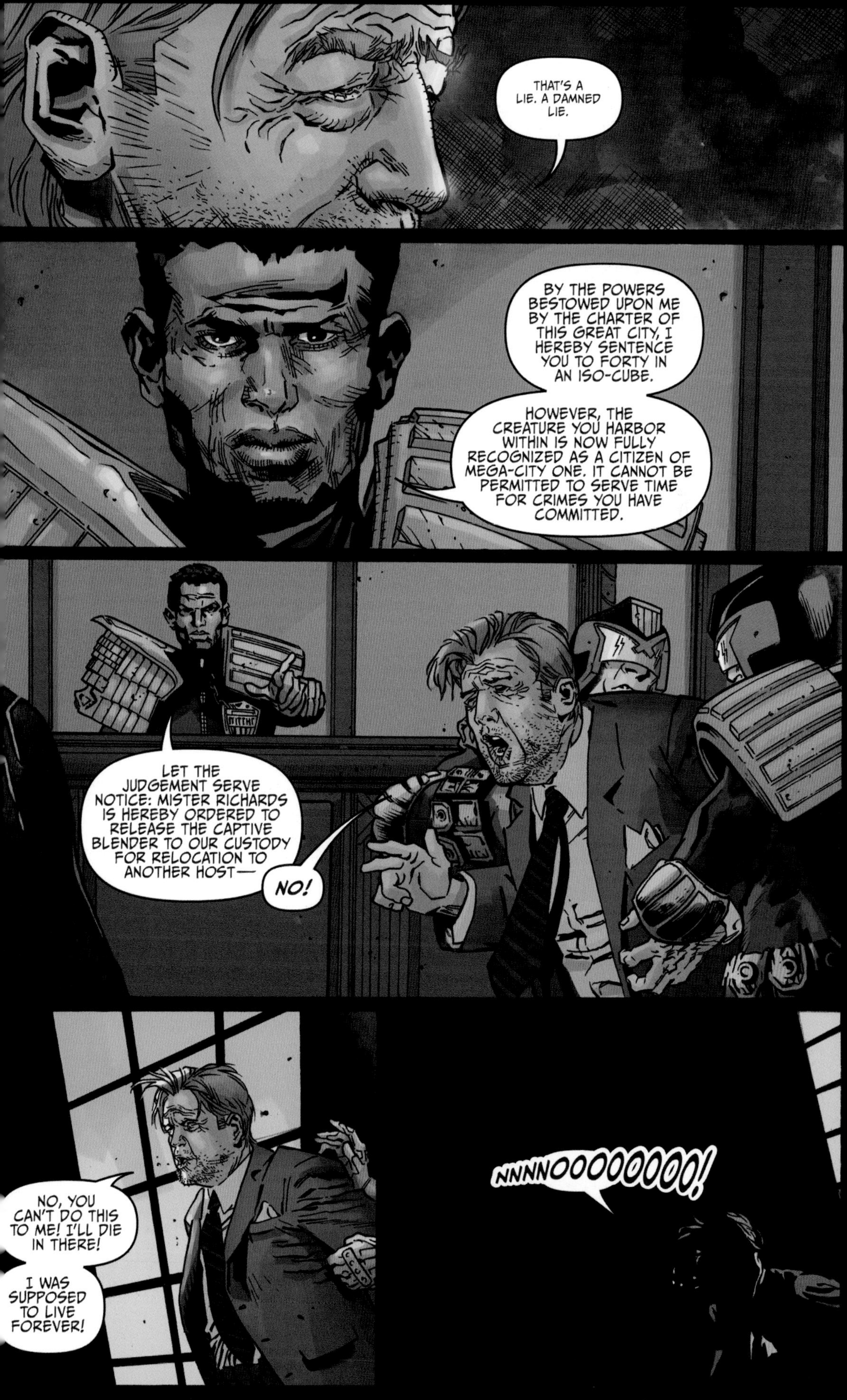
THAT'S A LIE. A DAMNED LIE.
BY THE POWERS BESTOWED UPON ME BY THE CHARTER OF THIS GREAT CITY, I HEREBY SENTENCE YOU TO FORTY IN AN ISO-CUBE.
HOWEVER, THE CREATURE YOU HARBOR WITHIN IS NOW FULLY RECOGNIZED AS A CITIZEN OF MEGA-CITY ONE. IT CANNOT BE PERMITTED TO SERVE TIME FOR CRIMES YOU HAVE COMMITTED.
LET THE JUDGEMENT SERVE NOTICE: MISTER RICHARDS IS HEREBY ORDERED TO RELEASE THE CAPTIVE BLENDER TO OUR CUSTODY FOR RELOCATION TO ANOTHER HOST—
NO!
NO, YOU CAN'T DO THIS TO ME! I'LL DIE IN THERE!
I WAS SUPPOSED TO LIVE FOREVER!
NNNNOOOOOOOOO!

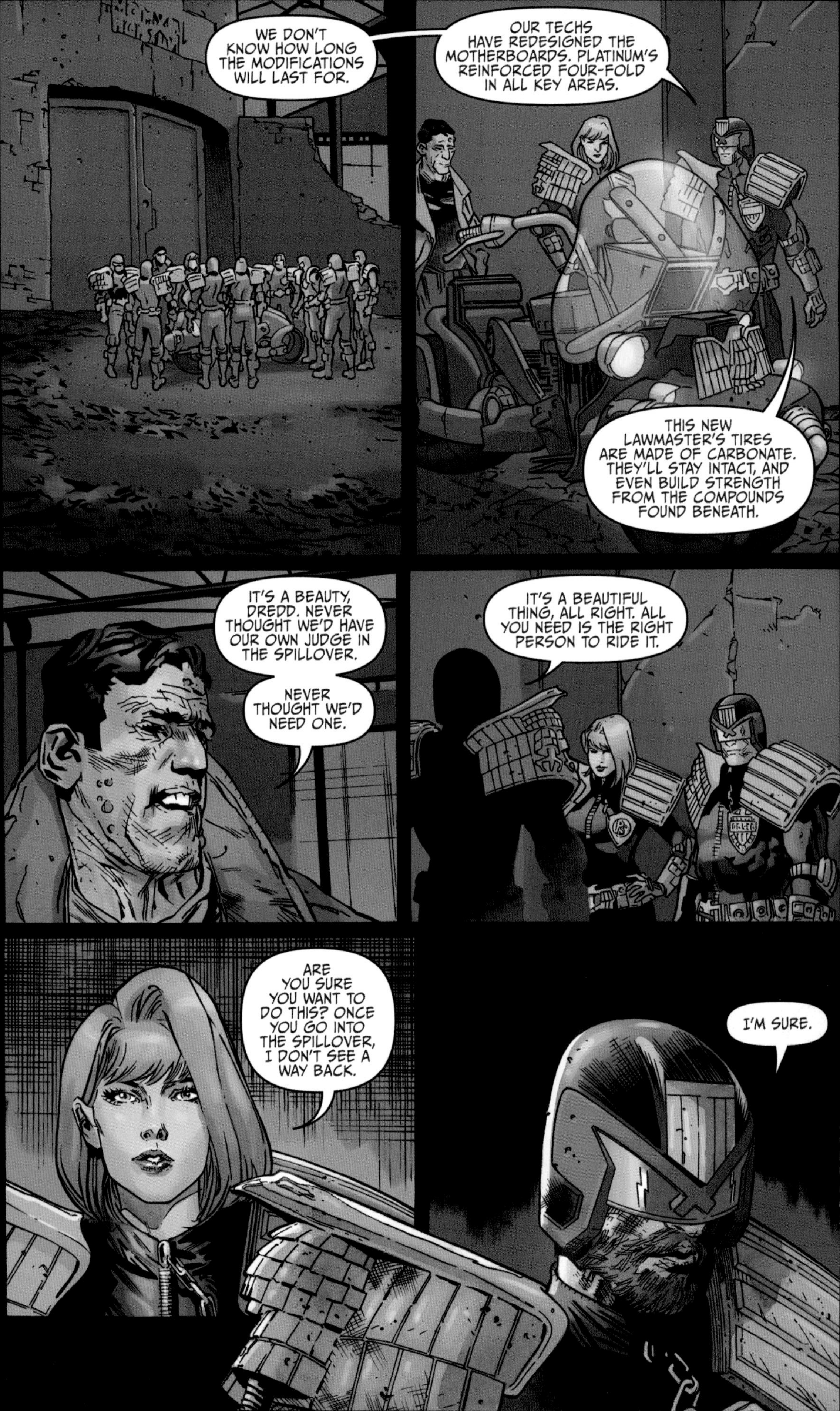
WE DON'T KNOW HOW LONG THE MODIFICATIONS WILL LAST FOR.
OUR TECHS HAVE REDESIGNED THE MOTHERBOARDS. PLATINUM'S REINFORCED FOUR-FOLD IN ALL KEY AREAS.
THIS NEW LAWMASTER'S TIRES ARE MADE OF CARBONATE. THEY'LL STAY INTACT, AND EVEN BUILD STRENGTH FROM THE COMPOUNDS FOUND BENEATH.
IT'S A BEAUTY, DREDD. NEVER THOUGHT WE'D HAVE OUR OWN JUDGE IN THE SPILLOVER.
NEVER THOUGHT WE'D NEED ONE.
IT'S A BEAUTIFUL THING, ALL RIGHT. ALL YOU NEED IS THE RIGHT PERSON TO RIDE IT.
ARE YOU SURE YOU WANT TO DO THIS? ONCE YOU GO INTO THE SPILLOVER, I DON'T SEE A WAY BACK.
I'M SURE.

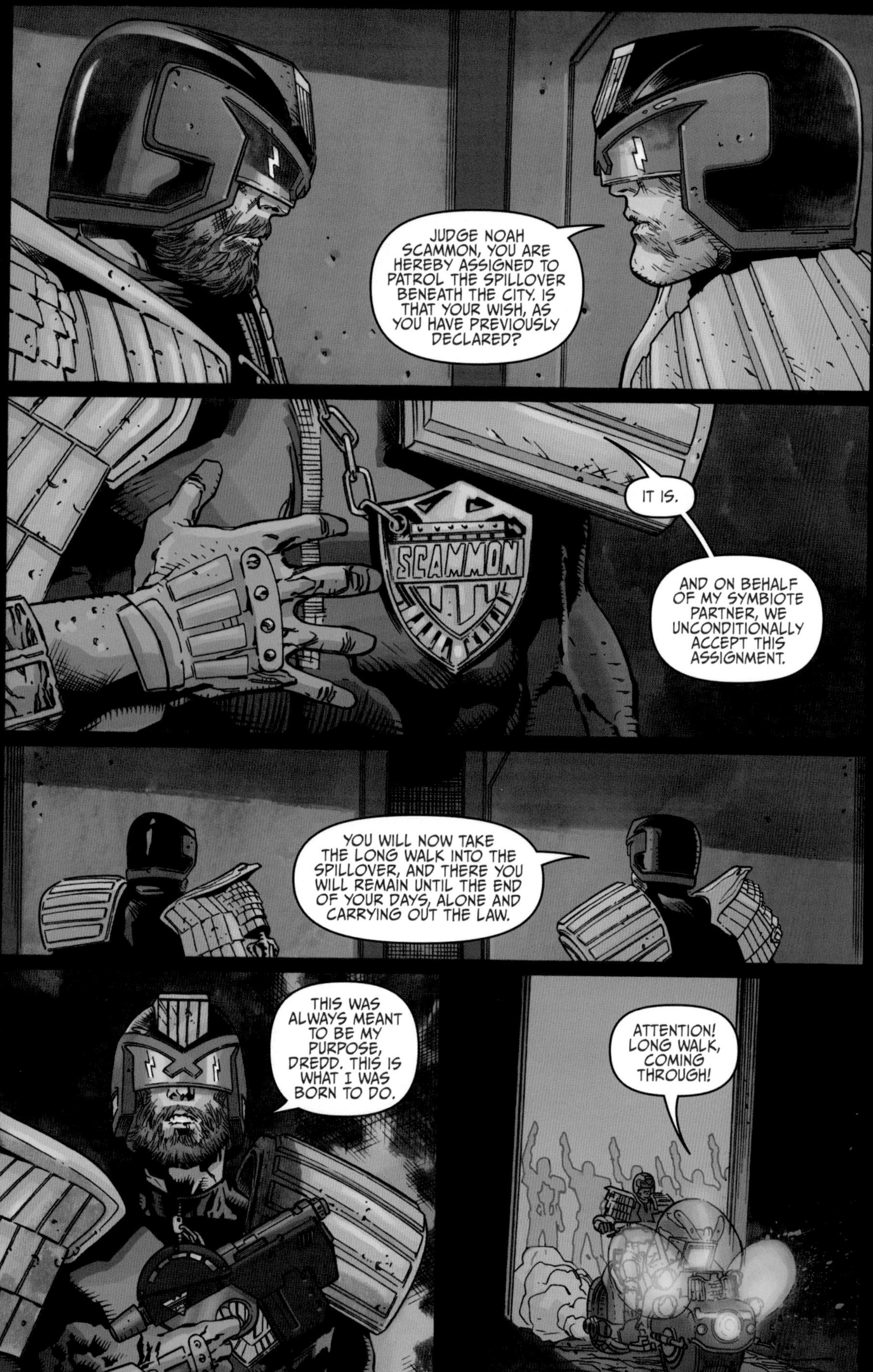
JUDGE NOAH SCAMMON, YOU ARE HEREBY ASSIGNED TO PATROL THE SPILLOVER BENEATH THE CITY. IS THAT YOUR WISH, AS YOU HAVE PREVIOUSLY DECLARED?
SCAMMON
IT IS.
AND ON BEHALF OF MY SYMBIOTE PARTNER, WE UNCONDITIONALLY ACCEPT THIS ASSIGNMENT.
YOU WILL NOW TAKE THE LONG WALK INTO THE SPILLOVER, AND THERE YOU WILL REMAIN UNTIL THE END OF YOUR DAYS, ALONE AND CARRYING OUT THE LAW.
THIS WAS ALWAYS MEANT TO BE MY PURPOSE, DREDD. THIS IS WHAT I WAS BORN TO DO.
ATTENTION! LONG WALK, COMING THROUGH!

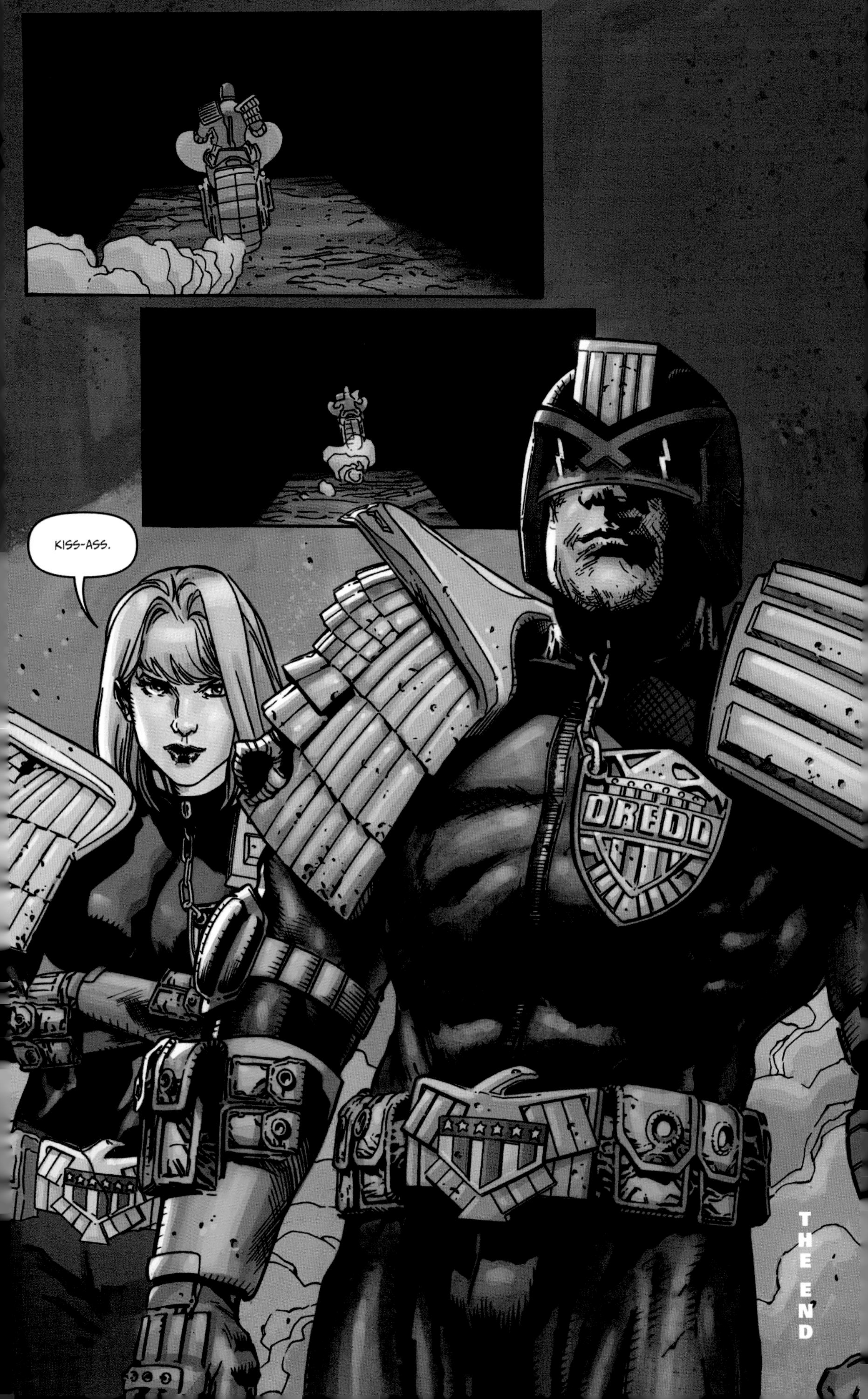
KISS-ASS.
DREDD
THE END

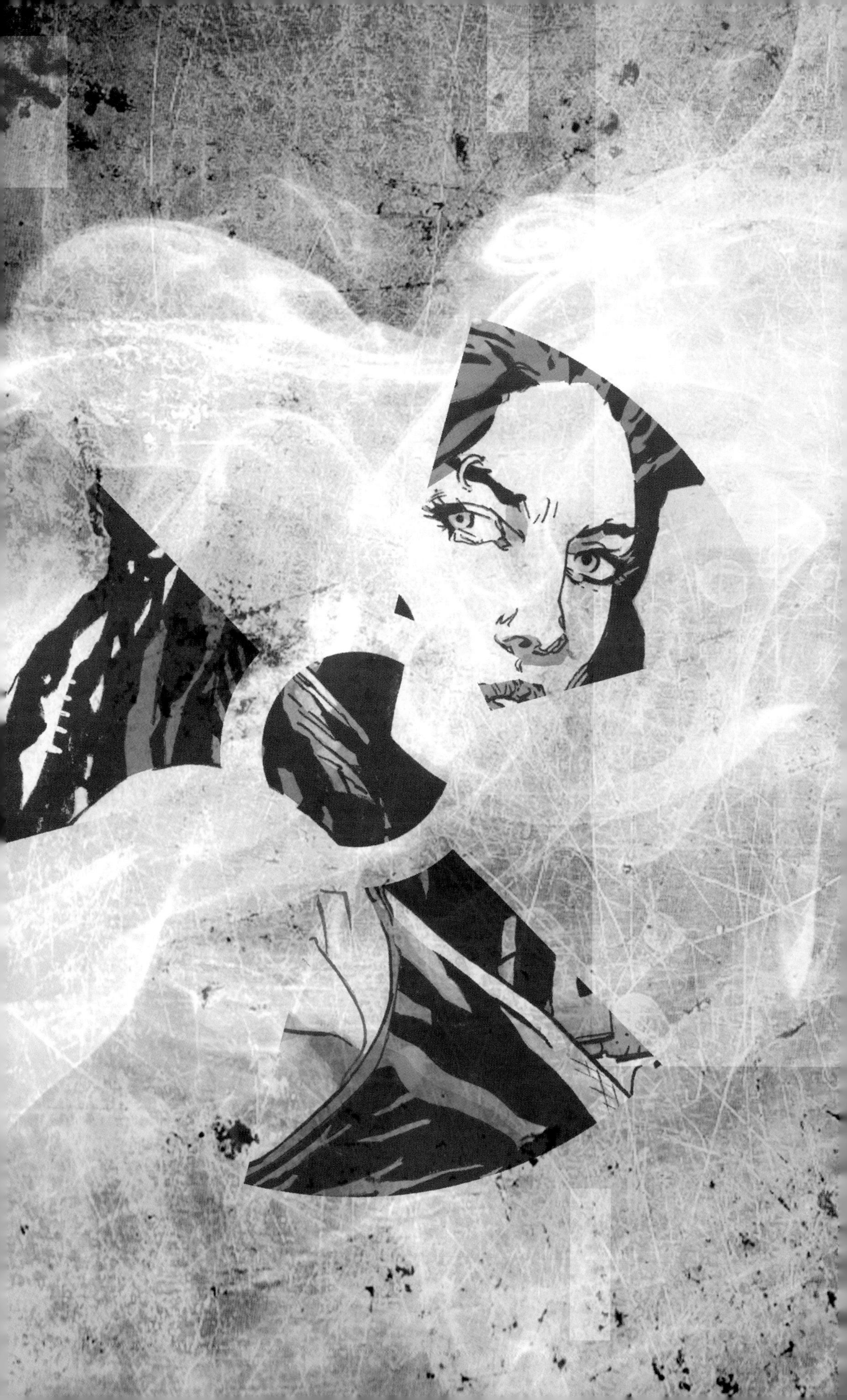

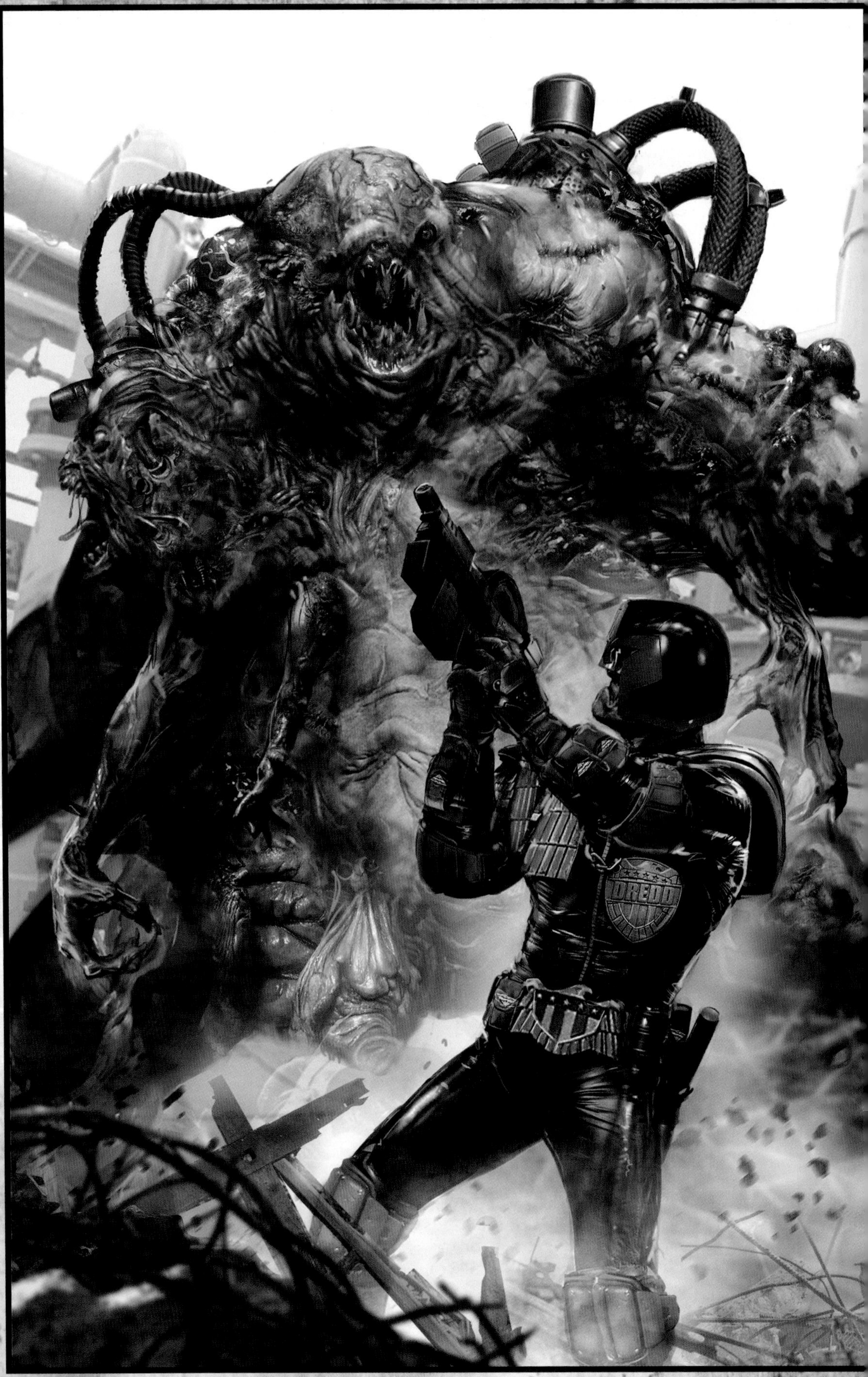
DREDD

ART BY **JOHN GALLAGHER**

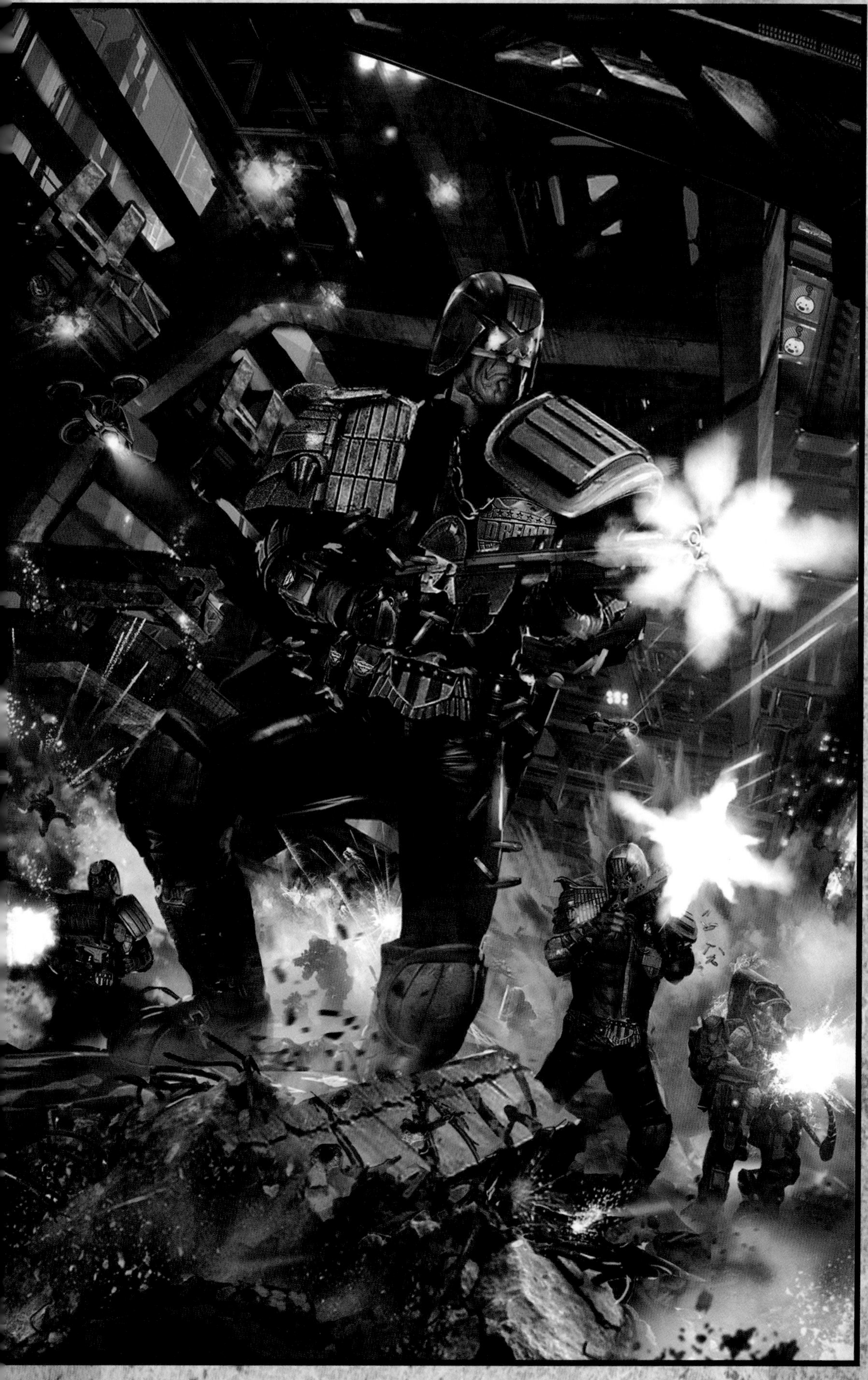

ART BY **JOHN GALLAGHER**

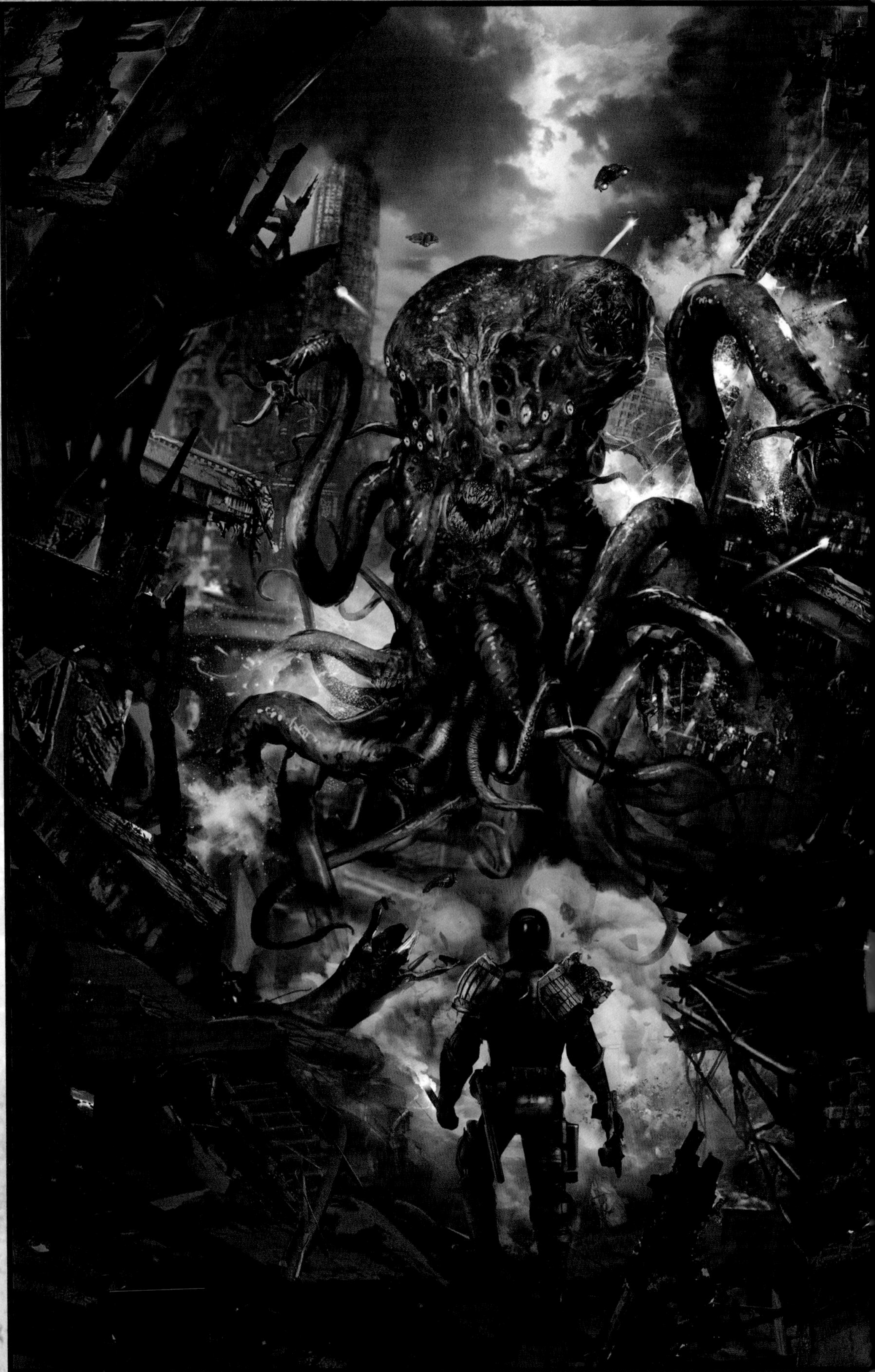

ART BY **JOHN GALLAGHER**

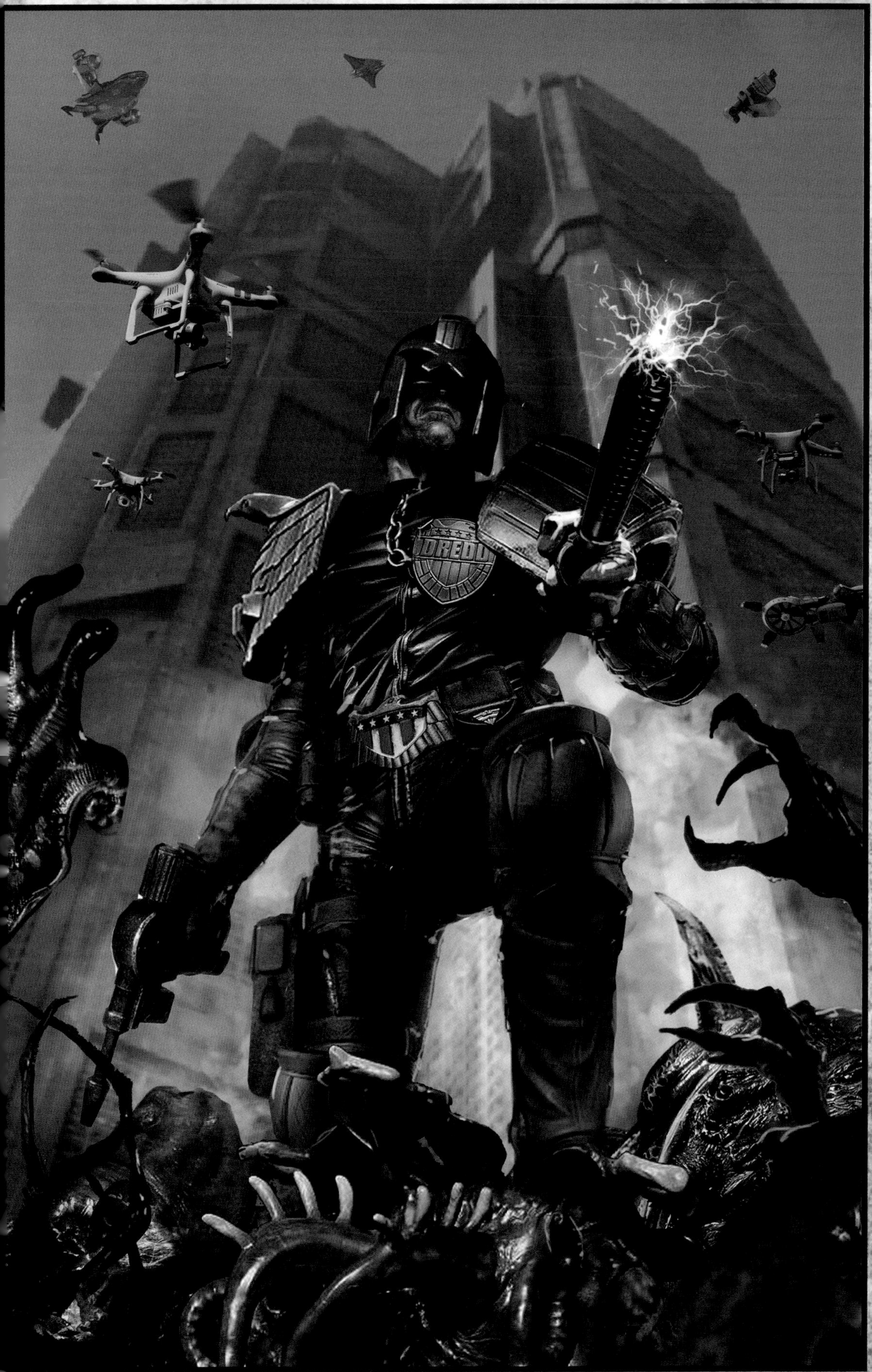
DREDD

ART BY **JOHN GALLAGHER**

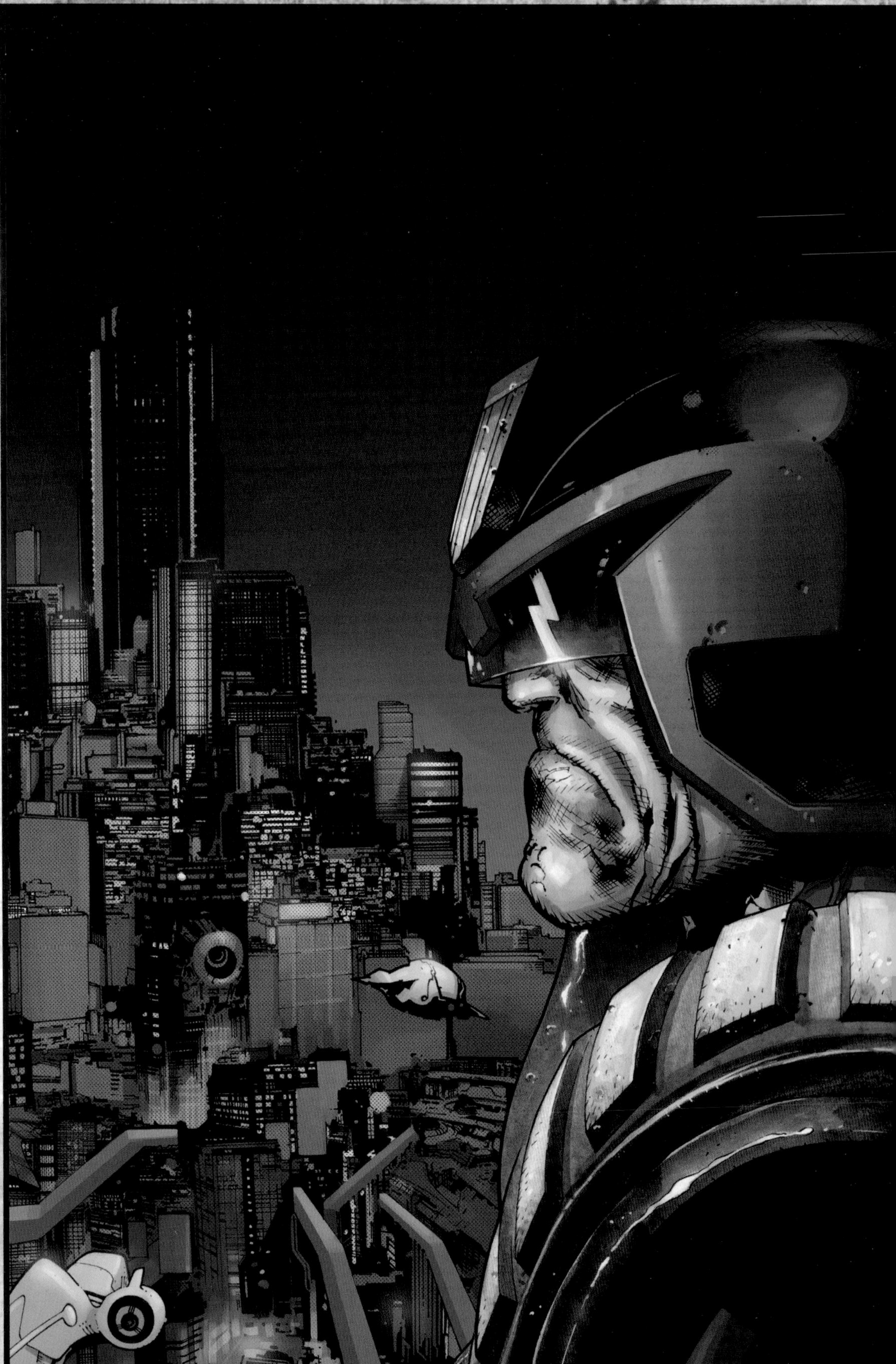

ART BY **MARCO CASTIELLO** COLORS BY **JASON MILLET**